THE AMERICAN GIRL GOES TO WAR

WAR CULTURE
Edited by Daniel Leonard Bernardi

Books in this series address the myriad ways in which warfare informs diverse cultural practices, as well as the way cultural practices–from cinema to social media–inform the practice of warfare. They illuminate the insights and limitations of critical theories that describe, explain and politicize the phenomena of war culture. Traversing both national and intellectual borders, authors from a wide range of fields and disciplines collectively examine the articulation of war, its everyday practices, and its impact on individuals and societies throughout modern history.

For a list of all the titles in the series, please see the last page of the book.

THE AMERICAN GIRL GOES TO WAR

Women and National Identity in U.S. Silent Film

LIZ CLARKE

RUTGERS UNIVERSITY PRESS

New Brunswick, Camden, and Newark, New Jersey, and London

Library of Congress Cataloging-in-Publication Data

Names: Clarke, Liz, 1981–author.
Title: The American girl goes to war: women and national identity
   in US silent film / Liz Clarke.
Description: New Brunswick: Rutgers University Press, [2022] |
   Series: War culture | Includes bibliographical references and index.
Identifiers: LCCN 2021016528 | ISBN 9781978810150 (paperback; alk. paper) |
   ISBN 9781978810167 (hardback; alk. paper) | ISBN 9781978810174 (epub) |
   ISBN 9781978810181 (mobi) | ISBN 9781978810198 (pdf)
Subjects: LCSH: War films—United States—History and criticism. |
   Women in motion pictures—History—20th century. | Women and war—
   United States—History—20th century. | Nationalism—United States—
   History—20th century. | Heroines in motion pictures—History—
   20th century. | Sex role in motion pictures—History—20th century. |
   Silent films—United States—History—20th century.
Classification: LCC PN1995.9.W3 C593 2022 | DDC 791.43/6522—dc23
LC record available at https://lccn.loc.gov/2021016528

A British Cataloging-in-Publication record for this book is available from
the British Library.

Sections from Chapter 4 and Chapter 6 appeared as "Doing Her Bit: Women and
Propaganda in World War I" in *Resetting the Scene: Classical Hollywood Revisited*,
ed. Philippa Gates and Katherine Spring (Detroit, MI: Wayne State University Press,
2021): 201–210.

References to internet websites (URLs) were accurate at the time of writing. Neither
the author nor Rutgers University Press is responsible for URLs that may have expired
or changed since the manuscript was prepared.

♾ The paper used in this publication meets the requirements of the American National
Standard for Information Sciences—Permanence of Paper for Printed Library
Materials, ANSI Z39.48-1992.

www.rutgersuniversitypress.org

Manufactured in the United States of America

For my mother and father, Donna and Gerry

CONTENTS

CONTENTS

ILLUSTRATIONS

THE AMERICAN GIRL GOES TO WAR

INTRODUCTION
The American Girl Goes to War

In 1916 Alice and Ruth DeVere, the "Moving Picture Girls," went to Oak Farms in New Jersey and filmed a war picture with their company, Comet Films. The film, called *A Girl in Blue and a Girl in Gray*, featured Ruth as an army nurse and Alice as a spy. The camera operator stated: "War stuff is going big now.... All this talk of preparedness, you know, the war in Europe, and all that. The public is fairly 'eating up' war pictures."[1] During production, Alice and Ruth DeVere befriended an extra, Estelle Brown, an accomplished equestrian who performed stunts throughout the climactic scenes. Neither this film nor the DeVere sisters exist. Ruth, Alice, and the film company they worked for were fictional creations in the juvenile book series, The Moving Picture Girls, which was published by the Stratemeyer Syndicate in the mid-1910s. However, *A Girl in Blue and a Girl in Gray* forms the central narrative of the final Moving Pictures Girls book, *The Moving Picture Girls in War Plays, or, Sham Battles at Oak Farms*. That the war genre is at the center of one of only seven books in the series demonstrates the popularity of war films and the prevalence of women's roles in the genre at the time.

Another popular books series about a young woman in film production, Ruth Fielding, also included a book about Ruth's participation in the war effort. *Ruth Fielding in the Red Cross* came out in 1918 and reveals the difference two years during this pivotal decade meant for women in depictions of war. In this book, Ruth sets aside her work in moving pictures so that she can enlist in the Red Cross. During her time at war, although occupied with caring for wounded soldiers, Ruth continues to investigate a group she suspects to be enemy spies. Unlike Ruth, the DeVere sister characters in *The Moving Picture Girls in War Plays* never participate in real war, but the various roles they and other female characters play in the production of the film within the book range from nurse, to spy, to horse-riding heroine. These two books, released during the 1910s, capitalized on well-known roles for women in war-themed films of the 1910. Heroic women, active participants, patriotic heroines: these were the women who filled the frames of war films during the 1910s.

This book, *The American Girl Goes to War*, begins with the popularity of American Civil War fiction films in 1908 and ends in 1919, the immediate post–World War I years. The Civil War films—as well as American Revolutionary War films, border war films, Mexican-American War films, and films that depict wars with Native Americans—often featured heroic female characters. Athletic, skilled, cunning, and quick-thinking heroines saved the day in many films during this period. Estelle Brown, the skillful equestrian friend to the Moving Picture Girls, is an exemplary of female characters in films of the early 1910s because she not only performs heroic deeds but does her own stunts. When the war in Europe broke out, these moving picture trends did not immediately give way to depictions of masculine heroism, as one might imagine. On-screen portrayals of women's involvement in war remained consistent even during American involvement in World War I. As we see with Ruth Fielding, however, the role for women begins to shift during the war. By the war's end, and immediately following it, masculine heroism became the norm, and by the 1920s various factors combined to solidify the war genre as primarily masculine.

However, we need to rethink our understanding of war films to break away from strict generic codes in order to make sense of the multitude of war films from the period 1908–1919. These films were sensational, sentimental, often melodramatic, although sometimes comedic. In this decade before genre norms were solidified, war was the subject or the backdrop of a variety of films. Opening up the analysis of war films to include these not-quite-war-genre films about war offers a new understanding of the history of war in film. Focusing on films from the period 1908–1919 allows for an in-depth interrogation of how films about war differed from the later genre of the war film in one distinct way: the frequency of heroic, female protagonists.

War films produced between 1908 and 1919 focused heavily on female characters and their heroic actions. The frequent depictions of female heroism in film of the late 1900s and early 1910s is not a rupture, nor unprecedented, but a pendulum swing of gendered representations of militarism. Film is part of a larger tapestry of media and entertainment forms, many of which provide a pre-filmic history of representations of American wars. Throughout the nineteenth century women's intrinsic link to notions of American national identity appeared in dime novels, memoirs, popular theater, and popular journalism. Each of these forms drew from the subject matter of girl spies, cross-dressing soldier-girls and women keeping the home fires burning as much as they represented men in battle.[2] In fact, images and narratives of women had historically been used to solidify and reproduce American myth, and they continue to be, even today. However, not all women are represented equally: this book reveals the way white women enacted narratives of American imperialism, militarism, and exceptionalism.

WAR AS A POPULAR BACKDROP: THE QUESTION
OF GENRE AND EARLY CINEMA

Today we think of the war genre as divided between masculinist combat films, such as *Pork Chop Hill* (Milestone, 1959) and *Saving Private Ryan* (Spielberg, 1998), and women-centered home-front films, such as *Mrs. Miniver* (Wyler, 1942) and *Coming Home* (Ashby, 1978). In combat films such as *Courage under Fire* (Zwick, 1996) and *G.I. Jane* (Scott, 1997), women characters usually only appear in narratives of women proving themselves in a man's world. Even though until recently many scholarly histories of the war film have included a (sometimes cursory) discussion of women, and the topic of women in World War II home-front films has a rich history, these versions of the war film's history never fully account for the very active and heroic women of American silent film.[3] More recent scholarly contributions have accounted for gender and women's varied representation in war films from various periods in film history and from different national contexts. My goal here is to fill the gap in scholarship about women and war in the silent era.[4] *The American Girl Goes to War* focuses on American silent film in order to make claims about the origins of the filmic war genre and its relation to ideologies of nationhood, national identity, and militarism. By bringing together silent film scholarship on women and archival research on war films from 1908 to 1919—particularly ones that feature women as soldiers, spies, action heroes, and home-front defenders—I demonstrate that white American women played active roles in early twentieth-century representations of American militarism and American national identity.

The majority of the films discussed in this study do not belong to what today we would identify as a genre of "the war film"; most often they use war merely as a backdrop or were released during an American-fought war and were marketed as "patriotic" despite the fact that no war takes place within their narratives. The early American films are difficult to categorize because they do not bear the signs of distinct genres.[5] In short, despite the fact that the films that make up the bulk of this study cannot be categorized as "combat films" or "home-front films," they indeed belong to the larger category of the "war film" in its earliest development. War is a central *topic* that connects these films and facilitates a coherent analysis of how those films engage with myths of American patriotism and heroism. This book offers up a new understanding of the history of war films—specifically, a history that acknowledges the importance of women in the early history of the genre.

At this time war in film was closely aligned, and perhaps even interchangeable, with depictions of the West in film, in large part because conflicts during westward expansion, the (Mexican) Border Wars, the forging of the frontier, and the American Civil War were popular subjects.[6] Jenny Barrett, in her discussion of the phrase "Civil War film," suggests that there is no specific genre of the Civil

War, for the films that depict the war have various "generic allegiances."[7] The most popular allegiance of Civil War films is to the domestic melodrama, as many of the battles are shown to be fought outside the homes of the very families whose lives were most affected by the war. Likewise, other wars also bear these generic allegiances—from wars of antiquity to contemporary conflicts that had recently been fought in the Balkan states, or even World War I. Serial-queen melodramas (a popular film format consisting of a series of weekly episodes featuring action women foiling a villain's plans) also incorporated wars and battles into their subject matter, particularly during World War I.[8] I am interested in films that derived from a variety of "generic allegiances," and that featured women in narratives of war, because such films reveal a vital link between women, militarism, and American identity that existed during the period of silent cinema.

A recurring theme throughout these films is women's perilous victimhood that leads to righteous violence framed as "defense." In the case of these films about war, no matter the battle and no matter the politics behind the war, story after story reconfirms the myth that American militarism of the time is in defense of safety and purity of American women. In other words, while victimhood in battle is a key trope that determines who the audience should side with, this tactic is made all the more powerful by centering women's victimhood and the resulting action. The most useful concept for understanding how this use of victimhood, defense, and morality functions is melodrama. Rather than being a genre, melodrama is a dominant mode of narrative film—and other popular entertainment forms—during this period. Linda Williams describes melodrama as "an evolving mode of storytelling crucial to the establishment of moral good."[9] Melodrama has been used throughout American film history to promote imperial ideologies, using what Jonna Eagle refers to as "imperialist affect, . . . the processes by which cinematic action has been constituted as something that *feels* good—both pleasurable and right, thrilling and virtuous."[10] In other words, Williams and Eagle see melodrama as an American mode of storytelling that conveys important information about morality, imperialism, and national identity in a post-secular age. For Eagle, American imperialism is conveyed in film through the melodramatic merging of "spectacular violence and pathetic suffering," or the centering of victimhood to justify militarism.[11] A majority of films referred to in this book contribute to the representation of U.S. imperialism through the lens of melodrama. This was particularly important in an era when imperialism, militarism, isolationism, and American intervention were hotly contested topics.

The melodramatic mode has a history in American popular entertainment—popular fiction, theater, film, television—as a narrative form that relies on sensation and sentiment. Jesse Alemán and Shelley Streeby distinguish between nineteenth-century sentimental literature and the "less respectable" sensational literature of the dime novels and story papers, but state that "both modes translate political, social, and economic questions into affect-drenched narratives of relations among individual and collective bodies and both make women's bodies allegories for races, classes, and nations, but sensational literature is more outrageous and less respectable."[12] Early films, particularly the films about war, were indebted to the influence of sensational and sentimental fiction of the nineteenth century, continuing the tradition of eliciting emotion through shocks and thrills. Authors such as Williams, Eagle, Alemán, and Streeby demonstrate how the political is articulated in the stories of a given culture. In the introduction to *Early Cinema and the National*, Richard Abel, Giorgio Bertellini, and Rob King compare early cinema to mass print culture, to demonstrate how Benedict Anderson's concept of the "imagined community" created by print can also be applied to film's early decades.[13] Alemán and Streeby, in particular, discuss the way the bodies of female characters became the sites on which the anxieties about imperial expansion were explored.

The women in these films are sites through which we can read the political context of the 1910s. White women in American war films served to solidify and bolster imperialism, white supremacy, and national myths tied up with ideologies of racial superiority. In the affect-drenched narratives, filled with shocks and thrills, these women emerge as the virtuous, moral centers that demonstrate ideals of American identity. In the narratives of the Civil War the women often bridge the gap between the warring sides, demonstrating the unity of the nation through familial and romantic bonds. In the films that advocated for military preparedness prior to American entry into World War I, the female characters defended their homes and their nation against foreign invasion when all other characters demonstrate complacency in times of peace. In all of the films, these women's whiteness and youthfulness stand in as signs of purity, meant to be read as the ideal American subject. While Richard Dyer argues in *White* that "there is something at stake in looking at, or continuing to ignore, white racial imagery,"[14] I add that we must acknowledge the whiteness of these early film heroines precisely because the subject matter is so intimately tied to national myths. The American Revolution and the American Civil War were both hailed as the "birth of the nation" and both were central subjects during this period. The whiteness surrounding the characters in these stories cannot simply be ignored as a "product of the time." White supremacy in film and in stories of national myth must be confronted as central both then and now.

Perhaps the most notable example of the peril and virtue of the white American woman is the infamous rescue scene from *The Birth of a Nation* (Griffith, 1915). However, we risk dismissing the underpinnings of white supremacy throughout the U.S. film industry as a whole by focusing too heavily on a key example, attributing the depiction of race to the writer and director rather than interrogating the way it was exemplary of the "sociopolitical practices [that] insured that the articulation of race in early cinema crossed studios, authors, genres, and styles."[15] Daniel Bernardi argues that whiteness is a "very particular something" with "identifiable properties and specific history.... In early cinema, the particularity of this discourse ranges from the representational—where whiteface becomes an enduring image—to the narrational—where stories of nonwhite servitude, of colonial love, and of the divine centrality and virtue of the white family/white woman dominate countless films."[16] However, I focus on one subject—war—in an effort to provide a wider analysis of studios, styles, and authors to demonstrate the pervasiveness of using women—specifically white women—to contribute to ideologies of American nationhood and militarism.

Due to the limited availability of films from the silent era, many overview histories of the war film focus on a select—and limited—number of now-canonized silent war films. Traditional accounts of the war film as a genre proper usually credit D. W. Griffith with developing early war film aesthetic and narrative patterns within the specific subject matter of the Civil War, particularly in his infamous film *The Birth of a Nation* (1915). The connection of *The Birth of a Nation* to his later World War I film, *Hearts of the World* (1918), takes on a particular importance to war film historians because it links the representation of the Civil War to that of World War I in the history of the war film's development. In *War Cinema: Hollywood on the Front Line,* Guy Westwell's brief chapter on silent war films focuses primarily on *Hearts of the World* before moving into a discussion of war in film after the coming of sound. Despite the use of actual footage from World War I in the film, Westwell argues, the overall aesthetic and ideological concerns of the film mirrored Griffith's already established conservative and Victorian values that are prevalent in his Civil War films.[17] In other words, *Hearts of the World* may be about World War I, but it is just another of Griffith's Civil War films.[18] The film concerns a woman who is threatened by a villainous German and saved by a heroic American soldier; in short, the racism against African Americans in *Birth of a Nation* is exchanged for anti-German attitudes of the World War I era in *Hearts of the World*. Moreover, in addition to the Victorian values of *Hearts of the World*, the film's visual aesthetic also remained tied to the early 1910s stylistic traits. Westwell notes that Griffith, in fact, traveled to the front lines of the war in 1917 but preferred the potential of staged representations of battle, rather than footage from the war, leading him to merely recreate the same aesthetic as with his Civil War films.[19] However, Westwell's analysis of *Hearts of the World* suggests that a more comprehensive understanding of the Civil War films from the 1910s is needed to understand the lineage of war film history. The later chapters in my book reveal a much broader and more complex history of the war film than Griffith's output alone would suggest. Civil War and American Revolution films made by companies such as Kalem, Lubin, Imp, Powers, and a handful of others amounted to hundreds of films about Americans in war. Archival materials such as trade press reviews and advertisements can offer up a much more convincing history of the influence of Civil War and American Revolution films on the later

World War I combat films. Indeed, extensive archival research was necessary even just to build a filmography from which to analyze the genre during the period 1908–1919.

Many histories of the war genre look forward, rather than back—starting during an era when films contained all the trademarks of classical Hollywood style and form, and looking for contemporaneous influences, rather than mining the archives for long-forgotten traces of a time before the genre took its shape. In other words, another popular belief about the war film genre is that it formed in the 1920s, or during the era of the rise of classical Hollywood cinema.[20] James M. Welsh's discussion of the war film genre in this period looks ahead to when the genre is firmly established when he states that "the war film was stuck throughout the 1920s in its primitive stages."[21] Although Welsh analyzes only two silent World War I films in his essay, his use of the term "primitive" to describe this era of the war film virtually erases the pre-1920 instances of war in film. Welsh is not alone in locating the "start" of the genre in the 1920s and in more easily accessible films such as *The Big Parade* and *What Price Glory*. Few American silent war films remain extant. Silent film research is a laborious project. However, the films of the Spanish-American War, the American Civil War, the American Revolution, and any films depicting battles between the American military and Native Americans will deepen our understanding of the development of this genre, providing a more nuanced overview of the war film's history.

Although film's origins in the 1890s are arguably masculinist, many recent studies on silent film audiences have focused on the effect of women as consumers and public citizens on the popularity of film's earliest subjects.[22] The female heroines of the war films addressed in this book were part of larger trends in American filmmaking and cinema-going as a leisure activity targeted at women. The prevalence of women audience members—in addition to women in roles of writers and directors—makes it unsurprising to find heroic women at the center of these films. They were not there only to be looked at; they in fact propelled the narratives forward. As the following chapters will show, these roles—of female spies, cross-dressing women in soldiers' uniforms, and gun-toting women ready to defend the home and honor of their family—were so commonplace they gave rise to criticism in the trade press regarding overused formulas and character types.

Archival materials show that the history of women in war films is the opposite of that which has been commonly told. In his study of the war film, Michael Isenberg claims that women in World War I films were presented "first in their traditional wartime role and then, as scenarists stretched for dramatic effect, as active participants in the conflict."[23] Yet, what are these "traditional" roles for women in the category of war films? Most likely Isenberg refers to the suffering mothers, home-front sweethearts, and patriotic nurses; however, women's roles in films about war always also included the possibility of active participation. By turning to archival materials of this period, I will demonstrate that there never was a "traditional" role for women in war films. If anything, this book will demonstrate that the opposite is true: that women were active participants first, and later fell into roles of suffering wives, mothers, and sweethearts. In other words, by expanding the study of war in films from 1908 to 1919 I show that women in World War I films were related to earlier female heroines. To understand how women functioned within films about war during this decade, it is important to understand the context of film and cinema-going in these years.

War and militarism were packaged and commodified as a subject matter in popular entertainment forms and marketed to men and women throughout the late nineteenth century and early twentieth. However, because film was an entertainment form with a large female audience, it tended to encourage female patriotism through narratives about women. Women's independence in modernity coincided with their presence in an increasingly commercialized leisure world—a world in which film was just one form of entertainment.[24] The growth of female audiences affected and influenced the popularity of particular genres throughout the 1910s.[25] Thus, patriotism, militarism, and jingoism were quite readily taken up by the new medium of the moving picture—but the way in which these concepts were tied up with female characters at the time is of particular interest.

The dominance of movie-going culture was related to the commodification of leisure and culture that had been taking place since the nineteenth century. During the mid-1910s the promotion of popular serials included pictures of actresses in fashion magazines and the use of designers available to the public. Furthermore, fan magazines grew to mass popularity in the 1920s, providing fans with insight into stars' personal lives, including hobbies, favorite new fashion trends, and romantic exploits, making one's connection to a star more tangible and intense. The promotion of stars often paralleled the active roles they played on screen—that Pearl White and Irene Castle actually performed their own stunts, for example. Many of the women watching these films were not able to enact active stunts, so instead ready-made fashion and consumer items were sold as a way for audiences to enact the part of the American Girl, and, during wartime, to enact the part of the patriot.

Concomitant to the development of movie-going culture was the rise of the burgeoning star system. The star system featured larger-than-life women, often performing stunts that tested their bodies and emphasized the realism of the new medium.[26] At times these women were used in narratives of war to emphasize the heroic message above and beyond the text itself. The star was produced within a discursive field and did not emerge simply from the films themselves.[27] The rhetorical and representational development of star personas in this era is important to the study of patriotic or national-myth-building films because, in many instances, the promotion of the stars mirrored or complemented the character types they most often played. Newspaper articles throughout the 1910s told tales of heroic acts—exaggerated to varying degrees—undertaken by the female stars who so popularly demonstrated heroism on screen. Furthermore, both on- and off-screen star promotion regularly drew upon ideas about modern femininity, or—as in the case of films about war—the physical capabilities of these modern women.[28]

In this book, through an examination of dozens of films from this period, their promotion, and the discussion of them in the trade press, newspapers, and fan magazines, I argue that there is a distinct link between women, American national identity, and militarism from 1908 to 1919. The possibility of military women that this decade allowed for can be attributed to a number of factors: the not-yet-entrenched generic expectations of masculine war films; the dominance of the female movie-goer; and sociopolitical factors such as expansionist discourse, changes to American national myth, and changing roles for women in the public sphere. Examining the complex connections among gender, nation, and militarism offers an alternative reading to the history of war films as a male-centered genre. I suggest that we should rethink the definition of war films to include an understanding of the feminized period of the 1910s. American foreign policy was at a turning point. A stance of isolationism or neutrality in the face of the European war was giving way to an understanding of the nation as a major participant on the world stage. The predominance of female characters in films at crucial times during this era thus reinforced domestic-oriented politics of the era and how this focus on defense soon led to an era of mobilizing the nation to patriotism and wartime participation.

THE GENDERED DISCOURSE OF NATIONALISM AND MILITARISM

If this book were expanded to include the entire silent period, there would be a marked difference between the 1890s, 1910s, and 1920s. Specifically, the 1890s and 1920s produced more masculinist representations of war, whereas the period covered by this book saw an abundance of war films with active female protagonists. American representations of war are central in the mythmaking of a hegemonic form of "American" identity, both then and now. In particular, during a period of imperial expansionism and changing foreign relations, and during the Jim Crow era, mass cultural texts—such as film, nationally syndicated newspaper tie-ins, magazines, and dime novels—presented an America filled with white heroes and heroines. The discussion of white heroism in American popular culture at the turn of the century could be expanded to include stories of the American West, detectives, adventurers, and other proto-genres; however, in this book I am concerned with narratives about or set during war. This period, and this genre specifically, laid the groundwork for Civil War memorialization that valorized Southern generals and the "Southern Cause" by obscuring the relationship between the American Civil War and the institution of slavery. This discourse continues even today with debates about removing Confederate monuments and replacing them with memorials to the many enslaved people who lost their freedoms and their lives. Concomitant with debates about monuments are ongoing discussions about white women's complicity in current structures of white supremacy. To look back to the Civil War and other films of the 1910s shows us how entrenched this legacy is in American popular myth and memory.

The relationship between women and militarism is understudied but essential to understanding how war was represented in American culture during the 1910s. On the one hand, women who took up nationalist ideologies and promoted militarism could gain more equality through their wartime efforts—during the Civil War, the Spanish-American War, or World War I. The appropriation of these ideologies thus often helped them to claim citizenship; on the other hand, the process also reshaped the ideologies themselves. American militarism was not left untouched, and the representation of women in popular culture also shaped how people conceived of war itself.

The Progressive Era saw dramatic changes in American politics in relation to foreign policy and America's global presence. Frank Ninkovich demonstrates that the seeds for change existed throughout the latter half of the nineteenth century, as a form of "liberal internationalization."[29] While these years are primarily known for American isolationism, Ninkovich points out that viewing this period "culturally" reveals that certain segments of the population—the middle- and upper-classes—demonstrated a strong curiosity about the world beyond their borders, alongside self-fashioning projects.[30] During this time, the drive to define American national identity was of central importance in many journals and magazines.[31] In fact, Alan Trachtenberg argues that "America" itself was understood in contradictory ways in the post–Civil War era: "The antagonism that concerns me more than any other centers on the word 'America': a word whose meaning became the focus of controversy and struggle during an age in which the horrors of the Civil War remained vivid. In the eyes of those farmers, laborers, and radicals who joined the People's Party of the 1890s, America incorporated represented a misappropriation of the name. To the Republican Party, swept to victory in 1896 under William McKinley, it represented the exact fulfillment of the name."[32] Trachtenberg's work demonstrates that the turn-of-the-century image of America was up for debate, yet the country was moving toward an identity rooted in industrialized capitalism. This newly emerging, industrial conception of nation affected numerous institutions as well as American myths about heroism and militarism. Militarism became intertwined with industry and commerce both in the depictions of the military and in the promotion of patriotism through consumerism—such as the promotion of particular fashion choices for women during World War I. In short, the discourse of defining what it meant to be American was entangled with how American militarism was understood—and both, in turn, were embodied in the types of ideal men and women that were portrayed as representative of the American nation.

Late nineteenth-century conceptions of American national identity were distinctly masculine. Gail Bederman argues that the rhetoric of nation building during the early Progressive Era defined the American race as male: Like Mayne Reid's *Boy Hunters* and other Westerns, Theodore Roosevelt's *The Winning of the West* told a story of virile violence and interracial conflict. Yet while the hero of the traditional Western adventure was a *man* whose race was implicitly white, the hero of Roosevelt's story was a *race* whose gender was implicitly male.[33] Throughout this book, I demonstrate that conceptions of American national identity in the 1910s were distinctly feminine.

By the end of the first decade of the 1900s, women, too, were woven into the narrative of a nation built through heroic deeds and military battles. Even though Progressive Era representations of both genders remained largely white, women (at least) became increasingly visible in the public and political spheres, and they became integral to identifying and defining the American identity of the time. The turn of the century was marked by a masculinist discourse, but this gave way to a brief period in which women were central to defining traits of American identity such as militarism and patriotism.

In *The American Girl Goes to War*, I argue that the presentation of women as representative of a "domestic foreign policy" is key to understanding the symbolic use of women in relation to militarism. Drawing from Amy Kaplan's *The Anarchy of Empire in the Making of U.S. Culture*, I link the use of female characters to the shift in the 1890s of American national selfhood from one of domestic expansionism (the Frontier) to one involved in imperial efforts (the Spanish-American War).[34] Kaplan argues the rhetoric of nationhood was challenged because imperialism brought up a number of fears and anxieties about what constituted "home," and who were considered "citizens." Empire building in the 1890s was depicted as a demonstration of male strength in political rhetoric and cultural texts such as film and fiction. Nationhood, masculinity, and empire were all linked in this time period through rhetorical efforts, not because of any natural link between masculinity and the American nation. The nation was actively aligned with the male body in political speeches and popular accounts. The result was that the crisis of masculinity that came with the closing of the frontier was stabilized through empire-building efforts overseas. These efforts also reinvigorated both the nation and the nation's perceived masculinity. By extension, then, my examination of the period 1908–1919 demonstrates that national rhetoric returned to domestic matters—containing the borders, confronting immigration, and determining who were popularly represented as "American"—and, thus, used women as central characters.

Similar to Kaplan's work, but with a different category of analysis, Linda Frost calls her work in *Never One Nation* "a study of Americanness by othered proxy," arguing that the concept of what it means to be American varied widely throughout the nineteenth century, and from region to region, but has always meant whiteness, as defined by a racial other.[35] Like Frost, my book acknowledges that there is no one way to understand American identity. The prevailing whiteness found in the films discussed throughout this book is paired with the central female characters to demonstrate the way that white women serve nationalist, imperialist, and white supremacist aims.

The American Girl Goes to War is about how heroic women in films about war contributed to the shaping of the national myth during the 1910s. The nation's strength continued to be reconfirmed even as women stood in as the bodies through which those narratives were written. In her book about the military woman in British culture since World War II, Yvonne Tasker states: "Let me be clear here: though women's military service was evidently culturally troubling, I do not argue in this book that it is inherently transgressive or subversive. Though alive to the military woman's deployment as a sign of modernity, we should not romanticize or simply celebrate her. It is clear that to a large extent a place appears for military women as and when their labor is required. In our current historical context of open-ended war and ongoing military interventions, that labor has been integral to American assertions of military authority."[36] Indeed, like the military women Tasker analyzes, the girl spies, cross-dressing soldiers, and other female characters of the 1910s should not be overly celebrated. Instead we should continue to situate them within a set of ideological constructs and national myths they serve to uphold. And while American identity may not be inherently bad, the version of it that these films repeatedly presented most certainly was. The Civil War films celebrated the Southern Cause as often as not, glossing over slavery and presenting all Black characters as former enslaved people who remained loyal to the white characters. In short, these films contributed to a popular image of American identity as white and white alone, while supporting and justifying expansionism and the exploitation of enslaved people.

Scholarship on women and militarism has challenged assumptions about war as a masculine endeavor and women as the bearers of peace. In other words, these films demonstrate the tenuous link between men and militarism and women and peace. Matthew Evangelista thus states: "Women in general and mothers in particular are responsible for inculcating the key characteristics that define a cultural or ethnic identity, including such basics as language, religion, dress, and cuisine. Women serve as 'boundary markers' between different national, ethnic, and religious communities, and thus might be expected to play an important role when such communities come into violent conflict."[37] The women in the films addressed in this book demonstrate this idea of women as "boundary markers," particularly in their role in defining and defending the nation. Women throughout war films of the early 1910s embody a specific idea of American femininity and defend American values quite literally in the defense of their homes during battle. In relation to the representation of active and heroic women in films about war, even in the years leading up to World War I, we can approach this phenomenon as a more abstract result of women's changing role in relation to nationalism and militarism.

Not only was American nation-building important to American-born citizens, but, according to John Milton Cooper, recent immigrants at the turn of the century also sought the promised "freedom" of a country much different from "Europe's aristocratic, inegalitarian traditions."[38] In fact, this feeling remained even as World War I began in Europe: "To many Americans the conflict seemed to confirm age-old beliefs in a moral, political, and cultural dichotomy between a despotic, warlike Old World and a democratic, peaceful New World. When the Panama Canal opened in August 1914, the same month as the outbreak of World War I, the normally sober *New York Times* crowed editorially, 'The European ideal bears its full fruit of ruin and savagery just at the moment when the American ideal lays before the world a great work of peace, goodwill and fair play.'"[39] American identity, therefore, was defined by what it was not: it was not the "old" World. Tied to this definition is the idea that anyone can become American if they enact the values of the nation. Many of the films discussed in this study allowed for recent immigrants to embody American identities. This, however, was fraught by the underpinnings of white supremacy that informed the American identity: only white immigrants could ever look the part in a culture increasingly ruled by visual representations of identity.

ARCHIVAL RECONNAISSANCE: THE AMERICAN GIRL GOES TO WAR

In this book I analyze many examples of women embodying differing ideals of American national identity. Participation in war and the military remain at the forefront of these narratives, demonstrating that heroic women were, for a brief ten-year span, central to imagining war on film. There were myriad roles women played in films about war throughout the first decade of narrative film in the United States. I have structured this book in a roughly chronological manner, with chapters focused on groupings of films about the same wars or same political issues. The use of women in war films changed throughout the 1910s in part because of the American entry into World War I and in part because of changing audience tastes. I seek to complicate current histories of the war genre—or more broadly, war in film—by expanding the types of films analyzed.

The films that I discuss throughout this book are mostly lost. Rather than textual analysis of films, I supplemented viewing films with reading synopses in the trade press—no small feat when the list of films to work from was nonexistent from the start. First I consulted filmographies, bibliographies, and encyclopedias that were already in print, the most important for my project being *Encyclopedia of American War Films* by Larry Langman and Ed Borg; Paul Spehr's *The Civil War in Motion Pictures: A Bibliography of Films Produced in the United States since 1897*; Kemp Niver's *Early Motion Pictures: The Paper Print Collection at the Library of Congress*; and Frank J. Wetta and Stephen J. Curley, *Celluloid Wars: A Guide to Film and the American Experience of War*. From these sources, I generated a list of films about war (many of which are lost). The titles of all of these films can be found in appendixes 1 (films about the American Civil War) and 2 (films about World War I), and an additional filmography of films about other wars. In researching for this book, I watched approximately forty films at the Library of Congress, sections of *Patria* (see chapter 4) at the Museum of Modern Art, *Joan the Woman* (DeMille, 1916) and *Arms and the Girl* (Kaufman, 1917) at George Eastman House, and a number of films that are available digitally. Finally, exhibitor trade journals (*Moving Picture World, Motion Picture News, Motography, Film Daily*), fan magazines (*Photoplay*), newspapers, copyright records, and the American Film Institute online catalogue helped to fill in the gaps and to paint a picture of war films during the 1910s. When possible, I have included plot summaries to bring back to life these forgotten films, many of which no longer exist. The use of evidence in trade journals is meant, not to prove these films' popularity, but instead to demonstrate the discourse surrounding their promotion and the frames through which these character types might have been understood at the time.[40]

Although this book begins after the American film industry had embraced narrative film, the historical precedent of women in popular representations of war reaches back further with the dime novels and popular fiction about adventurous American women. Cross-dressing women soldiers, "girl spies," and women actively defending their homes against enemy soldiers were widely accepted in film because they had a longer history in popular print and theater. Chapter 1 defines and demonstrates the use of the term "American Girl" at the turn of the century and into the 1910s. From newspaper stories to film advertisements, books, and popular art, the term was a frequently used phrase to invoke a particular woman. Chapters 2 and 3 focus on "wars fought at home"—predominantly films about the Civil War, but also films about the American Revolutionary War, battles with Native Americans, and the border wars with Mexico. The films analyzed in these chapters served two roles: first, to link growing female independence back to domestic duties—in this case, defense of one's home—and to revise and reconfirm the concept of the American nation for the Progressive Era. These films, however, are notable not only for their dominance of female heroines but also for their contributions to the erasure of any race other than white from constructions of American identity. This reflects an effort to subsume American femininity into the ideologies of American exceptionalism and notions of America as a white nation. This is most evident in the near-absence of Black characters in the films about the Civil War in chapter 2. Chapter 3, which begins with an in-depth analysis of American Revolutionary War films, shows how film contributed to the representation of American national ideologies and identities that were focused heavily on defining who was considered American and what positive traits they possessed. The conclusion of chapter 3 turns from American subjects to films about war at home in other nations, including the Balkan conflicts and *Joan the Woman*, about Joan of Arc in France. This section of the chapter demonstrates how the figure of woman as both defender of home and home itself was transposed across national boundaries, ending with border-conflict films about the revolution in Mexico. In short, this corpus of films is about nation building and imperialism, and the presence of female characters is evidence of white women's role within the representational building of the American national myth.

Chapter 4 shows a shift in emphasis that took place between 1914 and early 1917. These films are best described as the "preparedness" films, as they focused on a common debate at the time: peace versus military preparedness. As the war continued in Europe, American politicians, newspapers, and citizens debated whether to prepare the army for war or maintain an isolationist stance in world politics. Women in the films about preparedness frequently play the role of peace-at-any-cost advocates. Even though the films have different messages— for instance, Ince's *Civilization* is pro-peace, whereas Lubin's *The Nation's Peril* is pro-preparedness—the female characters argue for their nations to remain at peace. In pro-preparedness features, the women suffer because the nation was unprepared for war and invasion. Thus, this chapter demonstrates the various ways women were used symbolically in the debates that surrounded military preparedness. These films, regardless of their stance, continued to circulate for exhibition after the United States entered the war. Chapter 4 concludes by discussing how the promotion and exhibition of the films changed to encourage enlistment and to promote patriotism. Women as symbols of bravery and devotion to one's country remained central in the advertising that accompanied these changes.

Chapter 5 concerns film serials that also take up the question of preparedness. *Patria*, *The Secret of the Submarine*, *Liberty*, and *Pearl of the Army* all promote the need for a strong army to protect the United States against foreign invasion. The preparedness serials functioned to extend the patriotic participation of the on-screen heroines to a continuing patriotism of women in the audience. Serial narratives resist closure even though the texts themselves cannot continue indefinitely. Although these serials were only eleven to thirteen episodes each, the writers and producers manage to end the text-as-product without closing the narrative off completely. As a result, the lack of narrative conclusion is used to inspire patriotism and acceptable forms of participation by members of the audience. It was not simply the lack of narrative closure inherent in serialized media but, also, the intermedial nature of serial texts that included films, newspaper tie-ins, and star promotion in fan and fashion magazines.

Chapter 6 discusses wartime films featuring women, making connections to the earlier categories of films discussed throughout the book. The women characters in films made during and just after World War I are fundamentally different from the type of home-front women in World War II–era war films—and in order to understand the history of the war genre, we must revise our understanding of representations of wartime women to include the women of World War I. This chapter demonstrates that patriotic films of the early World War I era focused on female characters and female heroism as a result of the particular history of popular American film subjects and imagined audiences. Women in films during the World War I era uniquely invoke traces of the earlier action heroines discussed in earlier chapters. Rather than staying home and performing wartime service in industry (like World War II's Rosie the Riveter), the women film characters of the early World War I era were meant to inspire participation in the war effort—namely, recruitment—by doing it themselves.

Finally, in the conclusion I argue that the 1910s offers us a unique period during which war films were as much about women's participation as they were about men's participation. Beginning with films that were produced toward the end of World War I and throughout the 1920s, the masculinized combat films began to resemble the war film genre that would dominate the remainder of the century.

However, the first decade after the rise of narrative filmmaking in American cinema offers us a different vision of war in film. During this decade, entertainment cinema was often pitched at middle-class, white female audiences. As a result, many films narrativize the ideologies of nation and militarism through white, female characters. This book weaves together previous scholarship on women and silent film, the war genre, and American politics of the 1910s to contextualize and analyze the predominance of heroic American women in war films from 1908 to 1918.

1 · AMERICAN GIRLS AND NATIONAL IDENTITY

Our American Girl on the screen should spring from our social life, her spirit our spirit, her courage, her self-reliance, her independence of thought, her contempt for hypocrisy, her ability to take care of herself under trying conditions, that of the American people. It is our business to know her as she is and as she is at her best. It is our business to discover her traits, those of coming generations, and to place them on the screen as revelations of what is fine in our national life.[1]

This excerpt appeared in *Moving Picture World* in 1916 as part of an article in which Louis Reeves Harrison critiqued the overuse of formulaic heroines in serials and other action-driven films. In other words, the heroines at the center of this book. Harrison's critique, however, reveals that, whether he liked them or not, female characters on screen were a powerful form of representation of American women. These women on screen functioned as markers of a particular form of, not just American femininity, but American identity as well. Harrison lamented the lack of depth to female characters in American film, for, as he argued, the American Girl is every bit as much a part of defining national identity as is her male counterpart. In other words, the American Girl should be given her due, according to Harrison, and presumably roles of a more realistic nature. Harrison was likely not a fan of the films studied throughout this book; but he is correct in his assertion that the mythmaking of national identity in popular culture is as much about how a nation's women are represented as it is about representations of men.

What was the American Girl, though? Harrison, although powerful in his role of film criticism and film writing, was only one person, with one opinion on the concept. But what did the American Girl mean across film, print, and theater—more generally across popular culture—in the early part of the twentieth century? The American Girl was created through a tapestry of films, stories, newspaper articles, commodities, illustrations, and advertisements beginning in the late nineteenth century. For example, in 1906 a book entitled *The American Girl* was published by the well-known illustrator and artist Howard Chandler Christy.[2] Christy had become famous with illustrations made during the Spanish-American War, including a portrait of Theodore Roosevelt. This book, however, highlighted the type of woman Christy would become known for: the "Christy Girl" or the American Girl. His book is not just a series of illustrations, however; it also includes a prologue celebrating and defining the qualities that set the American Girl apart from other women. In it, the history of American women is laid out:

> If there has been a fault, it has been an excess of indulgence. She has been the petted child, the protégée, the loved partner, the trusted chum, of the men who have carved her nation out of the raw material. With them she has stood shoulder to shoulder in subduing the wilderness; hand in hand with them she has blazed her way through the forests; alternately with them she has stood on guard against their savage foes; she has even borne, by the aid of her superb physique, a nearly equal share in their Titanic labor of carrying forward into the wilds the standard of civilization.[3]

Though the next line states that this is not "the American girl of to-day," it follows that "there runs within her veins the blood of these mothers of her race."[4] While the many iterations of the American Girl were varied, in popular representations of war—particularly the United States' historical wars—she embodied the above description, standing shoulder to shoulder with the men who "built" the country. Of course, this should be read as an imagined history, which mythologized particular ideologies, celebrating white men and women as the makers of and natural heirs to the country. It was strategic, then, to repeatedly use the white woman to represent "America" at the turn of the century—when immigration continued to rise; segregation continued, and continued to be contested, throughout the South; the boundaries and borders of the United States remained in flux, with continuing imperial expansion; and Native American populations remained an invisible presence. Each of these represents a perceived threat to the hegemonic dominance of white supremacy throughout the United States. While the immigration of white Europeans could, theoretically, be enfolded into U.S. culture through "Americanization," the difference of race within American identity was met with anxiety in many dominant media.

The American Girl was never just one thing. This book might seem to provide an image of American womanhood with stable boundaries and precise meanings, but it was never quite so simple. In his dissertation on the American Girl, David Jeremiah Slater demonstrates that a broad study of art, literature, and popular culture at the turn of the century provides competing images: those that "reproduce and reify dominant ideologies" and others that "aim to undermine them."[5] The consistency of what the American Girl means in representations of war would break apart if more subjects and more media were examined. In films about war, the American Girl—young white women like Blanche Sweet, Pearl White, Mary Pickford, Vivien Martin, and Billie Burke, to name a few—was a dual symbol. She was both a heroine defending the home and the reason the home needed defending. She was at once a strong and capable figure who was also in need of protection. The white purity of dominant American identity that was under perceived threat was played out in the embodiment of the American Girl. Advertisements for films, despite the narratives, featured these stars and heroines, often as the central image. The American Girl was meant as both an ideal of American womanhood and an ideal worth defending.

THE AMERICAN GIRL IN POPULAR CULTURE

While active heroines were indicative of larger trends taking place in the film industry from 1908 to 1919, it is also useful to understand how these women functioned as larger cultural phenomena. Particularly, I am interested in the way the traits of the independent, strong-willed, athletic woman were channeled into nationalistic and militaristic ideologies in a period marked by the United States' changing role in world politics. First and foremost, film—as it burgeoned into a medium with a mass audience—presented narratives of national identity. Film drew from other popular media, most centrally popular theater and cheap fiction, but it also had connections to the fashion and music industries, allowing it to reach mass audiences. In particular, audiences throughout the decade were varied: white middle-class patrons and immigrant working-class patrons were reached to differing degrees. For immigrant cinema-goers, film was a form of entertainment that could be enjoyed despite language barriers. It also played a distinct role in demonstrating American culture to those only newly arrived.

Film, and the other popular entertainment forms to which it was related, presented and re-presented over and over ideals at the intersection of American identity and modern femininity. Scholars have used the term "the New Woman" to describe a particular type of femininity understood at the turn of the century, which was reflected in character types such as the serial queen.[6] As such, it is important to distinguish the American Girl from her counterpart, the New Woman. Viv Gardner demonstrates that although the New Woman drew upon real-life muses, in many ways she was more the creation of the press, which used the term in predominantly derogatory ways.[7] Furthermore, Jill Davis has highlighted the creation and proliferation of the New Woman in "New Drama" of the era, which she claims was an attempt by men to "deny those aspects of feminism which offered potential disruption to gender relations as a power system which privileges masculinity." Put another way, "the New Woman was made, in the New Drama, to 'speak her master's voice.'"[8] She was financially independent, educated, dressed in masculine attire, smoked, and ventured alone into the modern streets of the city.[9]

In contrast, the American Girl that Harrison identifies in 1916 had long been a figure within American popular culture—from the Civil War girl spies, to David Belasco's "Girl of the Golden West," and numerous dime novel heroines. As Leslie Ferris demonstrates, the American conception of femininity was quite different from that in other national contexts, particularly the UK, due in large part to the centrality of the frontier in American mythology; the frontier myth supposed that women's abilities in the "wilderness" were necessary for survival.[10] And in fact, women of the Western Territories won the vote much earlier than their Eastern counterparts, while as a whole the United States granted enfranchisement to women in 1920.

The "Golden Girl," introduced in a 1905 play, offered audiences the chance to see womanhood depicted in a particularly American context.[11] Belasco's "Girl" works in the Wild West in a predominantly male environment, yet maintains her "honor" throughout the play and is ultimately married and leaves the male-dominated sphere.[12] For Ferris, the American version of the New Woman was heavily influenced by the frontier and other such American myths, which resulted in a character type much different from Britain's New Woman. The key issue for our purposes, though, is that these traits were often attributed to the frontier woman's girlhood, which ultimately terminated in marriage, when she returned to a traditional, domestic form of femininity.

Like Howard Chandler Christy's description of the American Girl, this suggests that she was allowed considerable more leeway in pushing the gender boundaries prior to marriage or during an adolescent phase. However, the term "American Girl" was applied just as readily to married women too, as we see in the quotation that opens this chapter. While the term "girl" arguably indicates an infantilization of the subject, even in such celebratory pieces as "In Defense of the American Girl," it is equally likely that she was so-named in direct opposition to the "cult of motherhood" that dominated the mid-nineteenth century.[13] The term "girl" suggested a transitional period from childhood to adulthood, when adolescence allowed for a degree of independence before entry into the expected role of wife and mother in adulthood. Thus, the American Girl was controllable and acceptable, particularly when her independent and daring nature was directed toward American defense.

The American Girl was as intricately tied to the military and expansionist American identity of the times as any male character-type. In fact, it is her connection to nationalist ideologies that affords her such freedoms in displaying traits of athleticism, independence, bravery, and heroism. Likewise, an understanding of American militarism in progressive era films cannot be complete without interrogating and acknowledging the place of the American Girl. This is not to say that the American Girl must necessarily be a military figure; rather, it is to argue that the narratives of war, which were popular in the 1910s, emphasize the importance of military heritage in the construction of each American Girl's identity. These women act impulsively, independently, and publicly—all traits that were deemed negative in the New Woman but that were used to serve the purpose of American military efforts and national defense by the American Girl.

Belasco's play, Harrison's "Our American Girl," and Christy's *The American Girl* are just a handful of the many iterations of the American Girl that existed at the turn of the century and that reflect a connection to, but also a marked difference from, the New Woman. In American history, women also demonstrated their value as citizens through their efforts during the American Civil War, but also entered into public life through women's groups concerned with "purity, uplift, control, and reform."[14] Women's suffrage began in the United States in 1848, and numerous Western states had granted women the right to vote by 1914; by 1920 the Nineteenth Amendment was ratified, giving women throughout the country the right to vote.[15] The independence of women threatened upheaval of social norms, but women's entry into the political and public realms also made women a central part of wartime efforts and their promotion.

This term, of course, should be approached with caution, because the American Girl as imagined in this period was specifically white and middle to upper class. It is not surprising, then, that war films starring women proliferated at a time when what it meant to be American and what it meant to be a woman were in flux. During this period, border wars, ongoing battles with Indigenous people, expansionism and territory acquisitions, immigration, and Jim Crow laws necessitated both political discussions and cultural representations of national identity. Due to increased immigration, the idea of who was considered an American citizen was in flux, yet the cultural construction of nation and national identity remained ruled by white supremacy. Numerous examples in newspapers, film, and consumer products provide evidence that the term "American Girl" circulated throughout the 1890s and the first decades of the twentieth century. In many of these examples, the American Girl was explicitly or implicitly understood to be a white woman.

In November 1906 the *San Francisco Call* published an article entitled "In Defense of the American Girl," which was actually dedicated to discussing at length the perceived differences between husbands and wives in the United States and in Britain. Accompanying the article were two Punch cartoons—"The American Husband" and "The English Wife"—which lampooned the loss of powerful masculinity in the American husband, who was reduced to carrying his wife's clubs as she golfed boldly. The article, as the title implies, came to the defense of the American Girl and the American man—demonstrating that the dominant traits of one gender were reliant on those of the other in this heteronormative conception of the world. Indeed, the strength, athleticism, and independent nature of the American Girl could be fully appreciated, according to this article and numerous others from the same period, only by the American man, who was no less "masculine" for supporting such a woman. The author writes, "But the other girls, you'll find—girls who become the women of a nation, proud of their American birth and heritage—are, in nine cases out of ten, wives of Americans, strong, progressive specimens of manhood, who have made Uncle Sam one of the leading powers of the universe and Columbia the most courted and fascinating lady in the world—if I say so myself, who, perhaps, should not!"[16] The article concludes, "The American woman is most appreciated and best understood by the American man—who has made her what she is today and will be in days to come."[17] Of course, this was only one opinion among many in the debate over changes to feminine—and masculine—behaviors and roles.

Defining the American Girl through a variety of newspaper articles, popular fiction, film and other media was not only a method for establishing a certain ideal of womanhood within the United States; it also reflected the growing sense of what America was within the global sphere. In short, the turn of the century witnessed a curious trend of seeking to define womanhood in a distinctly American way, precisely because of anxiety about America's increasingly global role.

This study examines major character types as they appear in films about war by arguing that they are representative of gender ideals and tied to nationalist discourse during the first decades of the twentieth century. For example, in 1905 a newspaper article contained a quote that illuminates the way in which normative American womanhood was then conceived, by relating an amusing anecdote involving Theodore Roosevelt's female cousin. Maude Roosevelt was in Berlin when two American women were trying to open an American-style soda shop there. They were repeatedly told they could not open until they received the proper business permits; each time a permit was secured, they learned another was still needed. Roosevelt, according to the article, went to the permit office and demanded the shop be allowed to open: "But it is the spirit of Bunker Hill, Sumter, and Gettysburg handed down from a generation of fighting ancestors and evidenced in her daring eyes and dauntless chin that has caused one American girl, Miss Maude Roosevelt Le Vinson, to don shield and buckler and go forth as valiantly as any Crusader of old to give battle for liberty and—soda."[18] The article is at once empowering in its depiction of Miss Maude Roosevelt Le Vinson as independent, brazen, and aggressive, and at the same time belittling, as it attenuates the military comparison by making light of the object of battle—namely, soda. The active and valiant American Girls were depicted as using their power for newly defined feminine concerns, such as consumer goods.

In an article from 1892, printed more than a decade before Roosevelt's battle for soda took place, another author asked: "Is the American girl not enough a girl or is she too much of a girl?" The answer was complex, and involved explaining how the American Girl had been birthed by the American nation:

It is certainly true that the American girl accepts, in fact, assumes responsibilities that no other girl in the world would dream of doing, and the consequence is that she sometimes appears lacking in that modest humility and timid appeal to her elders which is one of the charms of certain other girls: foreigners, in fact, are apt to mistake her calm self assertion for boldness and want of self respect, and acting upon this mistake they sometimes meet with rebuffs so startling that they rush into another mistake and set down the American girl as a shrewd, a sharp tongued and sharp tempered vixen, and please themselves by saying that no man in his senses would ever venture to marry her.

And yet how could we wish this freedom of action and speech or this capacity for self defense and aggressive warfare less, when we consider that these very traits are the foundation of American character, and that these very girls are to become the mothers of the men of the future?[19]

The argument is that the American Girl is what she is because she is American. Defining femininity at the turn of the century was not just about defining traits of womanhood; more importantly, it was about defining what it meant to be American—the military past, the independent and self-made qualities, the urban present, and the conquered frontier. All of these things, which we often attribute to masculine endeavors, were at this point being used to define American womanhood. The American Girl had, according to the numerous iterations in popular culture, the "capacity for self defense and aggressive warfare," and, as is seen in numerous films throughout film's first decades, she was not averse to using them.

In addition to defining the American Girl in relation to qualities of self-defense, boldness, quick wit, and opinionated nature, her beauty was also a topic of great interest. In fact, the quest to define "The Perfect American Woman" was under way. Another article states, "In all the years of our national existence, no one has ever made a systematic search for the standard American girl—the girl perfect in symmetry." According to this article, in order to catalogue the features of the American Girl, a survey of physical characteristics was to be distributed to active American women in order to finally categorize perfect physical attributes.[20] The article focused on the athleticism of the American woman's build, rather on aesthetic beauty, although this was implied in the project. Notably, all visual depictions of the American Girl that accompanied these articles were of white women.

Others similarly defended the American Girl ideal, and in 1895 one newspaper published a graduation speech by a woman named Maude M. Fowler. The speech was primarily concerned with promoting the education of young, American women, but in so doing, it celebrated the traits common to the "American Girl." First, Fowler acknowledged the vast expanse of the nation and the resultant variety of girl-types—the New York girl, the Southern girl, the Western girl, the New England girl, and so on—but she ultimately settled on a discussion of what these women had in common. For Fowler, the American Girl was "of good health, because she takes plenty of exercise and delights in the out door air," "the desire to be beautiful is a marked feature of every American girl," she "has a desire and an ambition to push out into business," and "to be independent and self-supporting," and she "has her opinions—decided ones—and is ready at all times to express them . . . for she has always read the newspapers and all the new books."[21] Certainly Fowler's designation of the American Girl as opinionated, well-read, and self-supporting is a result of the context of her speech—delivered at a graduation—but her list (combined with the above-mentioned characteristics) also described the dominant female character type in early narrative films: the American Girl. Such a woman was headstrong, smart, beautiful (even when wearing male clothing), prepared for self-defense, self-supporting, athletic, and most importantly, an integral part of the American nation.

Important in this discussion is a distinction between national identity and identity as citizens, both of which are at play in representations of American women in the cultural landscape of the 1910s. Perhaps a useful concept for understanding the urgency of defining American womanhood during this period is that of citizenship. Ruth Lister describes citizenship as a "contested and contextualized concept," suggesting at its most basic level that it is "membership in a community (itself a contested concept)," or, more difficult to define, that it is associated with "rights" and "obligations" such as "a practice of civic virtue and participation in the polis."[22] Lister is primarily interested in citizenship as a gendered concept, most often represented as its ideal—the (white) male citizen. Women were fighting for the right to vote—in some states they had already achieved this right—and were vocal on civic issues, with a variety of active women's groups springing up throughout the nation. In part the swell in cultural texts that helped to define American womanhood with the concept of the American Girl were reactions to women's changing relationship to citizenship. However, this was also a period during which the nation and national identity were also in flux. Nira Yuval-Davis's essay "Gender and Nation" articulates a need for more systematic analysis of gender in relation to nationalism.[23] Yuval-Davis reminds us that women are "'hidden' in various theorizations of the nationalist phenomena" despite being those who "reproduce nations—biologically, culturally, and intellectually."[24] *The American Girl Goes to War* considers the female characters of early, narrative war films as citizens and reproducers of a particular concept of the American nation.

2 · FIGHTING FEMININITY ON HOME SOIL IN CIVIL WAR FILMS, 1908–1916

From 1908 to 1916 there were more than 300 films made about the American Civil War.[1] Many of those films featured dominant female protagonists defending their homes and homeland as war raged around them. This chapter examines what these characters, inspired by the real women of the Civil War, signified for audiences of the early twentieth century. These films were released during peacetime in the United States, and so, unlike in the more propagandistic films released during World War I, the militaristic ideologies were not about mobilizing a population for wartime effort and military support. Instead they belonged to a tapestry of cultural texts that reaffirmed the American identity—both male and female—with concepts of strength and virtue, ascribed to the white characters that filled the nation's movie screens. These American Civil War films simultaneously performed multiple cultural functions, none of which should be considered separate from the others: First, subsuming white women into American militaristic ideologies that grew out of the expansionist efforts of the late 1890s and early 1910s. Second, these films actively erased Black experiences and Black history from the Civil War memorialization at play. Finally, by extension of the last point, these films were part of a larger cultural push to rewrite the Civil War—as has been discussed by numerous scholars of post–Civil War memorialization and commemoration—and to reimagine the "causes" in popular memory. We should not underestimate the importance of the Civil War in public memory of the period, because the memorialization of the Civil War during this period was seen not only in the numerous monuments erected at the time but also in films, stories, and other elements of popular culture. The majority of the war films made during the period 1908–1915 take the Civil War as their subject, in part because that war functions mythically as the "birth" of the American nation: two sides of the same nation fighting against each other and finally emerging as a unified country.

So many of these female heroines were from the South, steadfastly in support of the Confederate Army. Here, white womanhood was used to soften the image of the Confederacy. These women were meant to be seen as sympathetic, even heroic, figures. Their femininity, fragility, and near-victimhood at the hands of the Union Army—they were, of course, only protecting their homes—is meant to distract from the war's purpose: from the Union side, it was to eliminate slavery and to free enslaved people. In these films, slavery is a shadow that is never the focus, a presence that remains hidden behind hoop skirts and crinoline.

Women were dominant in war films of this period not because they were supposed to maintain the home but because the *homeland* needed maintaining. Historically, women are often symbolically connected to domestic spaces. With a war that was "fought at home," such as the Civil War, the inclusion of female heroics is, in part, due to the domestic nature of the war. We should not, though, simply read these films as narratives about women at home. American foreign policy at the time was all about domestic defense and defending borders, and these issues were translated into film. In other words, U.S. history was one of expansion and imperialism, but represented as defense of the country's borders. Women featured well in the representational gymnastics of valorizing defense and victimhood while downplaying militaristic expansion. Additionally, though, the 1910s were a time when women were entering into politics and the public sphere, and therefore representing women as integral to the birth of the nation—in their frequent heroic roles in the Civil War films—was also a key use of popular film.

The female characters in the Civil War films of the early 1910s were depicted either as the moral center of the family unit or as the brave, heroic counterparts of cowardly men. The dominant American identity of the day was aligned with the militaristic endeavors that filled the latter half of the nineteenth century, and women's new place as citizens meant that they could be either excluded from or incorporated into the concept of American identity by enacting the martial spirit. These women demonstrated that the American woman was vital to America as a whole, even if she occasionally transgressed certain gender roles, so long as she did so for the defense of the country and home. The military woman of the Civil War films was not the New Woman emerging in a different national context—instead she was the American Girl, whose military heritage informed her active nature. This American Girl was consistently defined through dominant, white, American national myths like the conquest of the West, the Civil War, and the Revolutionary War victory over Britain. White American femininity, then, was strongly connected to the Civil War past because this allowed early twentieth-century American militarism to include the participation of both white men and women.

Women in these films function as moral and virtuous figures. The focus on defending the home and maintaining borders was not just geographical but also was about maintaining a clear idea of who was in the center of American identity and who was pushed to the margins—or even pushed out altogether. Of the more than 300 films about the war, most of the films are about white families and white romance. The sheer number of films about the Civil War, and their popularity in this period, suggests that they were extremely important in the cultural memorialization of the war during the 1910s.[2] The valorization of white womanhood cannot be understood without acknowledging the concomitant erasure of Black history. Very few feature Black characters are present in these films; those that are present are primarily the loyal, formerly enslaved persons who remain in the family home during the war. According to Thomas Cripps, the formula of Civil War films, dating back to *Birth of a Nation*, was to "structure out" the presence of Black Americans in the narratives.[3] The Civil War films of the early 1910s demonstrate a similar "structuring out" of the Black presence by promoting the idea that the American national identity revolved around the white family unit. The centering of white women in the national mythos was intertwined with the marginalization of Black experience and the legacy of slavery.[4]

These films were released at a time when American femininity was also in flux. They functioned to subsume the possible subversive traits of changing femininity into American ideals that served solidifying white supremacy in the myths of nation. The heroic traits of the American girl were replayed over and over in these films through the narrative of awakening independence and martial spirit, but incorporating these characteristics into a tamed and containable version of femininity. Female characters not only encouraged their male counterparts to perform heroic deeds; they also performed the deeds themselves when the men failed to do so. Therefore, women were not only keepers of the home front; because the battlefield was potentially close to home during the Civil War, they were also *participants* in the war. As such, women were frequently integral to the plots of these war films. The two main ways women proved active and heroic in these films were through harboring or protecting a soldier or actively participating in the war, by delivering secret messages, crossing enemy lines, or holding back incoming forces at gunpoint.[5] In these films, female protagonists often fought for the South, defending and preserving the ideals that upheld slavery. White women in these films were not just complicit in white supremacy— they were active in the fight to maintain it.

WOMEN IN THE CIVIL WAR: FACT AND FICTION

Two complementary influences led to the trend of strong female protagonists in many of the Civil War films of this period—the popular reimagining of history and women's places in history, and the growing efforts of the film industry to encourage the growth in female audiences. Although not all of the Civil War films featured female heroines, the number is significant enough to warrant

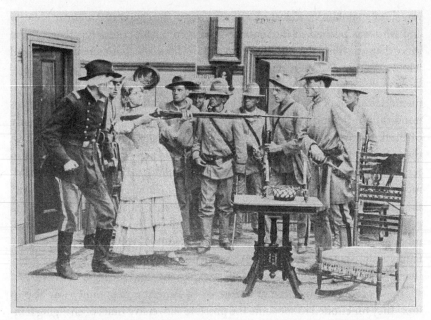

FIGURE 1. *A Daughter of Dixie* (Champion), in *Motion Picture News*, August 19, 1911, 11. (Courtesy of Media History Digital Library.)

further analysis; at least a third of all Civil War films featured a female protagonist, and it is likely that a third were about both man and women fighting or spying together (or as enemies). It was popularly known that women did, in reality, disguise their sex and dress as soldiers to fight during the Civil War, because the stories of such women appeared frequently in newspapers and memoirs after the war and even into the early 1900s. It follows, then, that these real and fascinating women would prove a popular subject for an entertainment industry intent on encouraging female audiences.

The films themselves were fictional but drew from an intense fascination with the real-life women who fought in the Civil War. Popularity aside, these women of war served another function: to tame the New Woman and make her into the American Girl, whose strength of character and daring ways were integral to the American nation. In sum, in an era when new roles for women—as workers outside of the home, as participants in politics and social reform, and as members of the public sphere—threatened the status quo, a specifically American femininity emerged in filmic representations. These characters were women whose active natures and athleticism served to maintain and defend the domestic space.

The female soldier who fought in the Civil War had long been a popular trope in fiction, song, film, and other popular entertainment forms precisely because women themselves were active participants in the wars. A number of scholarly texts have been written about women's participation in the Civil War.[6] These examples suggest that the female participants of war were likely a point of fascination for audiences in the 1910s precisely because they were well known. Real female cross-dressing soldiers in the Civil War were adapted into a myth of the past—they depicted not only a historical reality, but also a contemporaneous ideal of womanhood, one that in film's transitional period came to represent a specific type of American femininity. The reasons for women's participation in real Civil War battles varied: some wives joined their husbands in the camps, while others enlisted for patriotic reasons, and others still donned uniforms precisely because male attire and the war allowed for a mobility otherwise unavailable to women at the time.

Alice Fahs states that popular literature, during and after the war, shifted from focusing on female contributions to the war, to depicting events that privileged male heroics.[7] Fahs suggests that a significant percentage of literature about the Civil War, written directly following the war, focused on women's participation. Thus, she argues, the shift in understanding the Civil War as a man's event and "fought" only in the battlefields—and only by men—developed years later during the 1880s and 1890s. The years during and immediately following the Civil War included women—mothers, sweethearts, active heroines, girl-spies, and cross-dressing soldiers—in the wartime experience and the national identity. It is no surprise, then, that this focus on women in war should return—not wholly unique to the 1910s but reflecting the shifts and the changes in attitudes toward women in war that had happened in previous decades and continues to shift and change. In other words, the re-emergence of a "feminized" Civil War, during the Civil War film cycle, has more to do with the use of history for contemporary ideologies than with the history itself.

In these films, American national identity not only included women, it was shaped and defined by the traits represented in cultural texts featuring American women. In part this was because the Civil War was a defining moment in the mythos of the American nation. It signified the second birth of the nation, or even, for some, the "real" birth, because it represented the unifying of both North and South, or the moment when the nation became whole.[8] Jenny Barrett's book *Shooting the Civil War* offers a framework for understanding the importance of films about the Civil War in shaping American national identity. She argues that understanding the genre of Civil War films helps us to understand and "to question what is being 'said' about America as a nation, and so not to judge or read them according to an external referent (the war itself). . . . What the structure of the genre reveals here, through textual analysis, are ideologies of American national identity found in their representations of the American ancestor."[9] I adopt a similar understanding of films about war as representative of national identity at the time of their release rather than as texts that depict historical truths. Films about the Civil War, released prior to American entry into

World War I, tell a particular story of gender and the cultural drive to define American national identity in terms of whiteness.

The Civil War, as a subject, provided a stage on which to depict active, yet modest, vulnerable and family-oriented women, not only because female soldiers, spies, and other wartime women were a historical reality, but because they stood for American women defending the home. The Civil War was representative not just of militaristic ideals, but of *domestic* militarism and a war fought on the "home front."

In short, in the memorialization of the Civil War in the 1900s and 1910s, women were central to the mythic representation of domestic militarism. Gary W. Gallagher delineates four main categories of representing the Civil War in popular culture: "the Lost Cause," which valorized the South; "The Union Cause," which tended to see the North as focused on maintaining the country's unity; "the Emancipation Cause," focusing on the liberation of slaves; and "the Reconciliation Cause," which "represented an attempt by white people North and South to extol the *American* virtues both sides manifested during the war."[10] The films discussed in this chapter most often exemplify the "the Reconciliation Cause," by depicting the heroism of white Americans—North and South. Often central to these stories were romantic pairings across enemy lines, with the white woman functioning as a narrative device of union.

Arguably the war genre proper did not yet exist at this time; instead I want to emphasize that these films were domestic melodramas and to posit a link between domesticity and domestic militarism. Melodrama has its roots in eighteenth- and nineteenth-century theater and, according to scholars, is reflective of an American mythos that was central to the Civil War films from 1908 to 1916. Daniel Gerould argues that melodrama represents "American society and national character."[11] In contrast, Jeffrey Mason states that melodrama was a genre through which Americans performed America to themselves, in popular nineteenth-century theater.[12] Simplistic binaries are common in melodrama: "male and female, East and West, civilization and wilderness, and, most typically, good and evil."[13] This simplicity provided audiences with narratives that defined good and evil, pitting them against each other in sensational action. The Civil War films were more naturalistic than traditional melodrama; battle scenes were often filmed outside, and attention was given to the spectacle of battle. What does connect the Civil War films to sensational melodrama, though, is the relationship to the home and the virtues of domesticity, which was a central aspect of the films from this era.

Themes prevalent in traditional domestic melodrama include threats to the home and the ultimate victory of virtue over evil. Mason argues:

Virtue is defined in domestic terms—the family is sacred, women are canonized as mothers, and children are so innocent and pure as to be virtually saintly. The responsible man works hard (and enjoys his labor) in order to provide for his wife and children, who depend upon him for their livelihood and protection. The virtuous woman remains loyal to her husband in spite of any temptation or assault, so her chastity—sexual exclusivity, really—becomes not only an assurance that her children are her husband's rightful heirs but also a badge of her commitment. Her marriage is, precisely, a sacrament, and she becomes both the defender of sentiment and its paragon.[14]

Civil War films thus map the domesticity of the home onto the homeland; the American nation was envisioned as an extended household. This accounts for the prevalence of female participants in battle because they were equally important in defending the unity of family/nation.

The remainder of this chapter explores the common trends among these films: the moral guiding mothers, the linkages between past and present through the family unit, the active women who maintained feminine attire throughout their daring adventures, and the cross-dressing girl soldiers.[15] Examining the female character types across a large selection of films from multiple studios demonstrates the narrative function of women in the Civil War as national myth. A later section of this chapter will focus on one studio, Kalem, to emphasize the importance of the Civil War film in popular culture at the time. Finally, this chapter will also include an examination of the film *Her Father's Son* (1916), which reveals that by 1916 the cross-dressing, active heroine was no longer heroic, but had become comedic instead.

MORAL MOTHERS: THE CENTER OF THE NATION

Mothers played a key role as the moral center in films about the Civil War, including *Abraham Lincoln's Clemency* (Pathé American Co., 1910), *A Spartan Mother* (Kalem, 1912), *A Dixie Mother* (Vitagraph, 1910), *Grandmother's War Story* (Kalem, 1911), *Barbara Frietchie* (Champion, 1911), and *The Fugitive* (Biograph, 1910). Unlike their young and adventurous counterparts, these women performed acts of patriotism in symbolic form—flag waving, sacrificing a child or husband to "the cause," or modeling American morality for the younger generation—and in doing so, they guided the younger men and women into making the "right" decisions.

A Spartan Mother follows a young soldier who tries to escape from battle before his mother, enacting her loyalty to the Southern Cause, forces him to return. The following review from the *Moving Picture World* demonstrates that "patriotism in women" was common in films and other popular entertainment. The film might be classed as a Southern war picture, one of a series of similar subjects that have been singularly well portrayed by the Kalem players, and illustrates most vividly the virtue of patriotism in women, which has been the subject of song and story for ages.[16]

KALEM COMPANY—THE INTERNATIONAL PRODUCERS.

Guy Coombs   Helen Lindroth

Scene from

"A Spartan Mother"

Released Monday, March 11th

FIGURE 2. *A Spartan Mother* in *Kalem Kalendar*, February 12, 1912. (Courtesy of Media History Digital Library.)

The mother in this film, Mrs. Marye, had lost her husband and three sons in one of the earliest battles of the Civil War. Her son, seventeen-year-old Robert, enlists against his will. Mrs. Marye hopes that he will be the hero needed to lead the Confederate Army to victory. When an intense battle takes place near the Marye home, Mrs. Marye watches from a hilltop while the Confederate regiments are outmaneuvered into a position flanked by hills. Eventually she is forced to return to her home, which she discovers is burning to the ground. Mrs. Marye hides in the smokehouse with the people her family had formerly enslaved. Her son arrives at the door and she realizes that he had deserted the battle early that day. "'Get up, *coward!*' she called. 'If you don't, I swear before God that I'll shoot you and go out there and lead them up the hill myself!'"[17] Despite Robert's attempts to stay home, Mrs. Marye eventually shoots a pistol at him and misses, causing him to run. Due to the proximity of the home to the battlefield, Robert runs through the battle and, in fear, charges up the hill toward the Union Army. His fellow soldiers mistake his fear-induced charge for bravery and follow him up the hill to defeat the unprepared enemy. Unfortunately, Robert is fatally wounded during the charge. He is hailed a hero by the men, and his mother reacts with relief. When told of her son's death, Mrs. Marye responds: "And so he is dead—my brave, brave Bobbie! I am strangely happy, doctor, because of the way my boy died."[18] The doctor admits that the boy's final words were "It was my mother—my dear old mother—that saved our men and won the day."[19] In these final scenes two things play out: First, the mother demonstrates that the South—to which she is patriotic—is more important than having her family alive. Second, the son's admission that the heroism was his mother's alone also functions to give credit to women for their part in nation building. The print version in the *Motion Picture Story Magazine* opens with the acknowledgment: "Seldom do we read of the noble women who married men, and reared sons, whose lives took root in the core of their hearts, and yet who gave them to the cause—and lost them!"[20] Of course, audiences of the time *did* read about and watch women in these film narratives frequently throughout the early 1910s.

In 1910, Vitagraph's *A Dixie Mother* presented a similar view of motherhood. The *Moving Picture World* review hyperbolized the emotional impact of the film "A story of the Civil War embodying all the most important sentiments, the love of country, the love of home, the love of mother and the love of wife."[21] The plot involves a Southern man, killed during the war, and his immediate family. His parents, particularly his mother, are staunch supporters of the Confederacy, so when his brother marries a woman from the North, they refuse to welcome her into the family. It is not until they meet their grandson that they decide to reunite the family. Here, motherhood—both North and South—unite in one family, with the grandson symbolizing the new nation. In other words, this film demonstrates that the Civil War was understood in popular culture as the "birth" of the nation because it signified the merging of North and South through reconciliation and new family units.

Many films depicted the division of the country by showing families with opposing sympathies (brothers and sisters, or fathers and sons); correspondingly, a major theme throughout these films was that of the divided family.[22] A popular example of this type of film is Griffith's *Birth of a Nation*; however, I have chosen to focus on lesser-known films to provide a better sense of the

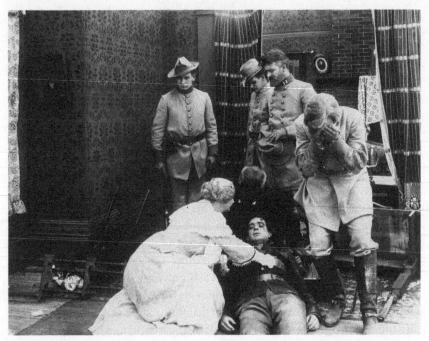

FIGURE 3. Film still from *A Dixie Mother*, 1910. (Courtesy of George Eastman House.)

trends of the period. Like *A Dixie Mother*, a number of the films about divided families portrayed reconciliation on account of a young child. The recurring storyline follows a son or daughter who was banished for marrying a sweetheart from the opposing side, only to return years later with a small child that led to the parents' forgiveness. *The Colonel's Oath* (Reliance, 1913), *Hearth Throbs* (Broncho, 1913), *Pride of the South* (Broncho, 1913), and *Quantrill's Son* (Vitagraph, 1914) each demonstrated the healing powers of a child, one who represented a newly united country. Much like the popular understanding of the Civil War in historical memory, the war—in film—brings two opposing sides together into a stronger whole. The child in these films represented the imagined progress of the nation after the strife and destruction of war, to the future of the United States.

Similarly, D. W. Griffith's *The Fugitive* (1910) demonstrates the ideal represented by women in the Civil War films: that is, that mothers and sweethearts are the unifying force that brings the nation back together. Much like how the mother in *A Dixie Mother* had to convince her husband—with the aid of her grandson—to welcome home their son, the two mothers in *The Fugitive* functioned as the symbolic link between North and South. The film had two introductory scenes, each depicting the departure of a son to fight for either the Union or the Confederacy. Griffith's cross-cutting is used throughout the film to demonstrate the similarity of the two families by portraying both mothers simultaneously reading the newspapers and both reacting positively. The climax of the film shows the Confederate soldier seeking refuge in the Union mother's house, although he had just slain the woman's son. When she learns of her son's death, and that he is her son's killer, she is tempted to give up the soldier to Union soldiers, but at that moment, a cut to the Confederate mother awaiting her son reveals that the Union mother is suddenly thinking of the other woman. When confronted with the idea that another mother might lose her own son, she decides to keep the soldier hidden. The film concludes with the Southern family reunited and embracing, and the final shot shows the Union mother hanging a sprig of flowers on her dead son's coat. This film demonstrates that it was the mother's moral fortitude that allowed her to overcome her hatred for the opposing side in the war. By extension, this suggests that this was how the country reunited after the war: through the love and forgiveness of American mothers. Symbolically, the nation is united through the shared experience of motherhood, both North and South. In other words, while the men were participants in the battle, stories that focused on mothers tended to emphasize the woman's place in teaching and guiding the nation toward reconciliation.

FAMILY: THE BOND THAT TRANSCENDS TIME

The use of the family unit to unite past and present was a common theme. Again, these films focus heavily on the loss of the South with sympathetic Southern characters. The suggestion is that the legacy of the South continues through the families that maintain its values. In these films and in the written stories in magazines such as the *Moving Picture Story Magazine*, this continued legacy and the unbreakable link between past, present, and future is a positive thing. However, it also demonstrates the way that the legacy of slavery remains a present force, then and now.

An example of a film that creates a link between past and present is *For the Cause of the South* (Edison, 1912). The print story in the *Motion Picture Story Magazine* is framed by a scene between two women. The younger of the two arrives to tell her aunt the good news of her engagement. However, Aunt Helen appears unhappy about the news. It turns out she is remembering her own lost love, a man she knew from her days at a seminary in the North. She tells the story of their love and their separation due to the Civil War. He joins the Union Army, while she is called home to her family, where her dad fights for the Confederate Army. Helen and her brother are home with the few remaining enslaved people in their home. Suddenly Helen's father returns home wounded and pursued by men from the Union Army. Through a series of battles within the home, the enslaved people are killed and Helen's brother cowardly retreats. Helen takes a dispatch carried by her father, intending to deliver it to Stonewall Jackson. Instead she and her father and brother are trapped inside. She holds a pistol and waits while more Union soldiers arrive. This time the soldiers are led by her beloved, Charles Dalton. Caught between love of her country and the love of a man, Helen is forced to choose. She chooses to shoot him and thus saves the battle and, in turn, saves Richmond.

The frame story is of interest here because it demonstrates the linkage between women of the 1910s and the women represented in these films. The frame story provides a representation of the legacy of the Civil War, though not necessarily in the romantic way it was intended: "There in the dusk their tears flowed into the same cup of understanding—half sweet, half bitter. Each could, with perfect understanding, look forward to the other's domestic felicity and children. Each could look back fifty years on the lover she had slain—such is the sympathy of women who have loved!"[23] The two women become one—or, in this sense, become one representation of white womanhood. They are mothers, wives, lovers, and killers at the service of maintaining their community, their homes, and their ideologies.

Another example is found in The Informer (Biograph, 1912). In this film Harvey goes to war leaving his beloved, Mary, behind. His younger brother keeps Mary company during his absence but continues to show affection for her. Eventually Stephen convinces Mary that Harvey is dead and that they should marry instead. As with most Civil War films, the war makes its way to Mary's house. Harvey arrives at the house, revealing that he is injured but alive and being pursued by the Union forces. It turns out that Stephen is a spy for the enemy. Mary is forced to take up arms to defend the house and the town. Her bravery and actions led to the Confederate victory of that battle. After the war Mary and Harvey are found in the garden, together again. The final words spoken by Mary in the print version found in the Motion Picture Story Magazine are, "We are still young, and will build our happiness upon the sweetness and the sorrow of the past."[24] This ending emphasizes the link to the past as the characters look to the future. While the films of this period glorify the link to the past, this version of history lays the groundwork for a legacy of ignoring the realities of the past—slavery and anti-Black racism—that can only continue if the past is obscured while simultaneously celebrated.

FASHIONABLY ACTIVE WOMEN

Young women were a frequent fixture of heroism in the Civil War films. Rather than the elderly mothers, the young sweethearts and daughters—approximately the same age as the men enlisting—were the most common heroic women of these films. One typical plot of the Civil War films of 1908–1916 involved either a Southern girl hiding a Northern soldier, or a Northern girl helping a Southern man escape capture. More often the young woman was from the South. The plot might vary in whether love of a man or love for her country reigned supreme.

With the sheer number of films produced in this relatively short span of time, there was no single formula but instead a series of character types and situations that repeated in different versions. Most often, though, the battle ended up at the woman's home. Each of the following examples demonstrates a variation on the trope of an active woman who, in varying degrees, must participate in the war.

For example, in *Fighting Dan McCool*, Dan McCool is sent to Reidsville undercover to find out information about their recruitment processes. There he meets Judge Reid and his daughter, Edith. McCool falls in love with Edith but she knows him only as a civilian and her heart and passions are for men who enlist and fight for the Southern Cause. In particular, she is in love with a man she has never met because she has heard about his heroism during war. This man is Dan McCool. She is also friendly with Bert, the leader of the Reidsville home army but is unaware that Bert is actually a spy from the North. Bert continually ensures a weak defense and alerts the Union Army of when it is best to attack. McCool discovers that Bert is an enemy and ensures that the Confederate Army arrives in time to defend the town from an attack. Bert runs to Edith for safety, but she points a pistol at him and keeps him at gunpoint until the Confederate Army can come and capture him. In the final moments of the film Edith learns that the civilian is, in fact, the heroic Dan McCool, and he pledges to return to her if he survives the war.[25]

In *The Soldier Brothers of Susanna* (Kalem, 1912), one brother, Joe, who had been to school in the North, joins the Union Army, while John remains loyal to the Confederate side. The rest of the family, including Susanna, their sister, remain home. During the war John is tasked with entering the enemy camp dressed as a civilian. When John falls off his horse and breaks his leg, Susanna goes in his place, managing to steal a map from the enemy camp. As she rushes back home, the men realize what she has done and pursue her in a chase. She climbs the wooden post of a bridge and manages to hide but is caught by one of the men, who had fallen behind. The man is her brother, Joe. Torn between his army and his family, he takes back the map and sets her free. He is caught and killed after trial by court-martial for the part he played in letting her go free. Due to his loyalty to Susanna, the family can remember him fondly, despite previously thinking of him as a traitor to the South.[26]

In these films the women demonstrate acts of bravery while maintaining their normal outward appearances, as opposed to the cross-dressed women who were also a common character type. Specifically, active women who *remained* feminine women throughout the narrative, rather than cross-dressing or gender-crossing, emphasized the positive traits of "new" femininity or "American Girlhood." These young women were athletic, daring, and willing to do whatever is necessary for the protection of the home. I call these women "active women" rather than "action women" because their athleticism and ability to perform stunts was central to promoting their star personas. In other words, these women were not in "action films"—they were in films with plots that celebrated their "active" natures.

Additionally, film reviewers increasingly commented on the stars' performances, mentioning the stars' athleticism and bravery as much as the athleticism of the characters they played. While audiences would see action women on screen, there was also a growing emphasis on how active the actresses were. Newspapers and trade journals presented readers with stories about women who would perform athletic stunts for their films. A review of Kalem's *Battle of Pottsburg Bridge* highlighted Marion Cooper's athleticism: "When General Stuart visits the home of the wounded soldier to congratulate him upon the success of his venture, he learns of the bravery of the sister. This part is played by Marion Cooper, a new Kalem beauty, who proves herself to be some swimmer. There is much good action in the picture."[27] The slippage from describing the character to describing the athletic abilities of the actress, Marion Cooper, aligns the character and the star with the concept of the "American Girl," who was lauded for her athleticism. W. Stephen Bush, in a review of the 1913 film *The Battle of Bloody Ford*, also featuring Marion Cooper, wrote, "This young lady, though still in her teens, is a splendid athlete, a good runner, a graceful and skilled rider and a perfect swimmer. She gives most delightful exhibitions of her accomplishments."[28] Athleticism came to signify an ideal for young American women, and this was reflected in the positive reviews given to actresses who demonstrated physical skills. Connecting the action of women in battle within the plot to the athleticism of the actresses who play the parts was a way in which promotional discourse could extend the significance of these women as role models for audience members. Although the young women of the 1910s would not be participating in battles, developing athletic skills could allow them to enact the role of the American Girl—to link their physicality with their patriotism and to link the idea of American national identity with whiteness.

In addition to female athleticism, active American Girls maintained close ties with the fashion industry. Films such as *My Lady's Boot* (1913) demonstrate that the accoutrements of femininity—in this case, her boots—became symbolic of the participation of women in war. In this film, a woman hides a message for General Lee in her boot, and is searched by a Union officer. Though the message could have been hidden anywhere, the conflation of femininity with fashion and women's patriotism with fashion is indicative of contemporaneous conceptions of women's interests. In other words, women were aligned with an interest in fashion, and, by extension, their active deeds were linked with their consumerist interests. Beginning in the 1910s the film industry would actually employ well-known fashion designers to further elicit female interest in movie-going. In the films set during the 1860s, fashion functioned to temper the active woman's transgression of gender.[29]

CROSS-DRESSING AMERICAN GIRLS

Recent studies have exposed the ubiquity of cross-dressing at the end of the nineteenth century.[30] Historically, cross-dressing afforded women opportunities outside the proscribed norms of femininity. Vern and Bonnie Bullough, in *Cross Dressing, Sex, and Gender*, delineate the progress and gains women made during the nineteenth century, but they remind us that "many women still found the easiest way to escape their restrictive assigned role was to pass as a man rather than to fight what they believed to be an almost impossible battle against male prejudice."[31] This historical reality, however, does not necessarily explain the popularity of the cross-dressing girl spy and soldier and other gender-crossing heroines in early American narrative films.

Film's cross-dressing heroines were deemed acceptable precisely because their motives were representative of traditional American values, such as honor, bravery, and the protection of home and family. The cross-dressed woman in early American film is the subject of Laura Horak's book, *Girls Will Be Boys*. Horak discusses three waves of cross-dressed women in the first decades of the twentieth century. The first wave, from 1908 to 1921, corresponds roughly with cinema's transitional era and concerns the films made in the period of development between non-narrative film and the rise of narrative film and a standardized studio system.[32] Horak demonstrates that during the early 1910s, American films, particularly the range romances and war films, "used cross-dressed cowboys and girl spies to appeal to cross-class, trans-regional audiences and affirm a virile national ideal."[33] There is a strong similarity between Westerns and Civil War films that featured cross-dressed women, and what is consistent across both subjects is the use of female strength and heroics to reaffirm a white, strong nation.[34] In other words, because these traits of heroism serve nationalist ideologies, these women should be read not as subversive proto-feminist heroines defying gender norms but instead as figures that uphold and reinforce nationalist ideologies.

One of the earliest and best-remembered Civil War cross-dressed heroines was Nan, the Girl Spy, played and written by Gene Gauntier of Kalem. In her autobiography, serialized in *Woman's Home Companion* in 1928–1929, Gauntier explained: "I wrote a picture called The Adventures of the Girl Spy which embodied all the difficult and sometimes dangerous stunts I could conjure up. In this I played a southern girl disguised as a boy of '61. It made a tremendous hit and exhibitors wrote in for more. Thus began the first series made in films and I kept them up for two years until, tired of sprains and bruises and with brains sucked dry of any more adventures for the intrepid young woman, I married her off and ended the war."[35] Gauntier's writing speaks to the popularity of the Girl Spy series as an early iteration of women in Civil War films. Central to these films was some kind of chase scene, usually involving Gauntier, as Nan, on horseback evading capture by the Union Army. Another central feature of these films was Nan donning the uniform in a transition from feminine dress to soldier's apparel.[36] The repeated formula of changing from women's clothing into uniform, followed by athletic stunts and horseback riding, was easily transferrable to multiple Girl Spy films. In this case the fascination, for audiences, was both in knowing that the woman was fooling the other characters in the film and in waiting to see what new stunts she manages to perform.

A synopsis in the *Moving Picture World* described Nan: "The daughter of a Southern family, left motherless in early childhood, her life had become embittered by the death of her father and only brother during one of the early struggles of the great conflict. She had consecrated her entire life to the cause of their beloved Southland."[37] Like the serial queens to come, the girl spy was motherless and young and, as Gauntier suggests, participated in her adventures prior to entering adulthood, or "proper" femininity, which was denoted by marriage. Cross-dressed characters such as the girl spy embodied a youthful fluidity of gender characteristic of adolescence that allowed for the slippage between male and female roles. The Girl Spy series was extremely popular and resulted in a number of films with Kalem: *The Girl Spy* (1909), *The Bravest Girl in the South* (1910), *Further Adventures of the Girl Spy* (1910), *The Girl Spy before Vicksburg* (1910), and *The Love and Romance of the Girl* (1910).

A handful of films used the trope of a cross-dressing character protecting one's family: *The Little Soldier of '64* (Kalem, 1911), *Wages of War* (Vitagraph, 1911), *Special Messenger* (Kalem, 1911), *With Stonewall Jackson* (Champion, 1911), and *The Drummer Girl of Vicksburg* (Kalem, 1912). A variation of this was women donning a man's uniform to protect the *honor* of her family. In *The House with Closed Shutters* (Biograph, 1910) a young man is proven cowardly during war and returns home to hide from the battle, despite having to deliver an important message about battle plans. His sister, described by an intertitle as "A Daughter of Dixie," would not allow her brother's cowardice to shame the family—she took the uniform and the letter from her drunken, unconscious brother. An intense scene followed as she, dressed as a young Confederate soldier, delivered the letter but was ultimately caught and shot by enemy soldiers as she attempted to return home. A letter was then delivered to her mother and brother, informing them of "his" death in battle, at which point the mother decides to keep her son behind "closed shutters" for the remainder of his life. It was the young woman's sacrifice that saved the family, demonstrating not just the bravery of women but the strong familial and patriotic values they should hold. In *The House with Closed Shutters*, the girl donned her brother's uniform not to demonstrate her own bravery but to save the honor of her family.

In another example, *The Darling of the C.S.A.* (Kalem 1912), the woman is an inspiration for men's bravery. The film is about Agnes, a prolific spy for the South,

A COMING FEATURE

Hal Clements   Anna Nilsson   Guy Coombs

The Darling of the C. S. A.

A ROMANTIC DRAMA OF THE CIVIL WAR

RELEASED SATURDAY, SEPT. 7th

This spectacular military production portrays the thrilling adventures of an intrepid girl spy.

Special one, three and six-sheet, four-color lithographs
for this headline attraction.

FIGURE 1 *The Darling of the C.S.A.* in *Kalem Kalendar*, August 1, 1912. (Courtesy of Media History Digital Library.)

wanted by the Union Army. In one scene she is watching a Confederate regiment as they lose a battle, and a young, cowardly man comes running toward her in an attempt to escape the battle. When a shell lands at her feet, he has a sudden burst of bravery and throws himself upon it. Although it looks like the Confederate regiment is losing ground and planning to retreat, she realizes that, like the boy who threw himself upon the shell to save her, she is the motivation the men need to continue to fight. She surrenders herself to the Union Army, but not until she leaves a note for the Confederate general, letting him know that she will be shot in the morning. He asks the regiment for volunteers to save her, and every one of them volunteers. The men attack the Union camp and catch them off-guard, saving her and winning the battle.[38]

Civil War films frequently depicted female participation in battle precisely because such films were always about defense of home and country. Perhaps no such character—real or imagined—was more fascinating in this regard than Pauline Cushman, a Civil War actress who then became a spy for the Union Army, plying her trade while she performed, often playing men in Zouave uniforms. In other words, Cushman played the role of male soldiers *on stage*, while spying for the Union Army *off stage*, only to be portrayed on screen during the transitional period by female actresses starring in American films. In fact, after the Civil War, Cushman's notoriety as a brave spy propelled her stage career, and she lectured—while in uniform—about her experiences throughout the East from 1864 to 1870.[39]

Cushman was the subject of the film *Pauline Cushman, the Federal Spy* (Selig 1913) as a result of this fame. The following review notes actress Winnifred Greenwood's performance: "One is fascinated by her daring, her coolness amid danger, and the swiftness and cautiousness of her movements. Not once is there displayed a sign of self-consciousness.... Miss Greenwood looks well on horseback, and her dashing 'get-aways' in the saddle, as Pauline Cushman, are full of spirit and create enthusiasm."[40] Cushman the character—performed by Greenwood—maintains femininity rather than convincingly masquerading as a male soldier, unlike her real-life counterpart, who was known for lecturing in male attire. This reveals an interesting reality about cross-dressed characters in films about war: women could perform masculinity only for as long as it took to achieve a particular goal. The active masculine disguise was known to the audience as just a disguise, to be shed for the feminine accouterments and domestic feminine roles of wife, mother, and sister when the battle was over. Paradoxically, maintaining femininity was key to donning masculinity in the Civil War films of the early 1910s.

KALEM: A CASE STUDY IN EARLY AMERICAN FILM STUDIOS

Different studios were known for particular subject matter as narrative film production grew. The Kalem Company was a major producer of Civil War subjects on film.[41] By focusing on one company's output, it is possible to see the privilege given to white women in narratives of the Civil War and how this informs a larger cultural narrative of normalizing whiteness in relation to American national identity.[42] That women's whiteness was central to defining a particular type of American identity hinges on a comparison to the other films made by Kalem. Their Florida Unit made the Civil War films, the California Unit made films about the border and relations with Mexico, another unit made Westerns. Romances with Mexican women were fairly common. Domestic contemporary comedies with characters in blackface appeared from time to time. Adventure stories about Native Americans were also made by Kalem units. Comparatively, of the fifteen Civil War films made in 1913, only one—*War's Havoc*—featured a Black character in a role large enough to warrant a place in the film's description.[43] While these clusters of films and representations of race in the early 1910s require further analysis, comparison across the company's output should be a reminder of Thomas Cripps's statement of the "structuring out" of Black history from American Civil War films.[44] In other words, Kalem did not shy away from subjects of American history that featured Native American or Latino and Latina characters, so the absence of Black characters from films about the Civil War is in itself central to how the war was framed as a cultural narrative of the country's rebirth. We cannot acknowledge the prominence of women in these narratives without recognizing their race—and we cannot tell the full story of that which has been erased from the representation of this war without acknowledging what has been emphasized.

In 1907 the Kalem Company was created by Samuel Long and Frank Marion (both from Biograph Studios) and financed by George Kleine (a distributor from Chicago).[45] Although the head office was located in New York City, Kalem soon began producing a variety of subjects by assigning film units—including a director, writer, cinematographer, stars, and so on—to different locations. The Gauntier-Olcott unit worked for a period in Jacksonville, Florida, and later traveled to Ireland and Egypt to make fiction films set abroad. Their Jacksonville films often used the Civil War as subject and, when they relocated and subsequently left Kalem, a new film unit led by director Kenean Buel, with stars such as Alice Hollister, Anna Q. Nilsson, and Marion Cooper, took over and continued producing Civil War films.

The company heavily promoted its use of multiple film units in its advertising pamphlet *Kalem Kalendars*. Kalem's advertising suggested that the multiple units provided a strong variety of films that would prevent audience boredom. However, the company still provided exhibitors with a continuous supply of films that repeated popular themes and subjects. Each unit specialized in a specific type of film—Buel's Florida unit made the Civil War films, for example—so that Kalem was able to cultivate a balance between standardization and variety. Developing the proto-genre of the Civil War film in the early 1910s was a strategy

for securing distribution and exhibition, even at a time when Kalem was promoting itself as a company that provided a multitude of film types.[46] Although
Kalem made comedies and other film subjects, its films about American history
remained central to their promotion. The year 1913 was the fiftieth anniversary of
the war, which many silent film scholars have attributed as the key reason for its
surge in popularity. However, this alone does not interrogate *what* aspects of the
war were commemorated, or how it was memorialized. In short, the Civil War in
film was a popular subject for reaffirming white supremacy in the shaping of
American national identity, particularly through the virtuous and heroic white
female protagonists.

The Civil War takes on importance even across the Kalem promotions. Kalem
referred to its Civil War films, in particular, as its "features."[47] It is clear in the *Kalendars* that Kalem privileges some films over others in its production output. The
Florida unit's Civil War films are frequently given more than just the usual one
page with a still and a synopsis. In the "News Items" section, some films are given
not just praise but anticipatory coverage: "Mr. Buel now sends in a subject, soon
to be announced, which contains enough thrills for a sumptuous two reel production, what with the old ante bellum railroads, a collision of locomotives on
the bridge, hair-breadth escapes and astonishing battle scenes. . . . Watch for the
release dates of these spectacular subjects! Then you will understand why these
productions, together with others equally striking—but of an entirely different
character—have caused Kalem to be known as the 'Company of Features.'"[48] In
addition, Kalem had an in-house composer, Walter C. Simon, who wrote scores
for a select number of Kalem films in 1912. The scores were written for Kalem's
Egypt films, Civil War films, and a film about the Mexican Revolution.[49]

In the Civil War films the female heroics were promotionally linked to the athleticism of the actresses employed by Kalem. Marian Cooper's page-long promotional biography in the February 12, 1912, *Kalem Kalendar* highlights her athletic
activities: "Miss Cooper's most recent appearance was in the spectacular production of 'The Battle of Pottsburg Bridge.' This thrilling drama would have been
quite impossible without an actress of Miss Cooper's extraordinary ability to
handle the difficult leading role and the manner in which she dived, swam, han-
dled the boat and climbed the bridge is only a sample of what this athletic young
woman can do. She is equally at home, riding a spirited horse and while she mod-
estly refrains from issuing challenges, there are few who care to put on the boxing
gloves with her."[50] In addition to athleticism, the actresses at Kalem were praised
not just for beauty but for traits in line with the ideals of modern femininity. The
New York Dramatic Mirror had this to say about the Kalem actresses in January of
1912: "*The Mirror* presents on this page a collection of ten pretty Kalem faces—and
they are not show-girl faces either. Each one of the collection shows sweetness of
disposition, strength of character, strong individuality, and undoubted brains.
Can more be said of lovely femininity? Let us particularize."[51] Following this

statement about the positive traits of femininity found in the Kalem actresses is a list of the names, along with brief descriptions of the usual roles they played. Gene Gauntier, "expert horsewoman"; Alice Joyce, "a daring rider and an earnest, capable actress"; Jane Wolfe; Ruth Roland, "a leading lady of one of the Western Kalems, a fine rider, fencer, and rifle shot, and an actress equal to all the varied demands of an exacting position"; Marin Sais, "particularly good in Indian and boy parts"; Anna Q. Nilsson; Alice Hollister; Eileen Errol; Marian Cooper, "daring and athletic, accomplished and petit;" and Helen Lindroth. While the women protagonists were active, brave, and propelled the plots forward, the actresses themselves were also promoted for such characteristics, highlighting that the ideal American woman was not just found in fictional narratives.

FROM MELODRAMA TO COMEDY

A decrease in Civil War films is particularly noticeable after 1914, as the American entry into war became an ever-increasing possibility—World War I began in 1914 but the United States did not enter the conflict until April 1917. *Her Father's Son* (1916) demonstrates a clear transition from the Civil War films produced between 1908 and 1916, and the World War I–era films from 1914 onward. This film is again about a cross-dressed heroine of the Civil War, but it plays to comedic effect rather than melodrama. The figure of the cross-dressing now woman posed a threat to the patriarchal order, and thus Vivian Martin's character, Frances, was laughable for "trying" to be a man. Whereas many of the films discussed in this chapter were domestic melodramas, films like *Her Father's Son* were comedies, changing the tone and making a joke of Frances's heroic actions. In the film, Frances Fletcher's father receives a letter from his brother shortly before dying. Frances's uncle, William Fletcher, agrees to "bury the hatchet" and make Frances his heir because he believes her to be a boy. In a grand gesture to play the part, Frances reluctantly cuts her hair in front of a large mirror and leaves for her uncle's plantation donning male attire. Her arrival at Uncle William's plantation is framed such that it emphasizes her slight stature amid a group of tall and muscular men. Throughout the film, the cross-dressing Frances is shown in humorous situations as a vehicle for lampooning Southern notions of masculinity that are based on the ability to perform certain actions, such as smoking and shooting pistols. Frances becomes close with her female cousin, with whom she has much more in common than with the Southern "gentlemen," and also falls in love with a man who seems drawn to the male "Francis." The film culminates during the Civil War when Frances must don women's clothing to cross enemy lines—knowing that she would be perceived as less threatening in women's attire—thus finally proving the bravery the men around her thought "Francis" lacked. Ultimately, rather than bravery, Frances is known for her physical beauty and her "feminine" appeal, which is so strong that it charms even the male

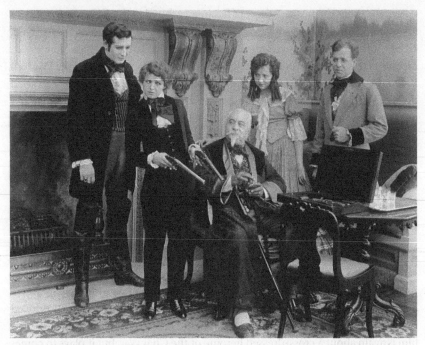

FIGURE 5. Film still from *Her Father's Son*. (Courtesy of George Eastman House.)

characters who believe her a man. While this film contains an example of a cross-dressing female, victory was achieved only when she donned women's clothing, demonstrating that femininity was her "proper" state and the only way that she could serve her country.

As a comedy, the film makes light of what are traditionally held to be masculine skills and feminine interests. Young men are supposed to be good at shooting targets, whereas young women should have an interest in fashion. But the comedic element of this film overturns those ideas: in short, because this film came later in the cycle of active women in the Civil War films, we are given to understand that active heroism can just as easily be achieved by a woman, as Frances proves in the final reel of the film. However, this film complicates the notion of cross-dressing because it is, in fact, *as a woman* that Frances finally achieves her heroic deed. After showing little interest in shooting practice, Frances instead finds friendship with her cousin, William's daughter. The daughter catches Frances trying on one of her dresses, at which point Frances exclaims, "Don't you think I'd make a jim-dandy girl?" The two hatch a plan to dress Frances in a gown for the upcoming ball, during which she fools everyone—including her future suitor, an enamored soldier—into believing that she is a young woman. Of course, the joke is that she *is* in fact a young woman, but this girl-as-boy-as-girl trope becomes central in the final reel. Again pretending to be a boy, though refusing to fight in the ongoing war, Frances finally realizes that she must participate when she tends to a wounded soldier and finds a package that must make it through the enemy lines. Rather than completing the task as "her father's son," Frances dons the clothing of a woman to make it through enemy lines more easily. That the task could be completed only by a woman is an interesting finale to this film, in which cowardice and bravery were traits so commonly discussed in regard to the male-Frances.

To finally prove her heroism, Frances returns to her feminine self. The feminine woman is capable of bravery and action. Even though Frances cross-dresses throughout the film, she proves incapable of fully embodying these so-called masculine qualities, while entirely capable of achieving results in her final mission, as a woman. This film, through its comedic approach to gender roles, encapsulates the very message that women heroines had stood for throughout the era of Civil War films: women, as women, were active participants in the defense of American ideals and homes. As much as Frances's success at the end of the film signifies that action women were indeed brave American citizens, the comedy throughout the film negates a truly progressive message, as the film suggests that women could not transgress cultural gender roles.

The shift from heroic women in melodramatic films to comedic roles can be understood only in its historical context. The year 1916 is marked by a rise in discourse about military preparedness brought on by World War I. Although Americans deemed it the war "over there," concern about the United States' place in foreign politics on the world stage became pressing issues. In other words, while the Civil War represented a domestic war, useful for representing battles about who claims national identity at home, changing fears shifted the enemy outside American borders. Melodrama films and serials about modern-day women and the threat of foreign invasion took on contemporary subjects. The heroic woman remained a key figure throughout the mid- to late 1910s; however, she appeared in films that were less about United States history and myth, and more about contemporary political issues.

3 · THE AMERICAN REVOLUTION AND OTHER WARS

The formula is well known and oft-repeated throughout war films of the early 1910s: A man is injured or retreats in fear, finding himself hiding or recovering in the home of a woman, roughly his same age—perhaps she is his sister or perhaps she is a stranger with whom he falls in love. She finishes the mission for him, if he is on the same side as her family, or she takes information from him and delivers it to a regiment with whom she shares allegiance. She saves the day. The information she delivers turns the tide of battle, or perhaps even the whole war. While this reads like the American Civil War film formula discussed in chapter 2, replete with its girl spies and cross-dressed women soldiers, the story was not isolated to that specific war. In 1908 and 1909—just as the formula was making its way onto the screen—a handful of these particular films were also about the American Revolution. If we believed all of the stories these films told, we might imagine that George Washington spent much of the war receiving messages from women who had risked everything to deliver information about the Loyalists' battle plans.

Even though American filmmaking in the 1910s privileged the Civil War, films about the American Revolution (or other battles in American history), and some films about other nations, shared a common theme: wars fought on home soil require the participation of all members of the family, including women. These include battles at the Mexican border, or fictional depictions of European wars, focusing on European women. Like the Civil War and the American Revolution, these narratives play out in someone's backyard. In the films of this period, female characters at home became entangled in the war at their doorstep not only out of patriotism but in defense of the home and in self-defense. In other words, these melodramas were about victimhood that justifies violence.[1] In the case of narratives about war, focusing on the family unit and wars fought on home soil centers the action around defense. This reaffirmed the American mythos about militarism as defense rather than expansionist or imperial.[2] As wars raged in American families' backyards and in neighboring forests and fields, on roads, and across rivers, America's women waited at home, not just to welcome home lovers, brothers, and sons but to defend the home as necessary. American films occasionally included European wars with female heroines that mirrored their American counterparts. However, these non-American women often reaffirm whiteness even as they remain distinct from American identity.

BUILDING A COUNTRY

Films served national mythmaking by representing the boundaries of American identity, whether it be the earliest days of the nation in the films about the Revolution, or the borders of what constitutes American soil in the films about battles in Mexico or battles against Indigenous people. Along with the Civil War, also a popular subject, these were wars that defined and shaped the American nation in popular myth—as a white nation—and these films defined what it meant to be American in a very specific and limited way. Subjects such as the American Revolution, the American Civil War, battles against Indigenous inhabitants of the land, and conflicts at the border with Mexico gave ample—yet somewhat repetitive—material for filmmakers to depict ideas about the "good American men and women" who built the country. These films work within a tapestry of media during the decade to define national virtues, to define its national citizens, and to rework history to build national myths.

One example of a war that served in national myth-building was the American Revolution. This war of 1775–1783 was also known as the American War of Independence and serves as the United States' founding war. This war was the subject of only a handful of films in the early 1910s as compared with the over 300 Civil War films. Interest in the Revolution remained more or less consistent throughout the first half of the 1910s, though it never became as popular as the American Civil War.[3] To suggest that the Revolutionary War films simply lifted the formula from Civil War films would be tempting, due to the vast number of Civil War films versus the relatively small number of Revolutionary War films of the period. However, this would be an oversimplification. Various companies experimented with the war formula in 1908 and 1909 using the American Revolution, when the Civil War films were only just starting to gain popularity.[4] Of the numerous films about the American Revolution, the only film that does not appear to have a woman as a central protagonist is Kalem's *The Swamp Fox*, while Kalem's *The Prison Ship* has an unclear description but a female character is seen in the film still shown with the *Kalem Kalendar* synopsis.[5] All of the other films featured women in central and heroic roles.

It is possible to read the presence of women in war films of this period through a number of lenses. First, women are included to add appeal to women in the audience. Second, including women in national mythmaking at the time was an important nation-building endeavor and, in a related sense, important to containing and directing new traits of femininity toward nationalist aims. Throughout these films, women are key to guiding men toward becoming good Americans. This enters into national mythmaking by the promotional discourse that foregrounds realism and historical accuracy even in films that are clearly following an established formula.

One of Kalem's films about the American Revolution, *The Governor's Daughter*, provides an interesting example of how a film company's promotion intersected with discourses of realism and authenticity. Like with their Civil War films, their Egyptian films, and others, Kalem's promotions often centered on the film creators (director, actors, writer, etc.) not just creating but also experiencing the adventures that appear on screen. In other words, in the promotion of films, stories of the adventures the players had while making the film, or traveling to make the film, augmented the sense of authenticity.[6] This strategy played into discourses of realism and foregrounded the storytelling aspect of narrative film. *The Governor's Daughter* takes a slightly different approach, still blending fiction with reality in a story about the story's origin. The *Film Index* published a complete lecture for *The Governor's Daughter*, and the following is the introduction that was meant to precede the film:

> During the past summer one of the members of the Kalem Company's executive staff spent his vacation with his grandparents at their home in a quaint little town in Eastern Virginia. Part of their house, an old rambling structure, was built before the Revolution. While rummaging through the garret one rainy afternoon he discovered a small table whose carved sides and strangely curved legs gave evidence of its great age. A close examination revealed in the back of this table a small drawer skillfully concealed from prying eyes. Here amongst a lot of old land grants, deeds and cancelled contracts he found a few torn and musty pages covered with the close, fine writing so common in revolutionary time. A perusal showed them to be a portion of the diary of one James Munroe Montague, a minister of the gospel, relating his romantic courtship of Lady Betty, the daughter of Virginia's Tory Governor. He forwarded them to the Kalem Company and the picture about to be shown to you is the same story faithfully reacted and presented in a series of nine beautiful scenes.[7]

The preamble to the historical story inserts the Kalem players into the overall narrative of the film: of its production. Although a promotional strategy, audiences are meant to believe—or at least suspend disbelief—that the story is taken from historical diaries and is representative of an actual incident of the American Revolution. It is most likely that audiences would have been aware that this was simply a frame to the story, as much a fabrication as the scenes they would see about James Montague and Lady Betty. The pretense of historical accuracy in these romantic war melodramas, though, is a key element seen throughout the trade press. These films were anything but historically accurate, with three basic story variations (and combinations of these stories) that existed: The first is that a woman saves the day by saving George Washington and providing him with key information. The second is that women, left at home while men are at war, must defend their homes from invading British and Hessian forces. The third variation is that a woman is in love with a British soldier and convinces him to convert to become American. The plots of most American Revolutionary films between 1909 and 1915 all contain one or all of these plot points.

FROM FACT TO FICTION: TYPES OF AMERICAN REVOLUTION FILMS

On the night of December 25, 1976, George Washington led his army across the Delaware River, attacking a group of Hessian soldiers, effectively precipitating the end of the war. General Cornwallis, of the British Army, later surrendered at Yorktown, his troops depleted. The tactical move of crossing the Delaware and making prisoners of the Hessian soldiers is an easily identifiable moment to mark the "turning of the tide of war" in favor of the Continental Army. However, this Thanhouser advertisement reveals the hole in popular historical knowledge that was exploited by early narrative filmmakers: "We all know of Washington's remarkable feat in crossing the Delaware River at Trenton with half of his command, surprising the Hessians and making them his prisoners; but how advance word of helplessness of his enemy reached the great general has ever been a mystery. The bearer of the message was the very patriotic maid here portrayed, who, with her American scout sweetheart severely wounded, cleverly disguises herself and takes her lover's message to Washington."[8]

It was not only Thanhouser that made a film suggesting that a woman delivered the vital information to George Washington. The first type of American Revolution film of the period featured a woman stealing through the night to deliver messages to Washington in various important battles during the war. Another example is Selig Polyscope's *Spirit of '76* (1908), which takes place in Philadelphia during the British occupation. Pamela Morton bids farewell to her lover, Harry Grey, a captain in the Colonial Army. A British major—Breen—decides to use Pamela's family home as his own residence during the war and, some months in, Pamela finds his plans and delivers them to the Colonial Army camp. The plans are then delivered to Washington, who then crosses the Delaware. The film ends showing Pamela and Harry Grey in an embrace.[9] Kalem's *Flag of Freedom* (1911) and Rex's *A Heroine of '76* (1911) present a similar story. Universal's *Washington at Valley Forge* (1914) is also about a woman who helps Washington, but in this film she pretends to sleep in his bed, thus taking a fatal stab wound meant for him. Another variant is in *Before Yorktown* (1911), in which a woman attempts to deliver a message to Washington, and, although she is unsuccessful at the time, he meets with her after the war's end to thank her for her bravery. Although not an overly high number of films, the similarities are striking, even among those, like *Valley Forge* and *Before Yorktown*, that veer from the formula. Again, these films follow a particular pattern yet are promoted for their educational value in representing American history. These films were key in establishing white women's place in the foundational myths of American independence.

The second type of film involves women who are at home when the British or Hessian army draws near. In these films the women have no choice but to take up arms and defend their homes against the invading army. The descriptions of Lubin's *Brave Women of '76* in both *Variety* and *Moving Picture World* demonstrate this plot variation of women defending their homes while men are at war. These films fill the melodramatic mode by establishing the women—and thus the white, American nation—as victims of invasion, thus precipitating the action and sensation. In this scenario the men from a small town are part of a single regiment that is fighting away from town. The regiment discovers that the enemy is near their town and they send a message to their wives. The wives take up arms. Those who do not have guns use whatever tools from home can stand in as a weapon against the Hessians. After the women win their own battle, they happen upon their husbands' regiment, which has shown up—too late—to help. The men and women embrace as the film ends.[10]

The film *1776, or, the Hessian Renegades* (Biograph, 1909) is about a family and the citizens of a small town banding together to defeat an oppressive force. The Americans valiantly fight to maintain their homeland and are victorious against the much larger enemy army. Like the Civil War films, this was therefore a film about defending the American home, a cause for which both men and women must fight. The men were the soldiers but the women's wit, bravery, and ingenuity were equally important in the fight. This was a key element in the American mythos of the American Revolution: the hetero-normative construction of a family working together to beat the enemies. In the Revolutionary War films, men and women worked together in defense of the home and ultimately defeated a strong, and organized, army.

In American Revolution films, families thus worked together to battle for the freedom of their homes. In *Hessian Renegades*, an American soldier is hiding in a family home while the British unknowingly shoot directly at his hiding place and he is killed. The family finds important plans hidden in his pocket, which they know they must deliver to his regiment. In order to distract the British soldiers to deliver the plans, the family members attack them. The women in the film play a variety of roles—decoy, distracter, and bearer of arms. At first a woman takes the enemy soldiers upstairs, while the hidden man is downstairs. Later she

George Robinson　　Stuart Holmes　　　　Hazel Neason

THE FLAG OF FREEDOM

An Incident of the American Revolution

FAITH TRUMBULL is in love with a Continental officer, Captain Strong, but her father, a Tory, will not countenance the match. He wishes to make an alliance between his daughter and Blent, a British officer. Strong, coming to the house, sees through the window that Trumbull and Blent are consulting papers, which he fears contain some plot against the Continental army. When he attempts to secure the papers he is captured, but escapes with the aid of Faith. Pursued by the British, Strong reaches the home of Betsy Ross, a friend of Faith's. Betsy, who is engaged with the making of the first American flag, conceals Strong in a chest.

Trumbull and Blent bury the papers but Faith watches them and secures the documents. She is startled to find plans of the Continental camp and particulars for the capture of General Washington. Faith hastens to Washington's headquarters and gives the General timely warning. She then proceeds to Betsy's house. Meanwhile Betsy has gallantly driven away Strong's pursuers with a musket and when Faith arrives, Betsy secures a minister. The minister is ready to perform the ceremony when he calls attention to the fact that another witness is necessary. At that moment General Washington arrives to learn of the progress of Betsy's work and he gladly consents to act as a witness, together with Betsy.

Special one, three and six-sheet, four-color lithographs for this headliner.

FIGURE 6. *Flag of Freedom* in *Kalem Kalendar*. December 16, 1912. (Courtesy of Media History Digital Library.)

escapes from the window and distracts a guard, allowing a man from the family to slip past. Again, this film emphasizes the community effort, the daring of individuals, and the quick thinking required of family members to outsmart an army that outnumbers them. In *Hessian Renegades* these characteristics were attributed to both the men and the women who made up the family unit and who successfully defended their home against enemy invasion. The enemy was seen as stronger and more organized, yet the underdogs won precisely because the family united in defense of their home. These films suggested that a united "America" was an impenetrable force, precisely because both men and women would join the fight.

Likewise, in the 1908 film *The Army of Two*, two sisters defend their home, a lighthouse, against the advance of the British after seeing a warship approaching. The sisters had been skillfully using guns since they childhood, and they managed to injure and capture an enemy soldier. One sister falls in love with him during his recovery, and he finally swears allegiance to the patriot's cause.[11] The narrative of this film contains two major tropes of the American Revolution films: first, the women who are left alone to defend their homes and, second, the love between an American girl and a British soldier that results in his conversion.

That brings us to the third, and final, type of American Revolution film: those of conversion: a British soldier becoming American through the devotion and love of a woman. An example is *Before Yorktown* (Republic Pictures, 1911), in which a wounded British soldier is brought to a doctor's house to recover from his wounds. Over the course of his recovery the soldier falls in love with the doctor's daughter, Beatrice. Later Beatrice tries to deliver a message to Washington, but she is caught by the enemy. Her lover helps her to escape from the enemy camp, and after the war Washington learns of her bravery and pardons her lover, on Beatrice's promise that she will make a good American of him. The films of conversion mark an important trope that recurs in films about American history: that of national identity, allegiance, and patriotism, particularly as represented in eras where the concept of nation is in development or change.

FROM FICTION TO FACT: WAR AND FILM AS EDUCATION

Eventually the trade press came to criticize the overuse of the Civil War films, suggesting that film companies exploited a tired formula, but this critique was often overlooked regarding American Revolution films due to their relative absence in American film and the supposed educational value of depicting this overlooked part of history, despite the similar reliance on formula, melodrama, and female heroines. For example, *Washington at Valley Forge* was mentioned in a response to a query submitted to *Motography*. A reader asked for film recommendations to start an educational film program in a small town, stating, "I am endeavoring with the aid of the principals and teachers of the schools in this and surrounding small villages to plan out a course to consist of five or six feature shows."[12] In response, *Motography*'s editors did not immediately suggest fiction films with historical or literary significance—as the writer had inquired about— instead suggesting "travelogues, industrial pictures, microscopic studies, [and] natural history studies," with which even film's harshest critics had trouble find- ing fault.[13] Rothapfel suggests how to bring skeptics on board with dramatic, fictional films that are based on historical events or literary classics: "Later on I would use a dramatic subject like those that you have mentioned, but not to begin with, because you will find that these subjects are very rare and no matter how well done they are there will be some who will find objections. On the other hand, no one can object to the other subjects I have mentioned and they will become interested. After they are interested they will not be so ready to object to something that may be a bit off."[14] The second half of the responding letter includes a long list of films that Rothapfel suggests can "awaken interest in even the most skeptical" and those films with that "something" that is "a bit off." The films listed are from a variety of companies—Mutual, Pathé, Universal, General, for example—and include travelogues, biblical pictures, adaptations of Shake- speare and Dickens and other authors, and historical pictures about the Revolu- tionary War, the American Civil War, and the Boer War. Included in this list is *Washington at Valley Forge*. The phrasing used here—"something that may be a bit off"—refers to the dramatization and fictionalization of historical events or the changes that take place in adapting plays, novels, and other well-known sto- ries to film.

This sentiment harkens back to what Jennifer Peterson refers to as a short-lived attempt to uplift cinema through educational film.[15] Peterson demonstrates that during the years 1910–1913 there was a failed attempt to legitimate cinema through the promotion of educational films such as travelogues and science films. Although, ultimately, it was the rise of the feature that solidified cinema's uplift, Peterson maintains that this brief period during which nonfiction and educa- tional cinema were promoted as the means through which cinema's uplift was possible sheds light on the connection between the early cinema industry and Progressive Era culture and politics.[16] What is interesting about the above letter to the editor is its date—1916—appearing three years after Peterson's time frame but demonstrating that a similar discourse around educational film remained in circulation. Further, the historical and literary films were aligned with education in an attempt to legitimate certain forms of "quality" filmmaking.[17]

The educational value of *Washington at Valley Forge* is also mentioned in a review from 1914, which suggested that the film stood out as unique in contrast to the plenitude of Civil War films. In other words, the American Revolution was as important to the sense of national pride as the Civil War and exhibitors might be interested in this film as a welcome change from the repetition of Civil War films. Danson Michell emphasizes the film's educational value: "Aside from the dramatic interest that it arouses, it is of value as an educational picture. It will do more to impress the wonderful story of the American fight for Independence upon the minds of an audience than any number of histories could."[18] However, the melodramatic plot of *Washington at Valley Forge* reveals just how far producers were willing to go in their efforts to promote dramatic films as educational pictures. The plot of *Washington at Valley Forge* is fairly typical. The film concerns Betty, who is staying at an inn, where she overhears the Hessian plot to attack Washington's army at Valley Forge. In disguise, Betty brings the information to her lover, a man she believes to be a soldier with Washington, although he is actually a British spy. He brings the message to the Hessians rather than to Washington and hatches a plan to murder Washington, who is set to sleep at the same inn where Betty is staying. When Betty learns of the plans, she convinces General Washington to switch beds, thus taking the fatal stab wound in his stead. After all is revealed, and Betty dies, her former lover is court-martialed and killed.[19] This film is clearly formulaic and melodramatic, and yet it serves as an example of a film that might be used to "bring the past to life" for audiences of the time.

Educational value is emphasized for various films about the American Revolution. Years earlier, the *Film Index* suggested advertising Selig-Polyscope's *The Spirit of '76* (1908) in a similar manner:

> It can readily be seen that this film is the greatest ever because of the many advantageous advertising schemes which can be worked, such as "Grand Army Day, or "School Children's American History Day," and with special invitation to school teachers to come and view with their own eyes something that heretofore they have learned from a book: in short, take them back almost two hundred years, to see face to face the great American generals, statesmen and early settlers who made it possible for a poor born lad to become President of the Greatest Nation on Earth. To meet face to face Washington, La Fayette, Schuyler and Jefferson, the men who installed the indomitable "spirit of '76" which has made this the most progressive and enlightened of nations.[20]

Here, rather than Rothapfel's caution against presenting dramatized history as purely educational fare, the dramatic aspects of the film are presented as its strength. In this film—as with other historical films—history is brought to life and made "more real" for its viewers because of the story, the actors, and the dramatic nature of narrative film. The review opens by calling the film "Love staged, a love story founded on facts, a tale of woman's heroism in the 'Days of '76.'"[21] The love story, which above might be exactly what Rothapfel means when he mentions that something is "a bit off," is instead a selling point, making history relatable to film audiences. The educational value of these films extended both to audience members whose families had been in the United States for generations and to the newly arrived immigrant audiences who found pleasure in the cinema-going experience.

EUROPEAN HEROINES

Film audiences in the United States during the early 1910s did not have a uniform concept of what it meant to be American. Immigrant audiences used film as a model for Americanness.[22] But additionally, some films used the same formula as discussed in chapters 1 and 2 to envision heroic European women. Some films even offered foreign characters as their heroic leads—for example, the Montenegrin peasant girl in *The Captive* (DeMille, 1915), or Joan of Arc in *Joan the Woman* (DeMille, 1916). Drawing from Robin Blaetz's argument that Joan of Arc was a popular archetype for American audiences, I propose that *The Captive* and *Joan the Woman* function in a similar manner. First, both the Montenegrin character and Joan of Arc appealed to immigrant populations who may have felt like foreigners themselves; and second, they mapped American ideologies onto foreign narratives to demonstrate that the American mythos could be enacted by anyone. These films served to incorporate immigrant populations into American identity categories that were defined by participation in the military.[23] The love of one's home and the right to defend it, these narratives suggested, was a natural right, and one that anyone could perform. Furthermore, many of these films presented underdogs successfully fighting against an imperial enemy, a theme that extends from the mythologization of the American Revolution.

The film *Joan the Woman* is indicative of early studio filmmaking: it is a Cecil B. DeMille epic, featuring a well-known female star (Geraldine Farrar), with a large cast and sprawling sets.[24] Ultimately, it was used briefly to encourage enlistment in the U.S. Army, despite its focus on Joan of Arc and a British soldier. The film, released in 1916, is about Joan of Arc's life and death, but it is framed by a story about a British soldier during World War I who finds her sword in the wall of a trench. He has a vision—which is the majority of the film—and is inspired by Joan's heroism and death. At the end of the film he volunteers to deliver a bomb, which results in his own death and sacrifice. The British soldier's sacrifice parallels Joan's and, in the context of using the film as a recruitment tool, also extends that parallel to men in the audience who were considering enlisting.

Robin Blaetz suggests that the story of Joan of Arc, and the DeMille film specifically, provided evidence of how Joan's story was manipulated to serve different national ideologies, precisely because there exist two versions of the film: the version released to American audiences and the version released in France. The major difference between the two film versions was the addition of a frame story in the American version: the British soldier finding Joan of Arc's sword and having a vision that he was the soldier responsible for Joan's capture. In repentance

FIGURE 7. Film still from *Joan the Woman*. (Courtesy of George Eastman House.)

for his past life's sin, the British soldier decides to volunteer to carry a bomb to the enemy trenches, thus resulting in his own death.

I will take up *Joan the Woman* again in chapter 4, as an example of a Hollywood feature that was given widespread publicity, but I introduce the film here because Joan of Arc is a key figure that circulated throughout American popular culture. Despite not being American, she influenced the representation of heroic American girls, and helps us to understand how non-American female heroines in film might have been understood by audiences at the time. Robin Blaetz suggests that the prevalence of Joan of Arc in American militaristic propaganda was an attempt to address immigrant audiences who could identify with Joan as an outsider and a defender of the nation.[25]

Joan of Arc was mobilized for American propaganda, as we will see in later chapters, but her use continues to reveal tensions regarding the representations of heroic women. Blaetz suggests that the frame story of the film separates Joan of Arc from the heroics of war: "Women are welcome to sacrifice themselves for the crusade but the deeds of war and the attendant glory are reserved for men alone."[26] This reading, however, suggests that the frame story negates all that happens in the majority of the film and fails to give credit to the female leadership demonstrated throughout the film by Joan, and in the star performance of Geraldine Farrar. Blaetz suggests that a female heroine is a threat to the patriarchal order: "As it stands, the institutions of patriarchy possess the meaning of

Joan of Arc whichever way she is beheld. Her dual significance as a self-sacrificing female martyr and a powerful woman who is reduced to her assigned role are invaluable to those for whom a true heroine represents a cultural danger perhaps greater than that presented by any war."[27] This cultural anxiety over the representations of powerful women may be the reason cross-dressing female soldiers and spies in films declined as a major character type roughly around 1915.

Films set during the Balkan conflicts (which had taken place just a couple of years earlier in Europe) provided a new militarized subject matter but presented the same themes that were discussed in American-based wars films to depict the values of homeland defense and the success of the underdog. Women in films about different wars were used to demonstrate the same characteristics that made the American Girls of the Civil War so popular—bravery, daring, wit, and impulsivity—but they had been transposed to different settings, such as a rural farm in the Balkans. In 1912 the Balkan War was being waged by Bulgaria, Greece, Serbia, and Montenegro against the Turkish Empire; by 1913 the Second Balkan War saw Bulgaria fighting against Greece and Serbia over land disputes. Like the American Revolution, it was a story of the underdogs and, like the films of the American Civil War, narratives presented women left alone at home to defend their domestic space.

During the Balkan Wars, film was a popular way for Americans to witness the conflict, the politics, and the countryside of a region largely unknown to them. According to Jerzy Toeplitz, the Balkan Wars were the first wars fought in Europe to be covered by film correspondents, which included views from various sides, shown in many countries.[28] The films sent to America were energetically promoted in the *Moving Picture World*, and a review for an Eclipse-Kleine release demonstrated one possible reason for the American fascination with the Balkan conflicts: "The whole world has been astounded at the fighting ability displayed by these armies of the Balkan states in their encounters with the Turkish forces; how they have beaten time and again the 'Terrible Turk,' who has been considered almost invincible upon the battlefield."[29] Much like the mythos of the American Revolution, the Balkan wars were presented to American citizens as the triumph of the underdog—in this case, the small Balkan countries against the Turkish Empire.

Further evidence of the American fascination with this war is the dime novel from 1911 entitled *Fighting for Greece, or, Three Yankee Boys against the Turks*, which was published in *Pluck and Luck*.[30] Furthermore, in 1915 *The Captive* reworked the trope of a woman defending her home into a story involving a Montenegrin peasant and a Turkish soldier of noble birth. In fact, the climax of the film involved the Turk protecting the girl and her younger brother against savage Turkish soldiers and recalled many of the Revolutionary and Civil War films that showed women as the moralizing force who showed unruly soldiers the true cause. The Balkan Wars—of fascination to Americans during the mid-1910s—reiterated for audiences the feminine-militaristic ideologies that had been circulating in American popular culture for some time. Blanche Sweet's role as the female protagonist in *The Captive* served to connect American values to the foreign conflict. Blanche Sweet played Sonya, a young woman tending to a small Montenegrin house with her younger brother. She must keep a Turkish nobleman captive during the war, and eventually they fall in love, despite being enemies in war. This film does not center around American protagonists, but it is played by American actors, and the subject matter was very similar to the Civil War films: The battle took place in Sonia's home country, and Sonya was both the protector of the home and the moral guide for her younger brother and her Turkish captive.

Women were the arbiters of peace and unity in the ideological construction of femininity emphasized in Civil War films and subsequently transferred to films about the Turkish-Montenegrin war. The following review reveals the impulse to familiarize the foreign through the common trope of "natural" femininity: "[In] 'The Captive,' a five-part picturization of a play by Cecil B. DeMille and Jeanie MacPherson, [Sweet] has a role of possibilities well in keeping with her personality and histrionic method. This time she is cast as Sonya Martinovitch, a Montenegrin peasant girl of an elementary, subdued nature; but underneath the rather coarse surface there lies a vein of feminine tenderness and plenty of fire and passion, once they are aroused."[31] This review emphasized the same aspects of femininity were lauded in these films: "tenderness" and "fire" are seemingly contradictory yet exemplary of how Americans conceived of the American Girl. Again, this review was more about Sweet, who was American, than it was about depicting Sonya as Montenegrin.

In *The Captive* Blanche Sweet reprised a character type she had played in several Civil War films: the quick-thinking, determined woman who, by matter of circumstance, must participate in war. Sweet had been the unnamed star of *The Battle*, a 1912 D. W. Griffith film in which she played the sweetheart of a man who tries to desert the army. Though her name was still unknown (as was typical of the film industry in the early 1910s), a reviewer from the *Moving Picture World* still praised her performance: "Did she weep, did she sympathize with this pitiful bundle of frightened humanity who had once been a man? She did not. She looked surprised, and then she laughed loud and long and heartily—half hysterically, half scornfully. And then her laughter left her and left her mad and she flew at that thing she had loved and called a man and tore at it and beat it, and ordered it from her presence; as well done a bit of acting in a very old and hackneyed situation as I have seen in many a day."[32] After Biograph released the names of its players, and Sweet had become a popular star in her own right, the *Motion Picture News* devoted an article to describing her "screen magnetism": "The wonderful fact of Blanche Sweet is that she does not act: instead, she lives through the experience of the stories which she is made to interpret with such fervor that the audience correctly believes it is not witnessing the illusion of life but life itself."[33] This passage reveals the developing strategy of promoting stars by emphasizing their similarities to the characters that they played on screen. Thus, the heroism and bravery of the characters on-screen is translated to supposed real-life attributes that the stars themselves possess.

Blanche Sweet is an example of how female star personas were crafted to include many of the traits their characters portrayed. In *Picture Personalities* Richard de Cordova discusses the promotion of these early stars, the "picture personalities," as an extension of their on-screen characters, rather than providing an insight into their personal lives. According to de Cordova, prior to 1913 personalities were wholly linked to the production of the film texts, while after 1913–1914, the popularity of "stars" was promoted with stories about their off-screen lives.[34] Sweet's "realism," which was emphasized throughout the article, echoed de Cordova's history of early stardom—"she does not act; she merely does things"—because her on- and off-screen personas coincided. Promotion of Blanche Sweet suggests that she was as much an "American Girl" in the narrative of the films was she is in her personal life and in her approach to acting. A newspaper article, "Reel Heroines in Real Life," mentioned that Sweet "rescued" a screenwriter who had wandered away from filming to scout out a new setting.[35] Here, the female star represented the ideals of active American womanhood both on the screen and off. Furthermore, though her name was unknown during her time as an actress with the Biograph Company, many of the films were re-released in 1915, boasting of the "star-studded casts," including Blanche Sweet.[36]

The re-release of the Biograph films would have coincided with Sweet's performance in *The Captive*, which was also released after her performance in the Civil War film *The Warrens of Virginia*. *The Captive* and the Civil War films had similar themes, and this was made clear through the figure of its star, Blanche Sweet: she represented the ideal, military American Girl, even when playing a Montenegrin peasant. In short, *The Captive* demonstrated that the active heroine protecting her home remained a model of femininity even as the popularity of the Civil War in film began to drop. Americanizing the foreign was an important ideological function for film in the 1910s; by rewriting other nations' histories according to American values, these films suggested that all women could be American Girls. Films were seen by many immigrant audiences and appealed to these audiences as a means through which they could "become" American. What stands in for Americanness, or the possibility for Americanization and assimilation, is further complicated not just by the representation of northern European women in these films but also by the representation of conflicts with Indigenous Americans and conflicts at the Mexican border.

BORDERLAND FILMS

The conflict in Mexico and along the U.S.-Mexican border was complex and provides an interesting counterpoint to the formula of the American Girl, so prominent in American war films of the early to mid-1910s. Film representations of battles fought along the U.S.-Mexico border were both about defending the home (and its boundaries) and also about looking outward, toward the U.S. involvement on a global stage. I have argued in this chapter that women stood in as a symbol of that which needs defending and yet also figured as active defenders of that home; but the ways in which this was tied up with ideologies of militarism and nationalism (imagining a white America) were always about the United States in relation to others. The border with Mexico, then, served as a symbolic space from which to look outward toward the world. In this case, however, it was very important that the U.S. involvement in the early to mid-1910s was one of military invasion.

In 1911 Kalem released a film entitled *The Mexican Joan of Arc*, which told the story of a woman whose husband and two sons were arrested by President Diaz and sentenced to death. The grieving woman, having lost her family, swears vengeance and ultimately pulls together a group of fighters, which leads to Diaz's removal from power. Stephen Bush compares the woman to the original Joan of Arc in this passage: "It possesses a tragic power greater than that of 'Joan of Arc.' The latter was impelled by patriotism, moved by heavenly visions to come to the aid of her king. . . . The widow Talamantes cared nothing about the insurrection in itself, she uses the insurrection as a means to an end and thereby lifts the whole story into a higher plane of dramatic force and interest. What must otherwise have been a common tale of war and politics now becomes a tragedy in the truest sense of the word."[37] The review belies Stephen Bush's attitude toward the conflict in Mexico. For Bush, there seems a need to distance the identification with the woman from her part in the Mexican insurrection. Rather than seeing her as a Mexican woman, he can only praise the film by emphasizing that she is a woman, motivated by "primal" drives. Perhaps Bush's review offers insight into how some might interpret or take pleasure in films about foreign characters. However, it is just as likely there might be others in the audience who watch the film for the positive depiction of the Mexican insurrection.

In her book *Borderland Films*, Dominique Bregent-Heald writes that filmic borderlands "expressed broader anxieties over maintaining gendered, racial, and national boundaries during the early twentieth century".[38] Borderlands, for Bregent-Heald, include the locations and communities around the U.S.-Mexican border and the U.S.-Canadian border. Of interest in this chapter are the films about the U.S.-Mexican border, the anxieties over the Mexican Revolution, and the formation of California. Throughout the era when Civil War films found popularity and the American Revolution was an occasional subject, the other battles that took place at home were depicted in films about border conflicts and the formation of California. The revolution in Mexico was also a topic of national interest that made its way onto the screen and into film advertisements. The Mexican Revolution, which began in 1910, played an important role in American foreign policy and the debates regarding the American military's preparedness for fighting in World War I. The murder of Francisco Madero, and subsequent takeover by Victoriano Huerta in 1913, precipitated the American intervention in Mexico. President Woodrow Wilson's government did not recognize Huerta, instead pledging support for the rebel faction, which in turn rejected American support for fear of becoming "a client state."[39] The conflict between the U.S. government and Mexican revolutionaries continued when the rebel faction's leader, Venustiano Carranza, took over after Huerta stepped down. This clash was then exploited by the leader of an opposing faction, Pancho Villa, who stoked the fears that Carranza was simply a tool used to further American interests. Villa's raids on border towns provoked Wilson to send 100,000 reserve troops to Mexico in mid-1916.[40]

The connection between Civil War and American Revolutionary films and the films that depicted or debated foreign intervention in the contemporaneous war in Europe is one of genre. The connection between films about the conflict in Mexico and the American entry into World War I is more straightforward. Jennifer Keene lays out four ways the Mexican Revolution affected the American attitude toward and preparation for their entry into World War I. First, the Mexican crisis illustrated the moral and philosophical underpinnings of Wilson's approach to foreign policy. Second, tensions between Mexico and the United States encouraged Germany to believe that an intensified borderland conflict would keep American from entering the European war. Third, German espionage in Mexico contributed to Wilson's growing distrust of Germany. Finally, the punitive expedition gave many men who would lead the American Expeditionary Force in France their first taste of leading men into combat.[41]

What this means for film, then, is that battles in and on the border with Mexico represented both concerns with and viewers' fascination with the Mexican crisis, as well as larger questions about what American involvement in the European war might mean moving forward.

The conflict with Mexico appeared in newsreels and actualities, as well as narrative films. In his 1914 review "Mexican War Pictures," in the *Moving Picture World*, Stephen Bush's discussion of the style of warfare was implicitly a critique of the Mexican people: "In the so-called Mexican civil war there is, as these films testify most eloquently, nothing of the glory and the glamour of war. The films convince us that the struggle in Mexico is down to the lowest level of human misery and sordidness: a lot of poor peons, more or less badly armed, fighting for they do not know what, and murdering each other like bands of savages."[42] Although this is a review of an actuality released by Mutual, it serves to clarify a thematic use of the Mexican border in film, which is later exploited in fiction films that served a propagandistic purpose. Bush notes that the Mexican factions are never called an army—"Villa's 'army' is at best a band of guerrillas"—and, he continues, they enact the lowest and least "civilized" form of warfare.[43] The type of warfare, the organization of the army, their actions, and the way they are represented comes to stand for the morality of the nation as a whole. On the opposite hand, of course, is the American "intervention," and likewise the American nation, which is framed in this review as the savior for wounded villagers and soldiers: "We have 'intervened,'" says Bush, "by treating the wounded soldiers of both sides who have sought refuge on the right side of the Rio Grande."[44] The Americans are the civilizing force bordering against a nation that needs saving, according to the popular representation both in films and critical discourse of the era. This framing of Mexican guerillas as uncivilized and lacking in moral righteousness, versus the American troops who are not only on the right side of the Rio Grande but also on the right side of history, continues to appear in films that either are directly about the Mexican Revolution or use Mexico as symbolic of the United States' need to prepare for war.

One final film about the Mexican Revolution brings into focus a number of factors, and returns us to a discussion of women in war. *The War Extra* (Blaché, 1914) is about a newspaper man, Fred Newton, working for the *Herald*, who goes to Mexico to cover the battles in Monclova. Once there, Fred and his telegraph assistant set up a wire to send information back to the newspaper. They also meet and save a young woman, Dolores, who had been adopted by Mexican shopkeepers. Battles take place all around them, and Fred and his assistant are captured as suspected spies. Delores rides back to the U.S.-Mexico border and enlists the help of Texan cowboys, who battle with the Mexican troops. As they try to ride back across the border to safety, more American troops arrive just in time to ensure that the newspaper men, cowboys, and Delores make it back across the Rio Grande. Fred returns home to New York and weds Delores, who is enthusiastically welcomed by his mother and sister.[45]

As the plot of this film shows, the male character is the central protagonist. However, Delores still saves the day. While Fred and his assistant are near death, injured and trapped by the Mexican forces, Delores manages to ride for help—embodying two symbols of American expansion: the cowboys and the ambiguously described American forces that arrive in the nick of time. Delores, importantly, is described as the adopted daughter of Mexican shopkeepers, thus intentionally leaving her heritage vague. Though she is likely Mexican herself, the ambiguity works to present her more as a blank slate, ready to be Americanized through marriage and the welcoming embrace of Fred's mother and sister. The cross-border romance, in this case, is also between an American man and a Mexican woman, a theme that historically has been used more frequently than the reverse. Shelley Streeby's study of sensational literature of the mid-nineteenth century offers a historical precedent to the character of Delores. Streeby writes about the character type of the cross-dressed Mexican female soldier, featured in sensational literature about the U.S.-Mexican War of the 1840s. The cross-dressing soldier would, by the end of the story, revert back to dressing as a woman, sometimes marrying a U.S. soldier. This fluidity of both gender and nation highlights the cross-dressing Mexican soldier as a "potentially assimilable foreign body" who "was frequently contrasted with other types of Mexicans who were viewed as decidedly nonwhite and inassimilable."[46] Delores *was* assimilable and did assimilate through her marriage to Fred and through her friendship with the two white women whose approval at the end of the film was necessary to represent her acceptance within white American society. In contrast, though not mentioned throughout the review or plot summary in *Moving Picture World*, the Mexican soldiers were those who must be kept apart and outside the boundaries (both the border, and the more symbolic imagined white nation). Here, then, we can imagine that the same attitude Stephen Bush expressed in his review "Mexican War Subjects" was meant to be applied to the faceless enemies in *The War Extra*.

The filmic representation of the Mexican border and the Mexican Revolution, and the contrasting depictions of the Mexican revolutionary armies and the American forces, are essential to understanding the pivot that happens between American neutrality in the face of World War I and calls to preparedness. This chapter and chapter 2 are focused on films that show war and battles at home, underscoring how militarism and American expansion was tied up with discourses around domestic defense. But the entry into World War I required American citizens to embrace militaristic entry onto a global stage. Chapters 4 and 5 will show how filmic formulas of the American Girl defending the home were perfectly fitted to the transition between neutrality and preparedness. The border with Mexico, as well as the nation's coasts, represented vulnerability and the need to prepare a strong military force.

4 · FEATURING PREPAREDNESS AND PEACE
America and the European War, Part I

Preparedness films mirrored debates happening in newspapers and in homes across the country about fears of foreign invasion and the need to prepare for war. There were films in favor of war preparedness—building a strong army—and films in favor of peace, or staying out of war. Although they were important at the time, these films have fallen into the shadow of *Birth of a Nation* in film history. More significantly, though, these films' melodramatic plots and gruesome violence stoked the fires of fear. Most of the preparedness films are lost, yet the surviving scenarios and synopses in exhibitors' trade journals bring back to life their narratives and significance. Like the films from previous chapters, the films discussed here mobilized the peril and purity of white American women, more often than not, to call the nation to arms. Unlike the films previously discussed, these films depicted more violent outcomes that might befall white American women. There is consistency in the underlying ideologies of the Civil War and American Revolutionary films of earlier chapters and the preparedness films and serials of this chapter and chapter 5. The preparedness debates were always presented to the American public as a question of defense of the nation rather than preparation to enter the war "over there," even though participation in the war was the end goal of many preparedness advocates. Thus, female protagonists—the defenders of the home—remained a mainstay of the genre in the years between 1914 and 1917.

Directors, producers, and writers communicated differing opinions on military preparedness through their films and serials, either by valorizing peace advocates or by showing the folly of peace through the grim possibility of invasion. Thomas Ince's *Civilization* (1915) was a plea for peace in light of war, whereas Lubin's *The Nation's Peril* (1915), J. Stuart Blackton's *Battle Cry of Peace* (1915), the Public Service Film Company's *Defense or Tribute?* (1916), and Thomas Dixon's *The Fall of a Nation* (1916) were more straightforward calls for military preparedness. A handful of serials, including *Pearl of the Army* (1916) and *Patria* (1917), also depicted the debate in their subject matter and advertising. In both examples, women played a central role within the narrative, demonstrating that preparedness must be unanimous and that every member of the nation was responsible for the defense of home soil. Serials will be the subject of chapter 5, as they offer up a different view of the film industry in the mid-1910s. Like the women in Civil War and American Revolution films from the early 1910s, women in feature films depicting the need for preparedness were sometimes active in the defense of their homeland. As a continuation of the active heroines of the earlier films, the women depicted in the preparedness films and serials foiled spies, disrupted invasions, and gathered armies to defend American soil. However, another character type emerged at this time: the peace-at-any-price advocate. Often aligned with women and feminist organizations—although sometimes the central peace advocate in a film was a man—the peace advocates in various films from 1914 to 1917 were mouthpieces for the opposition to militaristic spending.

The "preparedness" debates grew from an impulse to downplay foreign militaristic involvement by re-visioning current political debates as being concerned with domestic issues rather than foreign ones. As such, women continued to appear in these films—extending from the history of heroines and imperiled women from fiction and film about the Civil War and American Revolutionary War—as central protagonists for films about preparedness precisely because they were perceived to be the home's first line of defense. Direct descendants of the earlier film heroines, the preparedness heroines reconfirmed the concept that U.S. policy was about protecting freedom at home rather than expanding onto the world stage. The rhetoric of American foreign policy during the preparedness period emphasized domestic defense, and thus the trend of the female heroine as representative of domestic militarism continued. Again, this follows the definition of melodrama expanded on by Jonna Eagle in its relation to imperialism: Through the genealogy of melodramatic action that I trace, injury and suffering are linked to the mobilization of violent agency, soliciting identification with a national subject who is constituted as at once vulnerable and powerful, victimized and invincible. Nationalist violence is produced as both righteous and retributive, always already defensive in nature; the spectacular display of such violence, which both relies upon and refutes the premise of violability, is sanctioned as a site of mediated pleasure.[1] Eagle's book is about melodrama and American masculinity as tied to American imperialism. But the concept of melodrama as positioning the "hero" as the victim, in order to justify the turn toward violence and militarism, is evident in the films studied here and in the discourse surrounding preparedness in the mid-1910s.

Preparedness politics were framed by the contrast between Woodrow Wilson and Theodore Roosevelt, two prominent figures representing the two sides. The

FIGURE 8. Ad for Vitagraph Preparedness films, *Motion Picture News*, February 24, 1917. (Courtesy of Media History Digital Library.)

merits and shortcomings of Wilson's presidency (1913–1921) were heavily debated.[2] In particular, Wilson's stance on American foreign policy was not unanimously accepted; instead, it was the subject of many debates among politicians, journalists, political commentators, and the general public at the time. Roosevelt remained a strong detractor of Wilson's noninterventionist stance, and Wilson's reaction to the events taking place in Mexico and the submarine warfare of 1915 was often strongly criticized, both in the press and in the political sphere.[3] Leading up to his presidency, Wilson's priorities were largely focused on domestic issues, and it was only because of the conflicts that occurred in Mexico and Europe that foreign policy became such a defining feature of his time in office. During his years as president, Wilson redefined his political focus from privileging domestic issues to foreign policy because of the war in Europe, the revolution and civil war in Mexico, and the changing relationships between the United States and various Latin American countries.[4] As discussed in more detail in chapter 3, the conflicts in Mexico and along the U.S.-Mexico border were a significant turning point for President Wilson.[5] In the 1916 presidential campaign, the Democrats had lauded Wilson with the tagline "He Kept Us Out of War"; the Republicans criticized his "diplomacy," in reference to Mexico more than to the war in Europe.[6]

Journalists relied on exaggerated descriptions of a disinterested public and rhetorical fear tactics in order to steer readers toward support of preparedness: "It is the habit of the people of the United States to treat lightly the great questions of national danger and national defense. With a superb contempt for some of the most strikingly significant facts of our diplomatic history they are inclined, as a rule, to pooh-pooh even the possibility—to say nothing of the probability—of our becoming involved in war with a foreign country."[7] Articles about the lack of preparedness were commonplace in American newspapers during the first years of World War I, encouraging support for war preparation that bridged the gap between both political parties. Film, however, functioned to narrativize and give life to these political debates. Propagandistic in content and tone, these films placed their central characters in horrifying scenes to remind viewers of the perils of a foreign invasion. If anything, film was part of a tapestry of popular culture that fed fears of foreign invasion. In a reversal of the Civil War films and American Revolution films, these films created an enemy, a shadowy "them," known only in its stark contrast to the pure, innocent, and sometimes naive "us" represented by the American Girls.

A typical narrative of preparedness films involved showing one side of the political debate as flawed—witness the depiction of the peace advocates in *Battle Cry* as "silly" and "fanatic." The films would show these flaws as entrenched within society until a central character or event revealed the danger and convinced people to change their minds. For example, in *Civilization*, society is militaristic until Jesus appears and teaches the message of peace. Other films, such as *A Nation's Peril*, *The Battle Cry of Peace*, and *The Fall of a Nation*, told the opposite story: a country swayed by peace advocates is invaded and thus learns the importance of military preparedness. In *The Battle Cry of Peace*, a series of scenes take place during a Peace Meeting of "fanatic women and silly-looking men."[8] Most of the members of the audience, as well as the speakers, were pro-peace advocates, although one man interjected with questions about the need for preparedness and two participants were later found to be foreign spies. The peace conference erupts in a riot between members after the one man questions the effectiveness of peace and disarmament. A member of the conference escapes the building and finds a phone booth from which he calls the police, who in turn must come to break up the riot. The peace conference and its members are evidently a sham, hardly peaceful at all. The film asks audience members to see the folly of such individuals, to see their hypocrisy. Later a montage shows carefree Americans at cafés and dance halls, hardly aware of the looming threat of invasion. The scenes are contrasted to show the foolishness of peace advocates, the presence of foreign enemies, the way the peace advocates influenced political decisions that left the United States vulnerable to invasion, and finally, the relative naiveté of the American populace.

While the war in Europe remained a central concern, the discourse of military preparedness in the United States was framed by the threat of foreign invasion on home soil, a threat that carried greater weight. Most interestingly, female characters in these films were associated with pacifist organizations; some learned that pacifism would damage the nation's defense abilities, while others successfully spread the message of peace. Regardless of whether the film was pro-preparedness or pro-pacifist, the female characters functioned as the strongest advocates of peace. This, of course, was a complete reversal of the roles for women in the Civil War films of the early 1910s.

Women in both pro-preparedness and pro-peace films were often depicted as belonging to peace organizations, largely because of the prevailing belief that many feminist organizations were aligned with peace organizations. Writing about this period, Joyce Berkman states: "It is no mere coincidence that the peak of prewar peace activism coincided with the crest of the first wave of the women's movement. Each movement fed the other. Peace continued to be viewed primarily as a woman's concern—a consensus reflecting the established gender conventions among white Americans and Europeans. Some feminists rejected those conventions but attached themselves to 'peace' just the same."[9] Berkman's article demonstrates that the peace movement may have united feminists in the prewar period, but that during the war a division took place that caused massive ruptures along the pro- and anti-war lines.[10] However, during the years prior to U.S. entry into war, this woman-as-pacifist trend was the subject of several films. The films that advocated for peace and isolation often draw connections between feminist organizations and peace groups, depicting narratives in which female characters were exalted for their devotion to peace. Alternatively, pro-preparedness pictures sometimes aligned feminism and peace organizations so that they could later be proven foolish for their "naive" belief in "peace at any price." These narratives suggested that advocating for peace led to a weak army, which could only result in foreign armies easily invading the United States and causing destruction, and peril to the nation's women.

Lubin's *The Nation's Peril* is an example of the alignment between women and peace organizations, because the active heroine is at first a strong advocate of peace. She is duped into giving up plans to a foreign spy, but then kills him and helps thwart a foreign power's plan of invasion. Set in 1918, the film depicts the possibility that a foreign power—whoever wins the war "abroad"—would choose to invade American soil next. A review by Edward Weitzel in the *Moving Picture World* suggests the intended reception of the film: "The naval officer here receives the proper reward at the finish of this splendid object lesson to the peace-at-any-price adherents."[11] This review assumes allegiance with the cause of preparedness. In the film, the young woman, Ruth, is a staunch peace advocate and a member of an international peace organization. Through a series of events, Ruth's insistence on peace results not only in harm to others but also, in an invasion of America. Within its plot, *The Nation's Peril* reiterated the popular assumption that feminism and pacifism were connected: the character of Ruth is "under the influence" of pacifism, but she quickly learns that it will jeopardize her nation's safety. In other words, narratives such as this purported to reveal the "true" nature of women and men alike as fighters and defenders of the American nation, albeit after they learned a lesson about the perils of peace.

Two other films to take up the question of women and peace organizations, one (*Civilization*) in favor of pacifism, and the other (*The Fall of a Nation*) against it. *Civilization* was referred to as a "cinema-spectacle" because the screening was sometimes preceded by a prologue performed by live actors on a stage in front of the screen.[12] The spectacle was compared to Griffith's *Birth of a Nation*, which had been released a year earlier, but the review of the film in *Motion Picture News* did not engage an evaluative comparison, observing, "instead of rivaling it contrasts."[13] Whereas *Birth of a Nation* condones violence for the "right" cause, *Civilization* shows only the horrors. A central character in the film, Katherine Haldeman, belongs to an organization of "women pledged to suppress the war."[14] She convinces Count Ferdinand (of an unnamed European nation) to join her cause of peace. The film's narrative supports the women's cause, but Bush argued that although the spectacle was highly effective, the message of the film was lost amid the "confusion of ideas."[15]

In contrast, Thomas Dixon, the writer of *Birth of a Nation*'s source text, also wrote *The Fall of a Nation*, which attempted to show the "folly" of women who belonged to and promoted peace organizations by narrating the lesson learned by one such woman. The film begins with a prologue of short scenes that depict creation of the United States. The main plot of the film is set in New York City, where a millionaire named Charles Waldron poses as a peace advocate while actually working for a foreign power that was preparing to invade the United States. Charles works with Virginia Holland, who has political influence as leader of a peace group. Congressman John Vassar attempts to pass a preparedness bill but is outvoted. An invasion of the country at Long Island and the destruction of the Panama Canal lead to a successful invasion of the United States. The following act takes place after the foreign power has assumed control: Virginia Holland pretends to work with the new government while secretly joining forces with Angela, a woman who lost her husband in war. Angela and Virginia manage to recruit a number of women to help, and they ultimately build an army, with the help of Congressman Vassar, who has moved west and is training men far from the city. Together they defeat the foreign power and America is once again set free.[16] A review from *Moving Picture World* describes the women's army unfavorably in this passage:

> When it comes to reclaiming the country Mr. Dixon gives his imagination yet freer play by creating a band of loyal women, "Daughters of Jael," who secretly organize and then use their wits and charms to ensnare the officers or the dictators army, preparatory to a country-wide uprising. The final scenes, with their dash and spirit and the young women riding here and there and everywhere in their pretty white uniforms, recall the Ku Klux clan episodes in "The Birth of a Nation," except that in the present instance it is rather difficult to take the military operations seriously.[17]

In contrast to the Civil War and American Revolutionary films of just a few short years earlier, here we see a reviewer who finds warrior women hard to believe. Of course, active and heroic women were not universally popular, and the formula of women participating actively in these sensational scenes was divisive in the trade press.

It is possible that the contemporary setting and the topical themes influenced the reviews, assigning value judgments based on political opinions. For example, a review of the film in *Motion Picture News* refers to the conclusion of the love story between the main male hero and the woman: "John Vassar claimed Virginia Holland, who had atoned for her Peace-at-any-price folly by defying death to restore the sacred Union of States."[18] Later reviews of the Liberty Theatre screening in New York City again belied the bias of the reviewer toward preparedness over peace: "America's inadequate army is shortly overpowered, the eyes of the Pacifist and Peace-at-any-Price supporters are opened, and so, after two years of suffering under the yoke of the 'Emperor,' an uprising led by women succeeds in crushing the foreign power and re-establishing the republic."[19] In other words, reviewers highlighted Virginia's "folly" and suggested that peace advocates had their "eyes opened" to the real need for a strong army. The message of the film was that women's clubs across the nation should use their power of organization and influence to promote preparedness rather than pacifism. Dixon said of his film, "There is a strong feminist element."[20]

Both *The Fall of a Nation* and *Civilization* used female characters to convey different messages precisely because female characters could be used either as peace advocates or to demonstrate the need for preparedness due to the vulnerability of women at home.

FEATURING PREPAREDNESS

In mid-1915, Vitagraph was advertising its film *The Battle Cry of Peace* as a "Vitagraph Blue Ribbon Feature."[21] On the following page, in reference to a different film, the advertisement implies value with the statement "One of the most convincing arguments for the Blue Ribbon Features is the type of theatres who want them."[22] The term "Blue Ribbon Feature" was used in 1915–1920 in the Vitagraph studio's promotion of quality films.[23] The film itself stands at the intersection of promoting "big" pictures in a transition of the industry toward feature-length films, the use of politics and politicians as a promotional tactic for particular films, and a continuation of developing characteristics of the war film.

The Battle Cry of Peace was unabashedly propagandistic. The title demonstrates the way in which language is massaged to garner acceptance from those who might be on the fence between peace and preparedness. The film is touted as a "call to arms against war" rather than a call to arms for war. Throughout the various parts of the film, the idea is repeated: to have actual peace, one must be prepared for war. The foreign invaders, one might assume, will never invade a country with a strong military. Foreign spies work with peace advocates to ensure that military spending bills are voted down so that the foreigners can invade. In this film the fault lies with the naive and easily manipulated peace advocates. The message of the film is that peace is not possible by goodwill alone but instead needs to be enforced through strong armament. The film is based on a book and speeches by Hudson Maxim, an inventor of explosives and smokeless gunpowder. Maxim's connection to the production of explosives explains his connection to the cause of military preparedness. If the preparedness debate saw the formation of two mutually exclusive arguments—those in favor of America's isolationist policies, and those in favor of preparing the nation's army for war—*Battle Cry*'s writer fell firmly on the side of preparation. In a speech promoting preparedness Hudson Maxim said the following:

There is no one lesson which history teaches us more plainly than that the possession of wealth by a defenseless nation is a standing *casus belli* to other nations, and that always there has been the nation standing ready to attack and plunder any other nation when there was likely to be sufficient profit in the enterprise to pay for the trouble. Never have we seen any treaty stand for long in the way of such practices between nations. Treaties have always been mere scraps of paper, which, like the cobweb, ensnare the weak, while they let the strong break through.[24]

In sum, those in favor of preparedness argued that arming the country was simply defense against a possible invasion. Invasion was repeatedly invoked as a strong possibility, and supporters of peace and isolation were maligned for believing in diplomacy and treaties.

The film *Battle Cry of Peace* demonstrates how the debates were represented as both fact and fiction within film. The film consists of four parts: the first part is a speech of the need for military preparedness by Hudson Maxim, an inventor of explosives and gunpowder, who wrote the book of the same name; the second part is the fictional narrative of invasion; the third shows peaceful scenes from contemporary United States; and the fourth shows what is needed to build a strong military of defense.[25] The film is about two families who live in New York. The son from one family is dating the daughter from the other family. Her father is staunchly pro-peace, while the young man is pro-preparedness. Scenes contain arguments between the young man and the woman's father, as well as a lively debate at a pro-peace rally—particular characters take up the debates circulating throughout the United States at the time. There is, however, a spy who is working with the pro-peace groups to bolster peace advocacy so that he may call upon his countrymen to invade the United States after a bill for preparedness is voted down. The invasion is gruesome, with many deaths, explosions, and destruction of property. A society gala is blown up, with people frantically trying to flee the ballroom. The contrast between the pro-peace rally and the carefree dancing of unsuspecting, and unprepared, Americans is meant to highlight their foolishness as not listening to the warnings. Families die in their houses and in the streets. Women clutch their children as men are shot down or arrested. One scene depicts a puppy licking the hand of its dead owner. This is all to emphasize the gruesome possibility of invasion. It was not enough to say that invasion might happen; it had to be dramatized with the worst possible images of what might come. The threat of rape is consistent throughout. The young woman, Virginia, is trapped by someone from the invading forces and she give into him so that he grabs her and kisses her, which gives her the opportunity to take the revolver from his pocket and kill him. Her father is shot and killed; her lover is injured but later also dies while trying to fight against the invaders. In the final scenes of the narrative portion of the film, Virginia, her mother, and her younger sister are finally trapped. Fearing what will come for her daughters, the mother takes the revolver from Virginia and shoots them both. The story ends with the mother holding both dead girls in her arms. There is no triumph of American heroism or last-minute savior. Instead the savior comes in the form of the epilogue, or the following parts, wherein scenes from the United States are shown, followed by a call to preparedness and a list of facts about what is needed to prepare America against invasion.

In addition to their helping us understand how the plot and imagery of the film evoked fear of invasion, details about the promotion and exhibition of *Battle*

Cry and other preparedness features reveal the importance of preparedness as a topic. Many of the films under the preparedness banner were given the labels "event films," "features," or other terms that indicated the films' difference from the average film released at the time. The rise of the "feature" film is not as straightforward as simply longer-length films supplanting the one- and two-reelers in popularity. Chapters 2 and 3 focused on the transitional era, from attractions to the rise in dominance of narrative films; this chapter instead is situated in the context during which narrative films were common, when the film program—multiple short films—was the norm over one long film. Experimentation with longer-length films took place throughout the early 1910s and resulted in a number of films of roughly five reels during the middle of the decade. Sheldon Hall and Steve Neale note that early references to the term "feature" came from American film's vaudeville roots, denoting something special within the program, not always a specific film. By 1912 the term "feature" was used regularly, coinciding with the rise of multi-reel films.[26]

Battle Cry's advertisements in the trade press called the film propaganda and touted its importance not only in the current moment but also to American history. The assertion that *Battle Cry* would go down as an essential and long-remembered element of American history has not proven true but it serves as a starting point for understanding preparedness films. When the war broke out in Europe, the United States was not quick to take sides, and instead debates about isolationism, neutrality, and peace versus preparedness became the norm. Preparedness meant not only preparation to enter the European war but—more importantly, according to its presentation in the films—preparation to defend against foreign invasion on home soil. By 1916 these issues were debated at length in newspapers and political campaigns, eventually finding their way into popular entertainment as a subject of filmed and written serials and feature films. In short, the fear of foreign invasion was used to garner support for building a strong American military force—and the term "preparedness" emphasized the defense aspects of the military, to minimize the idea that the United States was an aggressive or imperial force.[27]

For *The Battle Cry of Peace*, as well as the other preparedness and peace films released in 1915–1916, the term "feature" was tied not only to length but also to the attempt to make these films "event" films. *Battle Cry* was not the only war-themed film that was promoted as a special feature, though it was one of the most overt in its propagandistic aims. One advertisement in the *Motion Picture News* stated, "'The Battle Cry of Peace' will find its way into the history of motion pictures as an epoch-making achievement—in the magnitude of its production, in the novelty of its appeal, in the idea that is behind it," followed by the statement that the film, in fact, "will find its way into the history of our nation."[28] As a propaganda tool, this film and the others billed as "preparedness" films, deserve a place in film history, at least. In an article about another preparedness film, *The Fall of a Nation*, a quote from the general manager of V-L-S-E demonstrates attitudes toward "big" pictures and films about preparedness:[29] "The successes achieved by exhibitors everywhere during the past year have proved beyond question of doubt the value of the big film as an added stimulus to business. . . . The prolonged runs of 'The Battle Cry of Peace,' 'The Ne'er-Do-Well,' 'Sherlock Holmes,' 'God's Country and the Woman,' etc., etc., and the advanced admission prices which they have made possible, show the demand of the public for such features. . . . Particularly have the Preparedness films been unusual in their drawing power."[30] This quote shows that preparedness and war pictures were not the only "big" films, but that producers, distributors, and exhibitors were aware that films billed as preparedness films were a draw.

These films were promoted as "big" films. In demonstrating the elusiveness of a definition of blockbuster films, Julian Stringer refers to size as central to our understanding of blockbuster as a category of film.[31] For Stringer, it is important not just to remember but to engage with blockbusters as a genre, because, as Rick Altman argues, "Instead of conflating the work of producers, exhibitors, viewers and critics, we need to recognize their differing purposes and the resultant differences in generic categories, labels and uses."[32] Two things must be clarified here: First, the term "blockbuster" was not in usage to describe films of the 1910s. Hollywood blockbusters are often discussed as a key feature of "New Hollywood"—*Jaws* (1975), *Star Wars* (1977), *Superman* (1978), and *Raiders of the Lost Ark* (1981) being key early examples. Steve Neale demonstrates that the term itself, first used during World War II to describe a bomb, was applied to Hollywood film as early as the 1950s.[33] However, if we shift focus from the term itself, understanding how the size of a picture enters into discourse surrounding promotion, exhibition, production, and distribution illuminates how we can enter into an analysis of these films. *Civilization* still exists to view; however, for the others—*Fall of a Nation, Battle Cry of Peace, A Nation's Peril*, etc.—only traces remain in the trade press, in synopses, in copyright records, and promotional materials. As such, much of my analysis focuses on the way these films were lauded for their size, for their lengthy runs in theaters, for the promotional stunts and event-like screenings. In other words, I am suggesting, not that the trade press articles confirm popularity, perceived quality, or box office success, but instead that the discourse around their promotion reveals the way these films were intentionally elevated above "regular" filmic production by the producers, distributors, and exhibitors. Whether they were elevated as event films *because* they depicted preparedness debates in narrative form or whether public interest in preparedness was used and exploited to garner interest in the films is beside the point. War pictures made for good spectacle. By the mid-1910s, spectacle was a key element of American films; and preparedness pictures delivered spectacle to expectant audiences.[34] Film histories continue to center *Birth of a*

Nation and D. W. Griffith as origins of American feature films, but I hope that this chapter illuminates a more complex understanding of the various films that were part of the history of "big" pictures. Preparedness films were but one of the many types of films that were given more coverage in the trade press, longer runs in theaters, and more elaborate promotional stunts. *Civilization*, for example, was promoted when Andrew C. Edison and Leo C. Harding took a cross-country motorcycle trip, wearing clothing advertising the word "Civilization" and distributing pamphlets and photographs along the way.[35] The elaborate promotion of preparedness films continued but was altered based on changing needs after the U.S. government entered the war.

PREPAREDNESS FILMS, WARTIME NEEDS

On April 6, 1917, the U.S. Congress declared war and officially entered World War I. Promotions of films quickly became laced with patriotic rhetoric, strong endorsement for support of the American military, and recruitment efforts. Films featuring active women that were produced, or even released, before the official entry into the war were reimagined and re-presented as recruitment tools to encourage male enlistment. Films such as *Womanhood, the Glory of the Nation* (Blackton, 1917) and *Joan the Woman* (De Mille, 1916) were sold to audiences not for their active female stars but instead for their depiction of men's wartime heroism. After April 1917, wartime heroism fell into two categories: women's sacrifice (for husbands, sons, or money to buy new clothing) and men's participation in battle. *Womanhood* and *Joan the Woman*, despite their central female characters, were used specifically to encourage male enlistment. However, the film themselves did not depict a masculinist patriotism or heroism; instead, exhibitors and distributors effaced the fact that there were active women on-screen and promoted the films as military spectacles meant to inspire men to enlist. In major cities the exhibition of these films included temporary recruitment stations set up at the theater so that men would be encouraged to enlist after having seen the patriotic subject matter on-screen.

In her book *Reel Patriotism*, about the production history of films shown during World War I, DeBauche states that the percentage of war-related films released during that time was actually quite low. The reasons for this were that the production time frame was three to six months, and the producers, exhibitors, and the public alike were split as to whether war films were even desirable.[36] However, even though the production of war-themed films took time to catch up with current events, the one aspect of the industry that was immediately adjustable was promotion. Theaters quickly adapted to allow for speeches of a patriotic nature, to encourage enlistment and the purchase of liberty bonds, and the motion picture advertisers showed an immediate desire to respond and to raise funds and patriotic awareness.[37]

Particularly interesting in this regard was the case of *Womanhood, the Glory of the Nation* (1917). Originally produced alongside other preparedness pictures, *Womanhood* was actively promoted upon its release as a recruiting tool necessary for a country newly at war. Shortly after the declaration of war, the trade papers began to suggest that exhibitors connect screenings of the film with official recruitment for the Army, Navy, and Marine Corps.[38] And, in fact, reports throughout April and May of 1917 suggest that the recruiting efforts connected to screenings of the film were successful, and that a number of the recruiting officers "requested that the run be continued."[39] The adjutant general of the United States also reportedly sent a letter of support and endorsement, and encouraged the use of screenings for enlistment purposes.[40] While not all exhibitors shared the same enthusiasm for the film, most seemed to indicate, at the very least, that attendance at screenings had been strong.[41] *Motography* reported that the distribution wing V-L-S-E was finding that interest in the picture extended beyond the usual forty-day average, and required the company to make extra prints to meet the continuing demand.[42]

The film is set in a fictional country and follows Mary Ward, an American woman who tries to leave Ruritania to return home, only to be caught in the middle of a war between the United States and the country she is trying to flee. Mary and her love interest, Paul Strong, work together to battle the tyrannical Count of Ruritania and his nation's army.[43] *Womanhood, the Glory of the Nation* is about a woman whose independence and quick thinking contribute to victorious ends; however, the review for *Womanhood* was more about masculine heroism:

> "Womanhood" is an inspiring appeal to chivalry, to manhood, to ennobling sentiments which lie deep and strong in the American heart, though almost smothered by material prosperity.... The Russian revolution had done much to transform our passive attitude into an active one, because the issue is fast becoming that of our own Revolutionary War; the issue of our Civil War. Those are issues we cannot evade, and they are suggested all too mildly in "Womanhood." The great world issue becomes ours when it is clearly defined as that of democracy in opposition to organized tyranny.[44]

The review appeals to (white) Americans by invoking the historical wars that had been mythologized in early films, dime novels, and popular histories. In other words, the narrative of the film must be taken together with the discourse surrounding its promotion, and the stunts used during its exhibition, to understand how it was framed in relation to contemporary politics and to bolster American patriotism.

The opening of the film, at the Broadway Theatre in New York City on April 1, was a scene of lavish patriotism: "The theatre was decorated with American flags from top to bottom, both inside and out, and militiamen were stationed in the lobby in honor of the occasion. The girl ushers were dressed as Red Cross nurses."[45] The reception of the film itself was mixed: Peter Milne, of the *Motion Picture News*, provided a critical review of the film, suggesting that "Blackton's preachments in behalf of preparedness have quite eclipsed his story" and that the film, as a result, lacked coherence.[46] However, a week later the *Motion Picture News* claimed that *Womanhood* sparked both patriotism and recruitment and was continually being shown to enthusiastic crowds.[47]

In these articles and reviews, a great deal was made of manhood and of Roosevelt's impact on the making of the film.[48] There was no mention of the female lead, Alice Joyce, or the reason for the choice of title. *Womanhood* thus owed its alignment with military preparedness and its heavy promotion, in part, to its connection with Theodore Roosevelt, who was credited with developing the idea for the film with J. Stuart Blackton. He also appeared in the film.[49] Indeed, the success of the film was due in large part to the effort made in the nationwide promotion for the film, and the elaborate efforts that connected the film with recruitment efforts in several major cities. The film's nationwide advertising campaign consisted of posters created by Vitagraph's distribution wing, V-L-S-E. According to an article in *Motography*, the campaign served two purposes: "The first to be of assistance to the government officials who want the preparedness picture presented in every city, town and hamlet in the country in order to arouse patriotic enthusiasm and the second to bear its share of advertising expense in order that the exhibitors in the smaller cities and towns will receive the patronage the picture justifies."[50]

Additionally, different screenings of the film were sponsored by different groups—the Military Training Camp Association, the Daughters of the American Revolution, the Junior Division Military Training Camp Association, and a number of others.[51] Along with the film itself and the related recruitment efforts, Greater Vitagraph created a contest entitled "How America Should Prepare," with a prize of $1,000.[52] The contest was advertised in theaters from April until the closing date in early July, at which point it was announced that 21,142 essays were received, supposedly twice the amount ever received in any other newspaper write-in contests.[53] In addition to the large number of entries, the contest seems to have had international appeal, garnering responses from Britain, France, Norway, Sweden, South America, Japan, and China.[54]

Perhaps in an attempt to tap into the popularity of *Joan the Woman* (1916), publicity stunts for *Womanhood, the Glory of the Nation* seized on the archetype of Joan of Arc to rally patriotic support. In an elaborate parade tied to a screening at the Chestnut Street Opera House in Philadelphia, both Joan of Arc and the "Spirit of '76" were represented—Joan by a woman on a white horse, the "Spirit" by a boy drummer, a father fifer, and his grandfather bearing a flag.[55]

Women meet the crisis by becoming Joans of Arc—See Womanhood.
Womanhood shows what Joan of Arc did for her country—See Womanhood.

Women make your men enlist—See Womanhood—See Womanhood.
Womanhood proves women have a place in War—See Womanhood.
Womanhood is a preparedness picture—See Womanhood at the Chestnut Street
Opera House.[56]

The presence of a woman in *Womanhood* was rarely mentioned in the trade
press; the above quote was one of the few times womanhood was even alluded to
in promotions. Other reviews focused primarily on how the presence of military
officials at the screenings aided in recruitment efforts. These film advertisements
ignored the film's title, *Womanhood*, and instead focused on the draw the film
would have based on its timely nature and its ability to convince *men* to enlist. In
fact, it was the co-star, Harry Morey—who was rarely mentioned as the "lead" of
the picture—who was reportedly used for public appearances by the Navy
Department in its efforts to encourage enlistment.[57] Notably, Alice Joyce, who
did get top billing in the film, was not exploited in the publicity, and her character's actions in the film were rarely mentioned in advertisements, save for the
aforementioned references to Joan of Arc. But this could be linked to the continued screenings of *Joan the Woman*, a film that was advertised as promoting patriotism and enlistment after the American entry into the war.

Prior to the U.S. entry into the war, the ongoing war in Europe was of interest to
the filmmakers only as subject matter, inasmuch as it offered the possibility of an
epic with big sets, battles, spectacle, and a well-known star. *Joan the Woman* is in
keeping with current trends of big-spectacle pictures that were sweeping through
Hollywood while screenwriter Jeanie MacPherson and director Cecil B. DeMille
were involved in pre-production. DeBauche provides numerous examples of letters between DeMille and Jesse Lasky in which they speculate about whether or
not the war would still be happening when the film was completed and released.[58]
These letters demonstrate that making a film about the war during the war was not
a motivating factor in producing the film. As this example demonstrates, the war
was a popular subject for films because it was another subject that enabled spectacle and battle scenes to increase sales and ticket prices. But of course, while Lasky
and DeMille might have been focused on the cost of the production or the appeal
of the film, after its release and the American entry into World War I the use-value
of the film to promote patriotism and recruitment changed drastically.

One interesting example of the use of Joan of Arc repurposed for American
recruitment was not a film, but instead a gimmick at a Chicago theater. Helen
Ketchum, a "lobby girl" (female usher), dressed up as Joan of Arc in an attempt
to ridicule "slackers"—men who quickly married to avoid military service—and
thus convince them to enlist. This, however, had a twofold purpose. In addition
to aiding recruitment, it was also, according to the press, "particularly apt as
advertising for Joan of Arc in 'Joan the Woman,' the Colonial offering, was no
'slacker.' She loved a man, Eric Trent, the gallant Brit, but she loved her country

April 21, 1917.   M O T O G R A P H Y   815

What Theater Men Are Doing
AN OPEN FORUM FOR EXHIBITORS

This is a department of, by and for exhibitors. We want YOU represented here. Other managers and proprietors of picture theaters want to hear YOUR experiences, your opinions and your advice. Write to this department telling us your story, how you started, how you grew and all about your theater and how you manage it. Mention your advertising methods and your lobby displays. If possible send in photographs of yourself and your house. Address, The Forum Motography, Chicago.

Presenting Geraldine Farrar Picture

PATRIOTIC appeal is the keynote in the presentation of "Joan the Woman," the stirring De Mille production, at the Colonial Theater, Chicago. The timeliness of the subject, just when the United States has taken its place in the world conflict, allied with the country for which Joan died, is impressed upon the minds of the audience in every way. While the lobby decorations recall medieval France, and the program girls wear costumes suggested by Joan's armor, in the theater the boxes are draped with the American flag, and the national colors form the basis of the decorations.

An effective introduction is given the picture when Miss Grace Hickox, a professional entertainer, reads the prologue of the play. After the curtain is raised and the house lights dimmed, one beam of light shoots across the darkened stage, and in this half-light, Miss Hickox recites the verse of the prologue, ending it with a plea to the audience to consider Joan's patriotism when they are called on to serve their country.

Norman E. Field, manager of the theater, had hoped to have Geraldine Farrar present at the opening night, but her contract with the Metropolitan Opera Company prevented this. In her place, Miss Jennie Dufau, of the Chicago opera company, sang "The Star Spangled Banner" during the intermission.

Chicago is receiving "Joan" very enthusiastically.

New $30,000 Theater

Contracts have been awarded for the erection of the new Strand moving picture house to be erected in Allentown, Pennsylvania, by O. H. Gernert, Miss Emma Gernert and Dr. Ben H. Stuckert. The contract price is said to be $30,000, and the building is to be ready for business August 15.

The theater will be two stories high, but the foundations will be built of sufficient strength to permit the building of other stories upon it when extensions are required. Plans have been prepared for the theater and call for the very latest conveniences.

A twenty-foot wide lobby will lead into the theater. The box office will be at the side. There will be a foyer, with retiring rooms for men and women on either side. In the foyer will be two drinking fountains. The interior will be a spacious auditorium with seating capacity for 800 people, with plenty of room between the rows of seats. There will be an orchestra pit.

Two Simplex machines of the latest type will be used.

The theater will be beautifully decorated in harmony with the building. There are to be nine exits. Heating and ventilating systems will be installed of the newest type and the lighting will be by the indirect system. When completed the theater will vie in beauty, comfort and convenience with any in the state.

Theater Girls Aid Uncle Sam

One of the most successful film publicity stunts ever "pulled" in Chicago was executed last week by the firm of Jones, Linick & Schaefer, which operates several picture houses. The stunt was arranged in co-operation with Captain F. R. Kenney, chief recruiting officer of the United States army.

Each of the seven Chicago papers devoted news-column space to pictures and stories of the patriotic tour.

The four Colonial Theater lobby girls, the Misses Helen Ketchum, Frances Burton, Elizabeth Walters and Gertrude Jacobs, dressed in duplicates of the armor worn by Geraldine Farrar as Joan of Arc in the filming of "Joan the Woman," which is running at the Colonial Theater, company with detailed officers of the recruiting service. They stopped on the important corners and with the military escort distributed enlistment literature and urged Young America to join the colors.

Lobby girls of the Colonial Theater, Chicago, aiding recruiting officers on the street.

Enthusiasm ran high, crowds were thick and enlistments came fast and furious. In front of the city hall, thanks to the courtesy of the police department, Miss Jacobs mounted a steed belonging to the traffic squad and encircled the square. It was an expression of the spirit which led the immortal Maid on to Orleans.

FIGURES 9 AND 10. Photos of "Lobby Girls" promoting recruitment at a Chicago Theater. (Courtesy of Media History Digital Library.)

better."[59] Furthermore, decorations in the theater were both French- and American-themed. As one piece noted, despite the contemporary appeal siding heavily with American patriotism, "the lobby decorations recall medieval France, and the program girls wear costumes suggested by Joan's armor, in the theater the boxes are draped with the American flag, and the national colors form the

872   MOTOGRAPHY   Vol. XVII, No. 17.

that only that which typifies the wholesome and true characteristics of life could live and give any art its fullest expression. His magnetic personality so keenly felt on the screen radiated from behind the footlights and his talk was greeted with constant applause. Following their stage appearance the players held an informal reception in the beautiful lounge room of the theater, greeting their many friends and screen devotees.

The novelty of the appearance of the stars and the spectacular stage scene made for one of the most successful productions created by Mr. McCormick at the Circle.

Lobby Girl Advertises Theater

Not all theaters have lobby girls. And if they do, they are not always so attractive and versatile as Miss Helen Ketchum of the Colonial Theater, operated by

Miss Helen Ketchum, lobby girl from the Colonial Theater, Chicago, in Joan of Arc costume advertising "Joan the Woman," now running at the Colonial. She is trying to induce some of the "slackers" getting marriage licenses to enlist.

Jones, Linick and Schaefer, prominent Chicago exhibitors.

One of the recent unique publicity stunts pulled off by the eternally vigilant press agent of the house was to get Miss Ketchum mixed up in the affair of the "slackers" who have been getting marriage licenses at the Chicago "marriage bureau" to the tune of several hundred a day.

Helen donned her working clothes and accompanied by a husky sergeant of Major C. R. Vincent's First Illinois Artillery, proceeded to the county building to heckle the "war bridegrooms" and drive them from the altar to the colors.

The stunt was particularly apt as advertising for Joan of Arc in "Joan the Woman," the Colonial offering, was no "slacker." She loved a man, Eric Trent, the gallant Britisher, but she loved her country better.

When the latter called she squelched her love and bade her lover adieu.

Unusual Projection Feats at Rialto

During the recent engagement of Sarah Bernhardt's "Mothers of France" at the Rialto in New York an impressively dramatic effect was secured by superimposing on the picture several excerpts from "Joan the Woman," the spectacular feature in which Geraldine Farrar is appearing at the Forty-fourth Street Theater. The famous prima donna, in the role of Joan of Arc, was made to appear as a vision to the stricken mother portrayed by Mme. Bernhardt.

Great masses of French troops, "the steel wall of France," also were shown, as well as a portion of a picture not yet released in which Napoleon appears, reviewing his triumphant troops. The effect was so undeniably thrilling that it brought the people in the audience to their feet time and again, cheering, waving their programs, and applauding with fervor perhaps never before heard at a motion picture entertainment.

So much comment was occasioned by this trick of projection and so many inquiries were made as to how much of what appeared on the screen was in the original picture and how much had been thrown on the screen separately that it may be interesting to exhibitors to learn precisely how the effect was secured. The credit for the innovation goes to S. L. Rothapfel, who was known as an expert on projection long before he made his reputation as an exhibitor. It was accomplished by the use of two machines, one carrying the feature picture and the other a reel of film made up of the selected inserts, with ten feet of blank leader between each subject. Mr. Rothapfel first measured the scenes in the feature on which he wished to superimpose his "visions."

Each bit of film for the visions was cut ten feet shorter than the scene on which it was to be shown, thus allowing five feet for a "fade-on" and five feet in which to "fade off" again. The title sheet in the operator's booth was then "cued" so that the operator running off the feature would know when to be ready with his supplementary machine. The motor on the supplementary machine was kept in operation constantly, so that the moment the first scene for which a vision was scheduled arrived on the screen, the extra film could be started at once.

When it was desired to produce the vision effect, the "douser" on the machine projecting the feature was pulled on half way and the one on the supplementary machine was pulled half way off, thus allowing only half the normal amount of light to come from each machine but producing a total illumination on the screen equal to what one machine would produce at full strength.

At the instant the dousers regulated the light, the film on the secondary machine was put in motion, with the result that two pictures, or in some cases a title and a picture, appeared on the screen at the same time. The result was not unlike a double exposure film, but far more vital and all embracing. Mr. Rothapfel first tried this experiment when he presented "The Girl Philippa" and it invariably called forth a burst of applause, but it was not until he elaborated the idea by using half a dozen added scenes during the projection of "Mothers of France" that the public recognized the impressive quality of the discovery at its full value.

Eileen Sedgewick, playing leading roles under Henry McRae, is having her first experience working with wild animals.

FIGURES 9 AND 10. (continued)

basis of the decorations."[60] The Colonial Theater's showing of the film included a prologue spoken by Grace Hickox, who ended "with a plea to the audience to consider Joan's patriotism when they are called on to serve their country."[61] During the same run, four of the "lobby girls" dressed as Joan of Arc and drove through the city with recruiting officers, handing out flyers about enlistment.

According to the reports, "Enthusiasm ran high, crowds were thick and enlistments came fast and furious."[62]

The popularity of Joan of Arc in wartime promotions was not as simple as the mere celebration of women's power. Robin Blaetz provides an apt observation on the use of Joan of Arc for American recruitment: "In retrospect, the use of images of Joan of Arc for propaganda purposes during the heightened years of the First World War indicates some uncertainty over the roles of the sexes in previously gender-specific arenas. Yet during the war, the freedom with which Joan of Arc was used (in comparison with her absence during the Second World War) suggests that the issue had yet to be recognized as a problem."[63] I would add that the anxiety over women's entry into the political sphere and the soon-to-be nationwide acceptance of women as full citizens was tempered by the use of Joan of Arc, an active woman who was both chaste and devoted to her nation. As discussed in chapter 3, Joan of Arc provided a model of gender crossing that was nonthreatening and that presented women as an inspiration to, rather than in competition with, men. What these publicity stunts reveal, then, is a distinct turn from the celebration of American women's active nature in the preparedness and Civil War films to a focus on male enlistment. Granted, recruiting was a necessary objective at this time, and theaters and distributors alike were committed to helping the U.S. government achieve its goal, but the active nature of the woman, in this case Joan of Arc, and in the earlier case of Mary Ward of *Womanhood*, was glossed over, removed from consideration, or mentioned only for the purpose of inspiring men to enlist.

5 · FROM SERIAL QUEENS TO PATRIOTIC HEROINES

America and the European War, Part II

Female characters as protagonists in films about war were nothing new in 1916 and 1917. They were part of a longer history of heroic American Girls in film that served nationalistic ends: *Pearl of the Army* (1916) and *Patria* (1917) both depicted active heroines who were patriotic and active participants in the defense of the American homeland. The serial *Liberty* (1916) featured a young American woman, Liberty, kidnapped in Mexico during an insurrection. Finally, in *The Secret of the Submarine* (1915) a young American woman, Cleo Burke, along with Lieutenant Jarvis Hope, of the U.S. Navy, worked together to keep a new technology out of the hands of foreign enemies. *Patria, Pearl of the Army, Liberty,* and Cleo fit within the history of active American women on-screen discussed in earlier chapters. In the early 1910s the overabundance of white-washed Civil War films shored up notions of American identity as primarily white. These later serials looked outward to reinforce American identity in an us-versus-them format. Like the melodramas that came before, these female-centered serials justified militarism through the fragility and the vulnerability of the potential female victim. Fear of the outsider—the foreign foe in each of these serials—was contrasted with the white heroines, each of whom was undeniably American. The juxtaposition served to remind viewers who the ideal American Girl was and who the "others" were who should be looked upon with suspicion.

These popular serials also depicted the debate in their subject matter and advertising. In each example, a woman played a central role within the narrative, demonstrating that preparedness must be unanimous and that every member of the nation was responsible for the defense of home soil. However, pre-existing genres, advertising, and exhibition practices were harnessed both before and during America's wartime participation to shape and reshape the narrative messages of these films and serials. In other words, in addition to the content of the films and serials, the methods of exhibiting the films, the popularity of their fictional tie-ins, the myriad magazine articles promoting these stars, and so on gave these texts fluid meaning that could be repackaged during wartime to promote patriotism where they had previously promoted preparedness, romance, adventure, and women's fashion in a military setting.

All of these serials were released prior to the American entry into World War I, and yet their promotion and exhibition continued well after the American entry on April 4, 1917. *Liberty*, for example, was advertised alongside other Universal offerings as though they were new—but repackaged as "Preparedness Pictures" almost immediately following the U.S. entry into World War I. Universal listed *Uncle Sam at Work* (1915), *The War Waif* (Holubar, 1917), *The White Feather Volunteer* (1915), *Court Martialed* (1916), and *If My Country Should Call* (1915) as films that would bring "home a real bank roll."[1] These serials shifted in meaning and use from subjects with war or foreign spies as the backdrop, to preparedness propaganda, to a call to patriotism for viewers.

SERIALS IN AMERICAN FILM OF THE 1910s

This chapter will demonstrate the way the political messaging of preparedness entered into a symbiotic relationship with popular seriality. Preparedness was exploited for sales, whereas at the same time these serials promoted preparedness and patriotism through the extended life of serial engagement and star promotion. I'll take *Pearl of the Army* and *Patria* as the central case studies throughout this chapter, although *Liberty*, *The Secret of the Submarine*, and *Neal of the Navy* were also promoted as preparedness and patriotic serials. The traits and the form of the silent film serial—with its links to sensational fiction and popular theater—worked in ways similar to the features of preparedness films: the good-versus-evil dichotomy so prevalent in silent serials only heightened the fears and anxieties regarding "the foreign" foe.

American serials of the mid-1910s were short films, frequently action-packed and featuring female protagonists, that were shown in weekly installments.[2] One of the earliest series film subjects was Kalem's "Girl Spy" films, featuring Gene Gauntier as Nan, the spy (see chapter 2). Unlike series films, serials had a continuous narrative that unfolded in the twelve to fifteen episodes, which were meant to be shown in theaters weekly. Film serials were often accompanied by newspaper tie-ins, which told a detailed version of the story that unfolded on-screen each week. Shelley Stamp argues that serials found a "ready-made" fan base of serialized fiction readers.[3] These tie-ins, combined with the weekly film installments, created an audience that was at once readers, viewers, and fans—with the participatory possibilities and outcomes—that we imagine as more common in a contemporary era of transmedia.[4] These serials deserve their own chapter because, despite the promotion of "preparedness," they differ dramatically from the feature films. First, the heroines of the serials are active, impulsive,

FIGURE 11. Ad for *Patria* in *Motion Picture News*, December 16, 1916. (Courtesy of Media History Digital Library.)

brave, and determined. These are not the peace-at-any-price advocates who bring about a nation's peril. Instead, the serial heroines take charge and save the nation from impending invasion. Second, this chapter is aligned with scholarship that does not see film serials as a stepping stone in the film-history progression to feature-length narrative film. Numerous scholars have suggested instead that we understand serials as a distinct form of film—a form that was central to cinema-going from the 1910s through to the 1950s.[5] Serials, by their very nature, provide repetition and variation. Ilka Brasch designates their recognizable and formulaic nature as part of what made them popular.[6] The preparedness serials of 1916–1917 take up the well-worn formula of serial heroines and add the much-talked-about discourse of preparedness debates. Third, as open texts, serials encourage extended engagement: they promote creative forms of fandom. In this sense, the use of serials for promulgating political messages was well situated to extend the propagandistic story on-screen into the lives of viewers and readers. And even though the heroines might not have developed "interiority," Richard Abel argues, the stars took on "life . . . outside the film," which included the interviews and features in fan magazines, and other ways in which fans might engage with the star persona.[7] Finally, film serials of the 1910s, and their tie-ins, are important for understanding film as a mass medium that united audiences in one pastime. Paul S. Moore argues that the serials were integral in moving pictures' transition from being a pastime with a fragmented audience to being an activity aimed at a mass audience. In short, the serial—through its newspaper tie-ins—became a way in which a number of different audiences could find "commonality," because disparate groups of people were reading the same stories en masse.[8] Serials, then, were an important form that explored the preparedness debates and cemented fears about foreigners while promoting a jingoistic celebration of American identity.

PREPARING FOR FOREIGN INVASION

These serials showed audiences across the country the grim possibility of foreign invasion and argued for the need to prepare an army.[9] Preparedness serials, for instance, presented fictionalized scenarios of the possible consequences—though far-fetched and sensationalized—of foreign economic interests in Latin America. We must again read these serials as both promoting military preparedness and depicting fears and anxieties over immigration and protecting whiteness within American borders. Film, then, was one medium among many that discursively wrote and rewrote the boundaries of national identity through narratives in which good and evil mapped out black-and-white ideas of "us" versus "them."

The fear of invasion and the threat against the hegemonic construction of American identity as white men and women figured centrally in these serials. The Mexican Revolution, American attempts to solidify trade with Latin American countries, and, finally, the war in Europe were reshaping the way Americans envisioned their role in world politics by extending U.S. turn-of-the-century imperialist aims. Popular at a time when the foreign inspired fear and curiosity, the genre of the serial—and more importantly the "serial queen"—not only provided an ideal outlet through which these questions of foreign policy could be played out for the pleasure of viewing audiences but also added to the heightened xenophobia that the invasion narrative stoked. This chapter examines how the serial genre functioned as an already popular format through which a number of debates happening in contemporary American politics were transformed into entertaining narratives aimed at female audiences.[10] These serials demonstrate that preparedness was largely pitched to the American public, not in light of events happening "over there," but more importantly in terms of the threat of invasion on home soil. But more than just conveying already existing political debates, these serials—and film more broadly—made the debates real to audiences, playing with tropes of suspense and danger to foment fear of the outsider.

The serials' ability to build and reach audiences throughout the United States made the serials in newspaper and film form an ideal venue for presenting sensationalized political messages. According to Roger Hagedorn, seriality as a narrative form is used when a new medium must find a new mass audience.[11] Hagedorn traces serial storytelling in cheap fiction (the dime novels and story papers), newspapers and magazines, film, radio, and television. Further, scholars Shelley Stamp, Ben Singer, Justin Morris, and others have shown that serials of the 1910s were a useful form for building middle-class, female patronage.[12] The popular genre in which the serial-queen melodramas existed drew from a rich tapestry of American popular forms, such as dime novels, Wild West live shows, cheap theater, and magazine fiction. It is precisely this form of intermediality that informs how I read Patria, and the other serial heroines, within the context of myriad media that engaged women in the sensational and melodramatic formations of American identity.

Both *Pearl of the Army* and *Patria* showed the "American" heroine—in both examples, descendants of high-ranking members of the U.S. Armed Forces—becoming entangled in the enemy's plot to invade the United States and threatening "peace" in the Western Hemisphere. The film serials *Pearl of the Army* and *Patria* promoted the need for military preparedness and were released with advertising that supported this idea. These serials *did not* depict a call to arms or demand that the United States enter the European war; in fact, the threat in both cases was foreign infiltration of North and South America, leading to attacks on the United States. The narratives were thus about a foreign invasion through Latin America, but the underlying argument for preparedness was directly related to the current war in Europe. Playing on popular anxieties and fictionalizing current political arguments and debates, these serials narrativized questions and concerns that were culturally significant at the time.

Liberty (1916) is a serial set on the border with Mexico. Like other serial heroines, Liberty's father dies in the first episode, leaving her fortune to the trustees, Major Richard Winston and Señor Pancho Leon. Early in the serial, Liberty is kidnapped by Mexican *insurrectos* and the Texas guard must enter Mexico to fight for Liberty.[13] The serial, although also about the permeability of the border, is a direct reference to the Mexican Revolution and the battles between American military and Mexican revolutionaries along the U.S.-Mexican border. Like *Patria* and *Pearl of the Army*, *Liberty* was billed as a "thrilling Patriotic" serial after the United States entered the war, with Marie Walcamp's face adorning full-page advertisements in the trade press.[14]

The Secret of the Submarine was about an experimental piece of technology that would allow submarines to convert the oxygen in water to breathable oxygen within the craft. Burke, the inventor, dies, leaving the technology to be tested by his daughter, Cleo, and Lieutenant Jarvis Hope, sent by the U.S. Navy. After Burke's death, the formula disappears, and the remainder of the chapters involves the adventures of Cleo, Hope, and his friend, Barnacle Hook, as they search for the missing information. Theses remaining episodes depict a race to see who will secure the technology: the U.S. Navy, a less trustworthy businessman, or spies from Russia and Japan. Billed as a "preparedness" serial, the serial formula—a young woman whose father dies in the first episode, new technology at the center of the story, a missing book with vital information—is evident, with the contemporary contextual information about submarine warfare as a convenient backdrop.

Each of these serials center American heroes and heroines keeping the home soil safe from invasion, keeping American inventions at home, and keeping American businesses thriving. Like in previous chapters, it is imperative to note who is served by this vision of America, and who is deemed American. In each of the advertisements, the female star is the focus. She is both the defender and that which needs defending. Again, the white, female heroine, centered as *the* American Girl, provides a dual purpose. She is ready to fight for her home, and she is simultaneously the image of home. Like with the Civil War films, the American Revolutionary films, and other military subjects fought at home, the American Girl is necessary both for defense and to win military battles. In the preparedness serials, though, the enemy is no longer an army regiment moving through a small American farm; instead they are foreign spies from all over the world, passing across borders and threatening the imagined stability of white, middle-class America. This was especially important—and particularly unstable—as the imaginary "America" of these war subjects on-screen was under constant renegotiation. For example, in both *Pearl of the Army* and *Patria*, the heroines' connection to traditional American military lineage serves as the most overt marker of American identity. It was their relation to, but distance from, the official American military that allowed them the freedom needed for the narratives to continue.

The female protagonists in each of these serials served dual roles: First, their assumed vulnerability as women symbolically emphasized a need for defense plans in case of foreign invasion; and second, their marginal—if not completely limited—role within the political and militaristic spheres allows them to transgress boundaries otherwise impenetrable by male figures.[15] In other words, both

Patria and Pearl could effortlessly move from interacting with high-ranking political leaders to engaging the men of the military who go to battle; and from hand-to hand-fights with foreign enemies in one scene, to communicating with secret government committees in the next. In short, these women were socially and politically mobile. Female characters presented an answer to the popular question of preparedness: namely, that endless debate and political discussions must give way to action. Each Patria, Pearl, Cleo, and Liberty solved the problems, through action, facing American audiences in the wake of U.S. entry into World War I.

PEARL WHITE, OR THE MODERN JOAN OF ARC

Pearl White's character in *Pearl of the Army*, Pearl Dare, embodies the American Girl as a citizen with American military heritage. But she simultaneously has the ability to cross the boundaries between the foreign and domestic, and between high-ranking officials and low-ranking military men. Furthermore, the military threat—and the subsequent need for preparedness—represented in this serial was, as always, the threat of European invasion on home soil through Latin America. Just prior to the film's release, the plot of *Pearl of the Army* was described thusly in an article from *Motion Picture News*:

> Her [Pearl White's] role is of an American Joan of Arc, stimulated with resolve to prove the innocence of a high military crime for which an officer to whom she was attached was degraded. . . .
>
> In her adventures "Pearl of the Army" discovers that secret foes menace our national peace, and eventually she reveals who they are and why they are plotting to destroy our national independence by wrenching from our control the most highly prized gateway to the commerce of the world—the Panama Canal—thus awakening us to our dangers.[16]

As noted in chapters 3 and 4, Joan of Arc was a prominent figure in American promotion of patriotism. According to Robin Blaetz, Joan of Arc represented the chaste outsider who functioned as a unifying symbol for new immigrants, due to the marginalization she experienced from her own French society.[17] Furthermore, when depicted by Geraldine Farrar, she was shown as a woman who could enact masculinity through cross-dressing in battle, while maintaining her feminine physical appeal, thus making her potentially subversive actions more acceptable.[18] Promoting Pearl White as Joan of Arc activated many of these underlying cultural associations: both Joan and Pearl were women who performed masculinity for their country while maintaining feminine qualities and, thus, remaining admirable and nonthreatening figures.

Also noted in the aforementioned article from the *Moving Picture News*, a contest was held to find a writer for this serial who could combine patriotism and romance in a popular format. This writer then featured Woodrow Wilson, Theodore Roosevelt, and Charles E. Hughes in the introduction to the first episode.[19] The introduction was said to present different opinions about the preparedness debate, while the story itself maintained "a strict neutrality."[20] Just like Patria, Pearl functioned as a boundary-crossing individual: she was both an active participant in battle and an important member in political debates. She was not relegated to the traditional feminine role of domesticity and motherhood, and could easily transgress the hierarchical boundaries that separated ordinary military men from the high-ranking officials due to her alignment with the idea of the American Girl. In one scene Pearl talks to a secret committee. It is evident that the committee men are entirely focused on her words and ideas—ideas she had developed from her own experiences in dangerous and active situations. In contrast, in the next scene Pearl moves into a separate room, where Adams—a mere orderly—is waiting. Due to his lower rank, Adams is not allowed into the room with the officials to discuss or influence any important decisions, despite the fact that he has been involved in every dangerous situation with Pearl throughout the narrative.

In an earlier scene, Pearl invades a meeting of foreign spies by hiding in a chest that is delivered to their apartment. Upon revealing herself to the group of spies, Pearl holds up a bomb and threatens to blow up the entire building should anyone attempt to move. These examples demonstrate Pearl's willingness to jump into danger when necessary. Although she is quite capable of joining the men who are debating and planning military preparedness, she is also willing to take action when necessary, despite the consequences or dangers involved. In the scene with the bomb and the foreign spies, Pearl calls her father to ask where the military is, only to find out he did not receive a message she sent informing him of her plans. Even so, despite Pearl's actions being depicted as verging on the impulsive, they work out in the end and save the United States from foreign invasion and domestic revolt.

The unnamed villain represents a threat to the Western Hemisphere and the political importance of the Monroe Doctrine in contemporary politics through his connection to Latin America. The Monroe Doctrine, a much-discussed political issue of the day, was even the name of one of the episodes of *Pearl of the Army*. Preparedness, although brought to the forefront of popular discourse by World War I, was just as strongly associated with American policies regarding Latin America as it was with any concern about the situation in Europe.

One of the ways that preparedness supporters crafted their argument was by encouraging fear of foreign invasion, thus tapping into the pre-existing narratives about the need for domestic defense that we have already examined. This was achieved by bringing the Monroe Doctrine into political debates. Mandated in 1823 by President Monroe, the doctrine was meant to justify American military action against any foreign power that attempted to infiltrate the Western Hemisphere. In particular, the Monroe Doctrine was central to Woodrow Wilson's policy on U.S. relations with Latin America during his first presidential term. In the 1900s Roosevelt had, however, converted the aims of the Monroe Doctrine from defense to expansion by justifying U.S. involvement in Latin American countries under the guise of keeping European influence at bay.[21] Later still, the fear of physical invasion gave way to the assumed threat of European economic dominance over Latin American countries.[22] The debate surrounding the Monroe Doctrine continued to escalate while the war in Europe was taking place. The following excerpt from a news story voices a popular concern about the war: "As a nation, we are less concerned with the European war itself, its causes, its course, than with its ending. Whatever the result of this war may be, whoever wins it, whenever it ends, the victor will be able to threaten the United States, and, if he chooses, to challenge the supremacy of the Western hemisphere."[23] It is through statements like this—which was merely one example of a handful of articles, editorials, and speeches about the danger of American unpreparedness—that support for building the American army and navy was garnered.

In *Pearl of the Army* the villain, a masked man known only as "The Silent Menace," is a mysterious and ambiguous foreign enemy: he stands for all foreign threats. However, one villain in the serial is given a specific national allegiance: Bolero, the leader of a revolutionary group, is from Grenada, solidifying and feeding contemporaneous fears for white Americans about Latin America. Further cementing the fear of invasion via Latin America, Pearl is the daughter of an army colonel who is responsible for the Panama defense plans. It is because Pearl lives amid the U.S. Army that she becomes entangled in the schemes of "The Silent Menace" and Bolero and must prevent them from invading the United States. The audience is reminded of Pearl's military heritage while watching the threat of foreign invasion through Latin America play out on-screen and in print.

In addition to the message of war preparedness on a narrative level, Pearl White's frequent publicity stunts—used to advertise her upcoming serials—were exploited as patriotic promotion. Even prior to *Pearl of the Army*, White was an extremely popular serial actress, frequently seen flying airplanes or performing other publicity stunts to promote an upcoming series. During the preparedness era, and then after the entrance of the United States into World War I, White's publicity took a distinctly patriotic turn. For example, she rode a steel girder to the twentieth floor of a New York skyscraper while throwing American flags to the crowd and then gave a speech about recruitment after she returned to the ground.[24] She posed for an Army recruitment poster with the slogan "Do You Think I'd Stay At Home?"[25] She also gave speeches as a "Four-Minute Man" (a nationwide effort to promote the war through four-minute speeches at theaters), supposedly making "a circuit of twenty-one theatres" in one night.[26] The

"Do You Think *I'd* Stay at Home?"

Howard Chandler Christy's Appreciation of Pearl White

No sooner had the distinguished artist, Christy, designed the appealing Navy poster, "Gee, I wish I was a man!" than the Army put in its bid for his services. Mr. Christy was ready to give the magic of his brush to Uncle

PEARL WHITE, THE AMERICAN JOAN OF ARC, IN PATHÉ'S "PEARL OF THE ARMY"

Sam, and asked Pearl White to be his model. The combined effort of his brush and the posing of "Pearl of the Army" has created "Do you think *I'd* stay at home?" which will soon carry its message thruout the nation. If you doubt that Pearl is able to sit an army mount and to be a suitable standard-bearer for Old Glory, here she is as the American Joan of Arc.

38

FIGURE 12. Pearl White in *Motion Picture Magazine,* October 1917. (Courtesy of Media History Digital Library.)

alignment between Pearl White and militaristic promotion was a natural progression, given that she was known for her daring, her stunts, and her traditionally masculine interests.[27]

PATRIA: AN HEIR TO PREPAREDNESS

Like Pearl Dare, Patria functions as a boundary-crossing character who embodies the dualities of American femininity: she is independent, yet eventually marries; she is active, yet feminine; she is a military woman, yet when not cross-dressing she dresses fashionably. Scholars such as Singer and Stamp have noted that often in serials the female protagonists are motherless and lose the male parental figure early in the series, commencing the woman's adventures.[28] This places the female character outside of the regular realm of patriarchy—particularly due to the lack of a mother figure, because of which the serial heroine is never associated with domesticity or the role model of motherhood.[29] Patria is no exception, as she has no parents, and her legal guardian is killed in the first episode. At the beginning of the series, Patria refuses a proposal of marriage from one man— thus rejecting the feminine role of wife—only to later fall in love with Captain Parr. The heterosexual coupling with Captain Parr toward the end of the series signifies Patria's exit from a life of adventure and her entry into the realm of socially acceptable female identity.

The final lines in the serialized fiction "Patria: A Romance of Preparedness" reveal not a marriage of the serial queen, Patria (played by Irene Castle in the film version of the serial), but a pledge of continued patriotic action: "Bending forward Patria tenderly set her lips to the lips of Donald Parr, dedicating anew her life and his, that was hers to do as she willed, to the service of their country, that it might be saved."[30] This conclusion comes at the end of an episode in which Patria commands an army of her workers against the invasion of Japanese and Mexican troops on American soil. Patria is within her rights as a citizen, the narrative suggests, precisely because she is defending her own private property. She never takes the battle—which is written about in terms that describe the trench warfare of the European war—beyond her property, and hence acts only in a defensive and nonaggressive manner. It is as a defensive strategy that Patria's military preparations mirror the calls to military preparedness that were being voiced in American politics at the time.

Throughout the series Patria has built up an army of more than half a million men—codenamed the Plattsburg scheme—entirely through private means. Rather than involving the government, Patria and Parr, her love interest, use drills and military units to create an efficient and skilled defensive military unit. But the final episode makes reference to the government and to the need for American military preparedness to defend against invading forces when private citizens are no longer enough. Though Patria pledges herself to the "service of [her] country," the final installment is not entirely optimistic about the government's ability to garner support for military preparedness. However, the final episode was released just a few weeks after the American entry into World War I. A close reading of the text alone (either of the few viewable episodes or the newspaper episodes written by Louis Joseph Vance) does not account for the way in which the meaning of the text altered from a call for preparedness to a call for recruitment and patriotic participation. In short, the open-ended nature of *Patria's* conclusion—which imagines her patriotic future continuing to shift alongside the ever-changing role of America in global politics—allowed for the serial, and its star, to have its meaning altered from a call for preparedness to a call for recruitment by changes in promotion and exhibition.

The conclusion of *Patria* resists narrative closure at the same time as it uses the common tropes: she is paired off with Captain Parr but not married into the domestic role of wife and mother. The concluding lines suggest that she will continue, with her love interest, as an adventurous heroine who also happens to defend against American invasion when necessary. Arguably, the very idea of the American Girl suggests an eventual domestication—girlhood is the precursor to womanhood, or becoming a wife. These "girls," including Pearl Dare and Patria, demonstrate active femininity only in the period preceding marriage. Even though Patria is ultimately domesticated, her relationship with Parr throughout the series revolves mainly around adventure, kidnappings, and running a military unit, rather than more-traditional activities of heteronormative courtship. Further solidifying her place within a traditionally masculine landscape, Patria is the descendent of a line known as the "Fighting Channings," a long line of military men, and thus heir to a munitions factory and a great fortune, meant to be used toward solidifying American preparedness. Patria is shown to be adventurous and responsible, carefree and entirely responsible, vulnerable and strong, embodying a number of seemingly contradictory characteristics. These contradictions represent the opposing sides of political debates that were narrativized in her actions and reactions and in the consequences that span the fifteen episodes of the series.

Echoing contemporary political discourse on threats to the Western Hemisphere via Latin America, the enemy in *Patria* invades through Mexico. The Japanese baron Huroki (played by Caucasian actor Warner Oland, who would later play famous Chinese detective Charlie Chan) and a variety of Mexican characters play central roles in the conflict with the Channing family and thus, ultimately, against the United States. In keeping with the dominant contemporary debates of foreign policy, *Patria's* narrative suggests that preparedness is a defensive strategy related to the threat of foreign invasion. Much like the opinions voiced throughout the decade on the validity, importance, and interpretation of the Monroe Doctrine, *Patria's* narrative highlighted for American audiences the possibility of a foreign invasion of the United States through both the character of Huroki and the portrayal of an invasion originating in Mexico.

The fictional tie-in in the Sunday papers provided both narrative clarity and further information about the need for military preparedness. In this case, readers were given information about the importance of preparedness by means of a description of a historical war and what could happen if the U.S. Army was not prepared to defend its homeland. *Patria: A Romance of Preparedness*—the title given to the Sunday paper's fictional tie-in—provides information that was left out of the filmed version. In the film version, audiences only knew that Patria was the descendent of a long line of Army men, and the heir to a secret fortune meant to aid American preparedness. In the fictional tie-in, readers see a letter written to Patria by her legal guardian. This letter, which film audiences would only have seen Patria reading, reveals why John Channing, the first of the "fighting Channings," felt so strongly about the need to set aside a fortune meant to prepare an army capable of defending the United States:

> When the war of 1812 broke out he resigned his ease and took the field as a colonel of militia. . . . In his military capacity John Channing 1st was an intimate observer of the lack of organization, military spirit, training, ability to fight, that characterized the American forces. Often and again he saw them break and run before the advance of British troops numerically inferior, but properly equipped and trained. He witnessed their futile attempt to withstand the British advance upon Washington. He saw—from a far hilltop—the burning of that city—a calamity that had never been possible had his countrymen been trained to fight in defense of their land.[31]

This description of the War of 1812 emphasizes a cultural anxiety that preparedness advocates used to garner support. The fear of foreign invasion on home soil, and the need to prepare an army ready to do battle and defend their land, became reasons to prepare the country's army to fight in a war across the ocean. This excerpt reveals a key part of the preparedness debate: Preparedness was pitched to the American public as defense of the homeland instead of as taking a side in the European war. The preparation of an army on home soil was then enacted by the female protagonists central to the films, serials, and fictional tie-ins that were popular during the years leading to the American entry into World War I.

Patria creates her army from the workers at her munitions factory, rather than befriending a pre-existing military unit like Pearl Dare did. Perhaps the most noteworthy example of this is in the Channing munitions factory strike. In episode seven, "Red Dawn," Huroki and his ally, Juan De Lima from Mexico, successfully convince a number of Patria's employees to strike.[32] While Captain Parr defends the factory, it is ultimately Patria who brings about a resolution to the strike by meeting with and offering the men military training for American preparedness. What is most remarkable about this scene is the aesthetic representation of Patria's "army": an image of the striking workers entering through the factory's gate in haphazard manner and disheveled clothing fades to black and is replaced by a shot of the same men in military uniforms marching in perfect unison.

The direct visual comparison between workers and the military is juxtaposed with the visual rendering of the Mexican "army" as a small group of mismatched and untrained men who ultimately fail because of their lack of organization—or, conversely, because of the success of American preparedness. Further, in a reversal of what Richard Slotkin refers to as the "military metaphor": "The military in this case is not used as an example of ideal forms of management, but rather, the pre-existing industries and companies throughout the industrialized United States become sources from which to create military companies."[33] Slotkin argues that after the Civil War, the structure of military units became a managerial model for large businesses. This ideology of military order was pervasive throughout the Progressive Era. In this serial, however, the military metaphor so commonly adapted to business practices was now used to demonstrate how successful business models should influence successful military preparedness.[34] The men were led by Patria, functioning as a bridge between corporate enterprise and military units.

HOW THE BEST-DRESSED, BEST-KNOWN WOMAN SOLD PREPAREDNESS

An advertisement for *Patria*, printed in the *Washington Post* on January 14, 1917, described Irene Castle (referred to as Mrs. Vernon Castle here) as the "Best Dressed, Best Known Woman in America." This advertisement is evidence that the serial was valued in particular as a genre that could showcase female stars—even if it was subsequently used to promote preparedness. The paragraph describing the film begins, "PATRIA is a romance of society and preparedness, introducing as its star the most talked of woman in the country" again reiterating the importance of femininity.[35] The wording implies that preparedness was placed between "society" and the star, indicating that it was the place of woman in high society that would draw the crowds. Another aim of the serial, and its advertisements, was to show women how to dress as American Girls, as well as how to act heroically. This type of promotion, however, was not unique to *Patria* and, in fact, reflected a number of changes happening in the film industry during the mid-1910s.

Film serials marked a shift from local advertisements by individual exhibitors to standardized advertising campaigns that were uniform nationwide, in part due to serials' longer running times in theaters.[36] Print advertisements for *Patria* could be found throughout national newspapers, and there was even in a short write-up about Irene Castle in *Cosmopolitan Magazine*.[37] Castle's feminine image and the concept of preparedness were commodified and sold to female audiences as part of the complex interplay between the serial's narrative and star promotion. American women were sold fashion as a way through which they could participate in, and visually demonstrate, their patriotism.

Castle was a movie star, popular dancer, and a fashion icon; she was also, as I will demonstrate, a person who embodied the connection between looking the part and playing the patriot. Articles and magazine spreads that featured Castle frequently displayed her clothing for female readers; they described either what she had worn to specific functions or the outfits she wore in various scenes throughout her films. As DeBauche reveals, the film critic Louis Reeves Harrison "bemoaned the link between clothes and [the American Girl]," but missed the fact that fashion was an increasingly important aspect of defining what it meant to be a woman in the United States in the mid-1910s.[38] Irene Castle enacted her American femininity in large part through the fashion showcased in her films and serials.

Castle's extra-filmic persona was quite different from White's. Castle not only showcased the active femininity that serial actresses were known for, but also promoted fashion and clothing as much as war preparedness during the run of *Patria*. Castle's star persona suggested that fashion itself was an extremely important aspect when it came to feminine displays of the American identity. A newspaper article about *Patria* stated that Castle "is made the embodiment, the somewhat slender if graceful embodiment, of patriotism," and so, much of the publicity surrounding *Patria* discusses Castle's wardrobe.[39] For example, The *Los Angeles Examiner* of November 2, 1916, featured a spread of pictures of Castle's costumes from the serial.[40] An article from an Oklahoma City newspaper of June 30, 1918, described rules for women's wardrobes during wartime.[41] The focus on dress continued throughout the war, and included a series of advice articles on how women should dress to support the war and to express mourning for lost soldiers without detracting from their fashion sense. After the death of Castle's husband and dance partner, Vernon Castle, an article in *Motion Picture Classic* detailed Irene Castle's plans to go to France to entertain troops, despite an injury she sustained on the set of a new movie.[42] Castle's devotion to the cause and connection with her husband, who died while training pilots, was emphasized throughout the article, which discussed her fashion choices and the loss of her husband in equal parts.

Patria explicitly linked militarism, consumerism, and fashion through the overt publicity involved in promoting the serial and the star, and also through a number of specific narrative elements. In the film, in a series of plot twists, Patria meets a dancer named Elaine, who appears to be her exact double (Elaine was also played by Castle). Elaine is then befriended by the enemies, Huroki and De Lima, and paid to act as Patria after they order Patria killed. Patria lives, unbeknownst to her enemies, and after Elaine is killed while playing Patria, Patria secretly steps in, and plays Elaine playing Patria. These plot twists were confusing, but the fictional tie-ins were a useful addition in ensuring narrative comprehension.

Patria-as-Elaine-as-Patria highlighted the narrative importance of the masquerade, which was as important as the trope of cross-dressing soldiers was to the Civil War films discussed in chapter 2. In very important ways, *Patria's* narrative and Castle's star persona stressed that donning the right clothes was an important step toward becoming someone new. Much like how the transition from workers to soldiers was signified in the changings of their clothing, the fluid movement between Patria and Elaine, then back to Patria-as-Elaine-as-Patria, placed significant emphasis on performance, costuming, and clothing. Therefore, despite the fact that the serial heroine represented an active form of femininity, what was actually being marketed to women was how to *look* the part— suggesting that the look was just as important as the act. When the serials were used to promote the concept of military preparedness—and their heroines turned to defending the nation—it was still in the fashion choices that female audiences were taught to show their own patriotic devotion.

Both the story itself and the promotion surrounding *Patria* alert us to the links between consumption, performing national identity, and patriotism. Much like how the film serials and their fictional tie-ins in the Sunday papers worked to create a mass audience, ready-made fashion fostered "American" audiences' participation. As Nan Enstad explains, ready-made fashion and cheap, formulaic fiction allowed for immigrant working women to enact American identities between the 1890s and early 1910s.[43] In particular, the narrative depiction of American heroines on-screen allowed immigrant women to fantasize their own inclusion in this identity category. According to Enstad, the act of purchasing fiction, fashion, and movie tickets was how these women enacted—affordably— the American Girl identity.[44] Additionally, as Kathy Peiss argues, the transition into the twentieth century was marked by an increase in commercialism that affected all classes.[45] DeBauche provides the example of Billie Burke's serial *Gloria's Romance* (Campbell and Edwin, 1916), which promoted the American Girl as "independent and sporting, as well as a model of haute couture."[46] The fashions that stars wore in popular serials and films served as a type of "fashion show" that revealed the upcoming season's new styles.[47] Whether it was the ready-made, cheap fashion that Enstad discusses, or the high-society haute couture explored in DeBauche's study, the fashion modeled in film allowed female members of the audience to observe and then mimic the look of the American Girl. Furthermore, when preparedness and patriotism were key themes, fashion choices became an emblem of one's participation in the war effort.

Patria, Pearl of the Army, Liberty, and *The Secret of the Submarine* were serials that featured female protagonists in narratives that valued action. These heroines bridged the gap between political leaders and policy makers, and the active participants in battle. In addition, the use of the fictional tie-in that was dominant during this era, and that accompanied all serials released at the time, provided additional information pertaining to the political arguments and contemporary references underlying the narratives. Thus, popular attitudes toward preparedness in the months leading up to American entry into World War I, as well as the ways in which this idea of preparedness was crafted and presented to the American public, were reflected in the serial film format. In other words, the film serial's well-known tropes and generic patterns were now commonly understood and thus served as an ideal form not only to present the ideas of preparedness to audiences but also to foment xenophobic attitudes toward foreigners through melodramatic depictions of foreign invasion.

6 · THE AMERICAN GIRL AND WARTIME PATRIOTISM

After the U.S. government declared entry into World War I, it was imperative that the message of involvement be spread by cultural industries; this included the film industry, which was a strong force by this time—firmly established and capable of marketing to a variety of audiences at once. With production times upward of six months, the American film industry had little time to make films anew, but the industry responded by changing the way it exhibited and advertised the films that had already been produced, so as to imbue them with the recruitment message. The active woman of the early and mid-1910s did not disappear during World War I, but she was tamed, controlled, and redirected for home-front mobilization. This chapter still focuses on women's roles in war films, alongside the way war films were pitched at women in the audience, despite the growing number of war films that centered on male heroism. In other words, the male combat film was starting to emerge as a trend among a variety of different formulas for war films. The trend of female heroics that dominated the earlier 1910s did not disappear, though, and this is evident in the variety of war films featuring stars such as Mary Pickford, Vivien Martin, Mabel Normand, and Billie Burke, to name a few.

The gradual masculinization of the war genre that would take place during 1920s was developing during wartime; however, the difference was that the political imperative of wartime was to convert *all* Americans, men and women alike, to patriotic support. Rather than a specific trend—as occurred in the preparedness period, when the feminization of the active defense of homeland emerged—wartime pictures during World War I offered myriad character types and betrayed a complex relationship between gender and wartime patriotism. Thus, even though there were still films featuring active women, the marketing and promotion downplayed women's involvement in fighting and shifted the focus to men's wartime duty. In addition, stars—both men and women—were mobilized to promote wartime efforts, including recruitment and the purchasing of Liberty Bonds. Closer to the war's end, when the production of films caught up with the current events, films about male heroism began to appear. These films continued to flourish immediately following the war.

In preparedness and wartime films, the process of promoting patriotism to women through female stars involved converting patriotism into consumable products—clothing—and the reverse, advertising consumable products as expressions of patriotism.[1] Could the commercialization of patriotism go too far? During American participation in World War I, the answer to that question seemed to be no. Particularly through the mobilization of stars and consumerism, as well as a direct pitch to female audiences, the film industry found quick ways to use pre-existing formulas to promote patriotism and film-going. As Leslie Midkiff DeBauche observes, a strong ethic of "practical patriotism" swept through the industry. Supporting the war effort—through selling or promoting war bonds, working in tandem with the government, and so on—was good for both business and the country.[2]

The government had to garner support for a full-fledged military engagement. The message in wartime films about war, and their promotional materials, changed from a call for preparedness (which had defined the period from the beginning of the war to the U.S. entry) to a call for male action (recruitment), as well as a justification for sending "our" men "over there." Central to this, though, was getting women on board with the message. Women needed to convince their loved ones to enlist and needed to be convinced that the sacrifice was worthwhile. Thus, film functioned as a useful medium—with its female audiences and its trend of women-centered narratives—to encourage patriotic support. In the weeks after the U.S. government declared war, the Committee on Public Information, headed by George Creel, was created to distribute propaganda in support of war efforts to the American people. Even though film production took longer to catch up, film theaters were quickly targeted as popular venues to reach the public. Speeches by Four-Minute Men promoted recruitment efforts and war bonds and provided information about the U.S. involvement in war. Even films produced prior to American entry in the war were exhibited as recruitment tools after the Americans entered the war in April 1917. As we saw in chapter 4, the United States had declared war on Germany in early April and *Womanhood, the Glory of the Nation* was being shown with recruitment booths at screenings.

Toward the end of the war and after, dominant character types at the center of American war films changed from active women to heroic, disciplined men. The masculinized version of the war film gained traction early, but into the 1920s film studios continued to produce female-centric depictions of war, such as war romances, war melodramas, and other women-led films with themes of war or military. It is important to remember these films and to situate them within the history of the genre and as part of the film industry's reaction to the realities of American participation in World War I. The remainder of this chapter will trace the dominant female character types that were used throughout the World War I years, even during the rise of masculine combat movies.

SLACKERS AND THE WOMEN WHO SAVED THEM

Slacker narratives were similar to those popular in the earlier cycle of Civil War dramas from 1908 to 1916, explored in chapter 2: a man controlled by a dominant mother, lover, or other eventually enlists in war and proves himself heroic. Films like *The Man Who Was Afraid* (Wright, 1917), *The Slacker* and *Draft 258* (Cabanne, 1917), and *The Gown of Destiny* (Reynolds, 1917) all depict narratives about men who can or cannot go to war and are shamed for staying out. *The Slacker* concerns a very particular period early in the war, when men who were married could avoid military duty.[3] The film is about a man, Robert Wallace (Walter Miller), who uses his recent marriage to Margaret Christy (Emily Stevens) as an excuse to stay home—until his wife's pleas and an incident with a group of children convince him to enlist. The final incident that convinces Robert to enlist is children playing with an American flag. A bully tries to take the flag from a young girl, and then a passerby also takes the flag. Robert fights the man who takes the flag from the young girl and is inspired to enlist.[4] The film shows both the displeasure of Robert's wife and the stirring incident with the young patriot as inspiration for Robert's final awakening. Like other melodramatic stories, the victimization of the young patriot is heightened by its being a young girl who holds the flag. The pathos over her potential loss of the flag is matched with Robert's call to action.

Promotion for *The Slacker* primarily focused on its popular star—not the slacker, but his wife, Emily Stevens. *Motography* describes the desired effect of the film: "In 'The Slacker' Margaret Christy, Emily Stevens, helps her husband to solve his own problem, as wives throughout America will help their husbands and friends to solve theirs. 'The Slacker' is a play that will build patriots."[5] The following review praised Stevens: "Until you have seen Metro's production of 'The Slacker,' you have not experienced the real, soul-piercing thrill of patriotism. Until you have seen Emily Stevens in the roll of Margaret Christy, you have not seen the soul of a woman, an actress, an artist, pour forth through its most inspiring channels, the terrible, crushing emotions felt by a mother, a wife—a patriot when the nearest and dearest to her heart—a 'slacker'—hears the call of his country and leaves for the battlefields of France."[6] Though the film was largely billed as an Emily Stevens picture, both the wife's encouragement and the husband's heroism were the focus of the advertisements and promotions for the film.[7]

Furthermore, Cabanne's next film, *Draft 258* was promoted as the follow-up, or unofficial sequel, to *The Slacker*, and echoed themes similar to its predecessor but further emphasized men's part in training for and fighting the war. Co-written with June Mathis, *Draft 258* "drives the message of patriotism home with sledge-hammer blows."[8] In this film "Mabel Taliaferro lends true inspiration to the part of Mary Alden, the girl patriot. The star was chosen for the role because she is a typically 'human' type of American Girl. Walter Miller, who played the part of the slacker in *The Slacker*, has a chance to redeem himself in the eyes of motion picture 'fans' in this production, for as John Graham he is patriotic from start to finish."[9] That Walter Miller's role evolved between *The Slacker* and *Draft 258*, as described in the above review, was indicative of the turn toward showing men's actions during war. The film is about Mary Alden (Mabel Taliaferro), her brothers, and her lover, John Graham (Walter Miller). Mary is a staunch patriot and wishes that she could go to war, if women were allowed to fight. Her brother Matthew (Earle Brunswick) is a pacifist who is being used by German spies to promote pacifism and prevent enlistment. Her other brother, George (Eugene Borden), is recruited early in the draft but is proud to serve because he had been inspired by Mary's many speeches. John Graham enlists voluntarily very early on. Mary is kidnapped by one of the spies, threatened, but saved by John and cavalry. Matthew is inspired to take up arms.[10] Again, the victimhood and threat on the female character inspires and leads to the justification for militarism and violence. Edward Weitzel states, "It is never overburdened with the atmosphere of war, the marching of soldiers and scenes from camp life. The news reels have shown us the genuine thing, and it is the story of one woman's fight for the honor of her country and her home that makes 'Draft 258' worthwhile."[11] Another review makes clear the message the film industry wished to align itself with: "Bravery and cowardice, patriotism and treachery, are frankly arrayed against each other in 'Draft 258,' and the right side wins."[12] The message of these films was that American men ultimately proved heroic when the time came—and the time was upon them. Of course, these men needed the encouragement, or possibly a strong nudge, from the women in their lives. These films demonstrated that early-wartime American patriotism was something that must involve all citizens—men *and* women. Even though in these films women functioned more as moral support and inspiration to male heroism on the battlefield, as opposed to being active participants in battle, they continued to be prominent in narratives about war during the American involvement in the war, both on a narrative level and in extra-filmic promotion of the stars who "did their part."

Mrs. Slacker (Henley, 2018) returned to a familiar plot of the Civil War melodramas. The film was unfavorably reviewed by Peter Milne, which may have been because of the outdated story. Robert Gibbs (Creighton Hale), a college-age man, marries Susie Simpkins (Gladys Hulette) in order to avoid the draft. Susie is disappointed and ashamed of Robert and decides to dress like a man and join the army in his place. She sees a group of German spies plotting to blow up a reservoir and tries to intervene but is kidnapped. Robert finds her and the spies, in the nick of time, and prevents the bomb from exploding. He is inspired to enlist.[13] The three films described above all provide examples of the same story: a woman or girl is patriotic but falls victim in some way, thus inspiring righteous violence and enlistment from the formerly slacker hero. This continues to reaffirm the narrative underlying the myth of American militarism and imperialism.

Another, but entirely different, film about a slacker, the 1917 film *Gown of Destiny* (Lynn Reynolds), begins with a renowned French fashion designer, André, living in New York City. He is ridiculed by the women who work for him, and he decides to enlist in the French army in order to prove himself a man. Unfortunately for the designer, he is deemed too "scrawny" for active duty. Instead he is told that he would serve better by staying home. With his masculinity in crisis, he decides to make a gown so beautiful that the women will owe him respect. His gown is indeed beautiful and inspires awe from each of his female employees, but it is sold to a woman whom the designer believes too ugly to wear his gown. While he spends the remainder of the film upset and dejected, the gown results in a chain of events that eventually come full circle. First, the woman who bought the gown wears it for their anniversary with her husband, who is no longer attracted to her. He is about to leave, having forgotten about the anniversary altogether, until he sees her wearing the gown and falls back in love. He is so overcome with emotion that he decides to finance a number of ambulances to send to France. The woman then sends the gown to her homely niece. When she wears the gown to a party, the niece suddenly becomes the object of affection of Neil Cunningham, a handsome Englishman who has previously had no interest in her. When the two finally declare their love for each other, Neil reveals that he is a slacker—a man who has not enlisted in the army—and that he cannot marry until he rights this wrong. Neil enlists in the British army, is welcomed back into the family by his father, and leaves for France. In France he helps to liberate a small French town, saving the mayor from execution by German soldiers. The mayor thanks Neil and tells him of his son, a fashion designer in New York City. The film ends, however, with André bitterly thinking about how he was unable to serve the war effort. The audience has privileged knowledge, but this does not help the tortured designer, who will never know that his gown saved his small hometown.

The Gown of Destiny works on a number of different themes that recur throughout the war period. While the slacker narrative takes over the second half of the film with the relationship between the niece and the Englishman, it is complemented with the narrative of André, the fashion designer, who is not a slacker but is not allowed to serve in the traditional manner. For those who had to stay home, for whatever reason, when the sentiment in popular discourse emphasized the importance of military service, it was important to tell a narrative that showed that even the most seemingly disconnected work was still important to the war effort. It's important to also consider the centrality of his position as fashion designer and the centrality of the gown throughout the narrative. It is an interesting narrative structure, as it follows an object—the gown—

from each loosely connected story. It is the gown that binds the three narrative threads, and the gown acts as a catalyst to spur each character into patriotic duty.

The focus on fashion as a key narrative thread in *The Gown of Destiny* serves to reinforce traditional gender roles in two ways. First, in a rather stereotypical manner, the job of fashion designer is meant to signify André's less than virile form of masculinity. A large portion of the first part of the film revolves around André's anxiety to prove his masculinity, his patriotism, and his fulfillment of his duty to country. But patriotism does not sit at the forefront of André's fears. Instead, he reacts to the laughter of women, in itself a useful motive. The film seems to straddle between suggesting to men: "Do not allow yourself to be laughed at" and "It's ok to stay home as long as you continue to live a productive life." The second way fashion is used to foment traditional gender roles is how the film suggests, somewhat problematically, that women can serve by inspiring men as long as they remain fashionable.

Finally, the slacker narrative is traditional: the Englishman cannot enjoy love, marriage, and ties to his family until he goes back to England to enlist for duty. In this film the men maintain a central role. The gown, while it functions as a connector, is only meant to stand in as the product of André's labor. This—and the short cycle of slacker films—demonstrates a shift in films about war that foregrounds men in battle and women at home. However, the depiction of female heroism that had thrived in American narrative film from 1908 onward saw continuing traces in films featuring the female stars of the era.

FEMALE STARS: AMERICAN GIRLS ABROAD AND AT HOME

Stars such as Mary Pickford, Billie Burke, Mabel Normand, Emily Stevens, and Lillian and Dorothy Gish featured in films about the war; they also "did their part" by appearing at various speeches, public events, and fundraising efforts in support of the war.[14] These actresses starred in films with female-centered narratives about American Girls at home or sometimes even stranded in war-torn villages in Europe. As discussed in chapter 1, the idea of the "American Girl" revised the idea of the "New Woman" into something more appropriate for an American context by valorizing the particular traits that better reflected American ideals, such as independence and athleticism. The perceived negative aspects of these traits (namely, that these women were uncontrollable and "unfeminine") were sublimated into participation in American military efforts. American-made films during World War I filtered the European conflict through American characters who exemplified this particular form of American femininity. For example, Pickford played a "little American" trapped in France during a German invasion, Lillian Gish plays an American in a French village, and Billie Burke plays an American stranded in a Belgium village. DeBauche argues that the war "afforded stars, as it did the companies which employed them, the opportunity to increase their prestige with the American public."[15] In other words, by promoting the war, female stars proved patriotic to their country and simultaneously further developed their personas as American Girls.

Mary Pickford made the films *100% American* (Rosson, 1918), *The Little American* (DeMille, 1917), and *Johanna Enlists* (Taylor, 1918) and appeared in public promoting the war effort.[16] In addition to films, Pickford's efforts included speeches promoting war bonds, and even donating ambulances to the Red Cross and encouraging other stars to do the same.[17] In July 1917, Pickford's public appearance in San Francisco reportedly led the 10,000 people in attendance to purchase $2 million in Liberty Bonds.[18] By May 1917, announcements for *The Little American* were already appearing in the trade press.[19] This means that preparation for and production of the film was under way prior to the American declaration of war. The use of Mary Pickford in patriotic pictures was discussed prior to American entry into World War I. This example is from a letter Jesse Lasky wrote to Cecil B. DeMille: "We have talked it over here and believe that at this particular time, when other countries are striving to catch the national spirit, by producing timely pictures with semi-patriotic titles—Mary Pickford in a production called 'The American Girl' would create a good deal of advance interest."[20] Pickford's war films vary in subject matter, but all revolve around an American Girl's participation—usually unwilling at first—in the war effort. In *The Little American,* Pickford is an American in France who becomes a spy for the Allied forces. In *100% American,* she plays a woman at home, doing her part to support the war—namely, by not spending money and instead buying Liberty Bonds. *Johanna Enlists* features Pickford as a young farm girl who meets and encourages a regiment of soldiers who are staying on her family's farm before shipping overseas.

The Little American is by far the most melodramatic and generic of the three and was part of a heated censorship dispute that delayed its Chicago release.[21] Pickford's films are about the American Girl and her place in the ongoing war. While *The Little American* is a sensationalized, melodramatic narrative that capitalizes on the perils of an American woman in the hands of the German foe, the other two films are about what the American Girl can do at home. *The Little American,* directed by Cecil B. DeMille and written by Jeanie MacPherson (the same pair who directed and wrote *Joan the Woman,* among other sensational, active women films and a handful of Pickford melodramas), is more firmly entrenched in the narrative and generic patterns of the female melodramas typical of the DeMille-MacPherson team than it was dedicated to promoting war enlistment. It differs from Pickford's two most explicitly propagandistic films—*100% American* is about Liberty Bonds and *Johanna Enlists* is about military enlistment—that I will discuss in this chapter precisely because they demonstrate how film producers and exhibitors used the star persona for the war effort. With *The Little American*, by contrast, rather than using interest in the film to sell the war, interest in the war is used to sell the film.

100% American depicts Americans as a nation of spenders. In particular, it directs its narrative toward female audiences by assuming that the consumer society was driven by female shoppers. American women were inextricably linked with these negative notions of national identity. An intertitle states:

Americans are extremists.
We may work hard, but we play hard—we also spend hard.
What we earn in six days, we spend in two hours.

This short film, about a woman who enjoys shopping but works hard to save her money for Liberty Bonds, suggests for viewers that even the most frivolous Americans can do their part. The scene in which Mayme learns that she should "Buy 4th Liberty Bonds now!" also includes a direct address to the camera. The man speaking to a crowd in the film points to the camera with an accompanying intertitle: "What are you giving right now?" The reaction shot is of Mayme and her friend, the central consumers and spenders within the film's narrative. The film consists of a series of incidences where Mayme's desire to spend, but resolve to be a "good American," is continually tested. Throughout it all, she maintains her willpower and buys the bonds, unlike her friend who continues spending. The soldiers' return is marked by a social dance, which can be attended only by soldiers and girls with bonds. A final moment of self-sacrifice sees Mayme give her friend the bond so that she can attend the dance. At the last moment, Mayme's sweetheart comes home with two tickets to the dance.

Although the narrative ends there, the film does not. An epilogue scene involving a stereotypically dressed German walking a tightrope carrying cases with labels such as "Militarism," "Autocracy," and "Brute Force" cuts to Mayme with a baseball labeled "4th Liberty Loan." She then throws the ball at the German, who falls into a giant vat of soup. Mayme turns to the camera and speaks, with an intertitle displaying her words: "Yours may be *the* Bond to knock him off his perch!" The importance of direct address combined with narrative should not be underestimated. According to Ine van Dooren and Peter Kramer, direct address was employed in feature films during World War I "to create heightened dramatic effects and/or to explicate the film's message, often for propagandistic purposes" precisely because of its "rarity and disruptive quality."[22] Pickford's films employed this technique precisely because her star persona was well known for the war efforts she participated in, including speeches and fundraising at public events. The direct address allowed citizens across the country to witness Pickford's speech through the medium of film.

Johanna Enlists is about a young girl living a monotonous life, each day doing chores from morning until night, in a rural community. Johanna's dream is to

FIGURE 13. Film still from *Johanna Enlists*. (Courtesy of George Eastman House.)

find love and model herself after the women in fashion magazines, but all this changes when a group of soldiers set up camp on her parents' farm. By the end of the film she becomes an honorary member of their regiment. Although her parents constantly call her simple and imply that she is a useless member of society, in the military atmosphere she finds value. This film also includes a moment of direct address comparable to the scene from *100% American*. Near the conclusion of the film, the colonel stands on a platform and tells the regiment they are shipping out, followed by a shot of the men waving their hats and an American flag in the center. Next, Johanna stands on the platform and says, "And don't you come back 'til you've taken the germ out of Germany!" Pickford/Johanna then waves her fist and speaks directly to the camera, causing a distinct slippage between the character and Pickford herself, as she is speaking both to the men within the film and the imagined men in the audience. The next intertitle—"God bless them and send them safely back to us"—accompanies this shot of "Colonel" Mary Pickford with Colonel Ralph J. Faneuf, the commander of the 143rd Field Artillery, both in uniform, saluting the camera. Now "over there" are all the soldiers who took part in this picture. They are the 143rd Field Artillery, of which regiment Mary Pickford is godmother and honorary colonel.

Unlike the controversial melodrama *The Little American*, Pickford's other wartime films were predominantly comic. Despite the portion of *Johanna Enlists* that addresses the audience and calls for *recruits*, the film itself was received as a lighthearted star picture: "That there is no necessity for somber mood in stories of present-day military atmosphere is delightfully illustrated in 'Johanna Enlists,' and she actually does enlist as Mary Pickford in the American Artillery regiment which gave her support in the play. . . . The story is more than a vehicle but is so little more than one that only a Mary Pickford could make full use of its leading characteristics."[23]

This sentiment—"that there is no necessity for somber mood"—is reflected in the general transition of women in war melodramas from active heroines to comic relief. Clémentine Tholas-Disset refers to Pickford's trilogy of war films as "an epic romance, a buffoonish comedy, and a semi-documentarian short advertising piece" that demonstrate how "the war film becomes then adaptable to address diverse audiences."[24] However, she goes on to discuss the importance of humor in Pickford's work, which is also in her book co-authored with Karen A. Ritzenhoff, *Humor, Entertainment, and Popular Culture during World War I*. Tholas-Disset and Ritzenhoff examine the use of humor as a coping mechanism in the face of the horrors of war.[25] Comedies to depict wartime subject matter include Pickford's *Johanna Enlists*, as well as films by Mabel Normand, Margeurita Fischer, and Vivien Martin (of *Her Father's Son*). Further, as Kristen Anderson Wagner argues, "female comediennes defused their perceived threat through comic portrayals" and helped to open up the category of New Woman, beyond simply the active heroines discussed earlier in this book.[26]

The characters in many of these films were adolescent girls: old enough to embody patriotism and young enough that their subversion of gender roles is nonthreatening because it is only temporary (until they are married and become women). These girls were actively patriotic prior to entry into traditional womanhood. An example of this is *Her Country First* (Young, 1918), which involved a young American woman leading an "army." In the film, Dorothy (Vivian Martin), aged seventeen, organizes a regiment of girl aviators and ultimately thwarts a German invasion. *Her Country First* is both comedic and sensational, involving humorous situations and adventures akin to the serial genre. The regiment, the GAC, has no airplane, but they do have uniforms and a drill sergeant. Although without an airplane, she organizes a girl's aviation corps whose duty is to watch over her father's munitions factory. The members order proper and well-fitting uniforms and go out in the countryside to drill. They're shown how to wigwag (signal with flags) by a farmer who served in the Spanish-American war, and have a number of funny experiences.[27]

This film demonstrates that the active female character is less threatening as a teenager, not yet required to enter the realm of domesticity. In fact, save for the military theme, the film has little to do with the actual war, which was currently taking place. Martin's character, Dorothy Grant, provides humor and thrills precisely because she is in an unthreatening phase of adolescence. Throughout the

FIGURE 14. Film still from *Her Country First.* (Courtesy of George Eastman House.)

film, Dorothy's family and close family friends tease her for taking up patriotism as a lark. However, by the end of the comedic film Dorothy and the GAC manage to disrupt the plans of German spies, posing as domestic servants. Dorothy has instructed her recruits to keep watch for spies. Ultimately Dorothy "catches" the wrong spy and is then kidnapped by the real spies. Finally she is saved and declares her love for Craig (J. Parks Jones), who has just joined the army. The shooting script lists the final dialogue:

CRAIG: You'll wait for me?
DOROTHY: Yes, Craig, our country first!

It is Dorothy who convinces Craig to enlist, and the change from "her" to "our" in the title phrase is indicative of the inclusion of women in the propagandistic efforts of the World War I era. *Her Country First* had no actual war combat scenes, but capitalized on the popularity of young, female characters in spy genre and of war propaganda at the time.

Similarly, *Joan of Plattsburg* (Goldwyn, 1918) is about a young American orphan who reads about Joan of Arc and then dreams about discovering and fighting against a German spy. Plattsburg was an American training camp that would have been a common point of reference for audiences. This film was

FIGURE 15. Film still from *Joan of Plattsburg*. (Courtesy of George Eastman House.)

directly marketed to American men and women by using the star appeal of Mabel Normand, who wonders, "What can I do for my country?" According to *Motion Picture News*:

> "Joan of Plattsburg" provides the answer. Mabel Normand as Joan, the little girl living near a great military encampment, sees for the first time in her life the pictured story of France's Joan, the greatest feminine heroine in all history. She hears the story of Joan and asks, "Can any little girl of today be a Joan of Arc and influence the future of her country?"
>
> And the answer is: "Yes; you can build up love of country. You can build faith and courage in your men. You and all other girls and boys and men and women can by your faith intensify and strengthen your country."[28]

By 1918 the active woman of the preparedness phase was gone. With American men abroad, these films confirmed that the patriotic duty of women firmly remained at home, as moral support for their men and as assistants in developing a "love of country." Furthermore, Robin Blaetz suggests, Normand's well-known star persona and sexual appeal were at odds with the spiritualism inherent in the narrative of Joan of Arc. As a result, she argues, "the film reflects the dichotomy between the virgin and the whore; the spirit of Joan of Arc provides men with the rationale for fighting, while the body of Mabel Normand makes it all worthwhile."[29] Or, as Maggie Hennefeld argues, Mabel Normand had a history of combining a "contradictory duality between excess corporeality and ethereal spirit into a figure who is at once hyper-vulnerable and fantastically indestructible."[30] Rather than appealing to women through the figure of an active woman thwarting spies and defending the nation, the film focuses on Joan, a young orphan, being awakened to the patriotic possibilities of those still at home. The film itself was deemed unique and unlike the patriotic pictures that preceded it. "'Joan of Plattsburg,' with a general appeal to both sexes, is directed nevertheless to the women of America. Men may react to false rumors, have their efficiency reduced through propaganda, but the faith of woman is endurable and constitutes an impregnable fortress in times of national trial," declares the Goldwyn statement.[31] This review reiterates that women were the moral center of the nation, while men took up the active battle.

In addition to films about American Girls in the United States during the war, there were also star pictures set in Europe, with American or European women at the center of the war narrative. Billie Burke starred as an American woman in *Arms and the Girl* (Kaufman, 1918), a film set in Belgium at the outbreak of the war. Olga Petrova's film *Daughter of Destiny* (Irving, 1917) used patriotism to garner attention for her own star persona as is evidenced in this review: "Using the war for a background and centering on German intrigue in a neutral kingdom of mythical origin, though suggestively called Balmark, 'Daughter of Destiny,' Mme. Petrova's first picture with her own company, makes a strong bid for popularity, particularly before those whose patriotism is aroused by the somewhat obvious method of flag waving."[32] The various war-related films in which female stars were featured—for timely, political, or simply financial reasons—served the purpose of defining women's part during war. They also revealed the diverse female roles that could emerge during wartime, as well as the cultural anxieties that accompanied changing roles for women in American society. Women promoted the war, and the war effort provided an avenue through which women could enact their own part in the American nation.

CONCLUSION

In this book I have shown a history of the war film that focuses on women's heroism, athleticism, patriotism, and bravery. Due to the norms of the film industry—female stars, serial queens, melodrama as a dominant mode of storytelling—war films from roughly 1908 to 1918 featured women in central and heroic roles. But these female protagonists were much more than that. They reinforced national myth and the ideological underpinnings of both historical memory of American-fought wars and contemporary politics. They served within a tapestry of popular cultural texts and discourses to define white American identity as *the* American identity. They erased from view those who didn't fit this narrow image, and they promoted fears about those who were different or foreign. This is an important period to remember and an important reminder that women, too, can enact or be used symbolically to reinforce racism, jingoism, and xenophobia. At best these women were patriotic supporters of their country; at worst they contributed to a national myth that excludes and vilifies others. Even as the years that followed this decade led to a masculinization of the genre, looking back to the 1910s helps understand women's roles not only in war films but in political engagement and popular culture then and now.

THE MASCULINIZATION OF THE WAR GENRE

Changing norms in the film industry and attitudes toward war, gender norms, and national identity led to a masculinization of the genre from 1919 onward. There are outliers to this generalization—see *Corporal Kate* (Sloane, 1926)—but the war genre as we now know it took shape in the 1920s.[1] The "masculinization of the war genre" reminds us that it was a process, not a de facto state of being.[2]

Arguably, the masculinization of the genre began with a handful of non-narrative films soon after the American entry into World War I. Much like the films that portrayed male military training in order to promote jingoism and the Spanish-American War, a number of films that depicted a military, masculinist power were released in 1917 to convince men of the benefits of enlistment and to justify the war despite increased knowledge of the horrors that accompanied it. Very soon after the United States entered the war, a variety of non-narrative films appeared that presented life in the military: *Uncle Sam at Work*, *How Uncle Sam Prepares* (Grant, 1917), and *Manning the Navy* (Mutual, 1917) are notable examples.[3]

How Uncle Sam Prepares was supervised by army officials and was shot over a series of months. It was advertised for its patriotic appeal: "There is no red-blooded American who will not be stirred by this picture, with its visualization of what the men of our army are going through in order to fit themselves properly to defend the country's honor. The scenes are complete to the final detail, and show that the United States has at command men who will live up to the record of the American Army in the past."[4] Similarly, *Uncle Sam at Work* was lauded for showing in a positive manner the minute details of Navy life: "Sailors are shown in their various forms of drill and in the duties that are expected of them aboard a man-of-war. Among these are the loading and firing of guns, signaling to distant ships, and stripping decks for action and releasing torpedoes. Life aboard submarines and torpedo boats is represented including the particular work cut out for the firemen, stokers, bakers and other men below decks who help so mightily in the efficiency of our navy."[5] These early wartime films were exhibited soon after the American declaration of war, but they also looked ahead to an important type of film that was released later in the war.

Films about the male experience of war, such as *The Unbeliever* (Crosland, 1918) and *The Lost Battalion* (King, 1919), focused on valorizing male action in battle. In a letter dated January 3, 1918, L. W. McChesney, manager of the Motion Picture Division for the Edison Company, wrote to distributor George Kleine about a possible collaboration with the War Work Council and the YMCA in showing the film *The Unbeliever* to new recruits. The explanation was this: "They wanted 'THE UNBELIEVER'" in preference to the millions of feet of available old film because, according to their statement, it seems to be the first motion picture which deals with the things they are trying to impress upon enlisted and drafted men—first, that character is moulded in war; second, that even war has its compensation; third, that most of the men who go to war are likely to come back."[6] This letter points to how the film was interpreted by military agencies. It was further elaborated upon in a series of letters exchanged between Kleine and the Edison Company regarding the partnership between local theaters and local recruitment centers as the film was distributed and exhibited across the United States. Kleine's resistance to an official collaboration with the Marines' recruitment centers rested upon his idea that the film would earn more if marketed as a commercial product rather than a military one.[7] Both of these positions—belief in the recruiting power of the film and belief in the commercial power of the film—presume the same things about the effects of war on men. That is, that narratives about boys becoming men through war—specifically, American heroes—were popular.

The Unbeliever opens with an intertitle that echoes this idea of growth through battle. It read, "The forge in which the very soul of man was tested," and was followed by a shot of men charging across the screen. Then the audience is introduced to the Landicutt family. The playboy son, Philip Landicutt, lives a carefree life of leisure. Philip is inspired to enlist but he remains steadfast in his beliefs that all Germans are evil and that there is a marked difference between people of the lower and upper classes. During his time at war, Philip befriends the Landicutts' chauffeur, Lefty, who later dies in Philip's arms, telling him not to judge others based on class. Throughout the film, a secondary story concerns Virginie, a young Belgian woman whose mother and brother are killed by a group of German soldiers led by a character played by Erich von Stroheim. Virginie escapes and works as a servant in a town where the Germans and Americans have a battle. Philip finds Virginie and gives her his mother's address, telling her that she will be safe in America. After a near-death experience on the battlefield, and a vision of Jesus, Philip becomes a believer and ultimately lives to return to his mother and to Virginie, whom he loves despite her peasant background.

While films about active women were still produced and released, *The Unbeliever* suggests a turn toward the masculine landscape of war in the following decade: narratives implied that battlegrounds were the sites where young male characters could become men. Even though discussions of *The Unbeliever* in the trade press highlighted the actress who played Virginie, she was not involved in action or battle scenes and instead served as the romantic anchor that tied Philip to home. In the films of this period, women came to represent the home front as a space of safe return, rather than a place in need of heroic defending. A review states Marguerite Courtot, the actress who played Virginie, had French heritage and an innocent nature: "There is about her the fragrant innocence of sheltered youth and this is revealed in startling contrast to the brutal lust of a Prussian lieutenant. Raymond McKee plays the spirited young marine private who finally transplants the Belgian flower to the more fortunate sun of America, and Miss Courtot makes her inevitable surrender a victory of love and gratitude."[8] Quite different from the active women of the American wars, Virginie experienced a victory of love and gratitude that was in every way subordinate to masculine heroism, even as the review focused entirely on the actress instead of the male lead. This again confirmed that female stars continued to be a driving force of the film industry in the late 1910s, and that even films of war needed a "feminine hook." It would not be until the mid-1920s that producers, and subsequently exhibitors, would begin to experiment with male-only narratives.[9]

The valorization of the masculinity of these war heroes, apart from their female co-stars, was derived partly from a turn toward privileging realism when filming and promoting films: "Alan Crosland, who directed, with the co-operation of the United States Marine Corps, has shot the actuality in registering the backgrounds. When he sends the hero into the trenches, trenches they are—not props. Every detail conforms to the actuality from the French type of helmet adopted by our troops in France to the bobbed-wire entanglements barricading the approach of the advancing army."[10] A similar effort was made in *The Lost Battalion* (1919), which featured the men from the 77th Division playing themselves on-screen, and the film presented the homosocial sphere of combat, bringing men together as a microcosm of American society. The scenes in the film's opening sequence show the numerous backgrounds—in terms of class, religion, former national heritage—of the men who ultimately come together to be part of the 77th Division's battle of Argonne. An intertitle reads: "Men from forty-two different races and tongues flowed into the melting pot." *The Lost Battalion* was successful and pointed the way toward a period of gritty realism in the war genre in the 1920s. One review read:

> That the W.H. Productions Company feature, "The Lost Battalion," is meeting with unprecedented success is illustrated by the number of telegrams, letters and critical reviews following each showing and lauding this unique production. Re-enacted by the survivors themselves of one of the bravest exploits of the American doughboy in the Argonne, this is a picture of marked originality that is being demanded by people who look daily to motion pictures for entertainment. It contains the intimate touch that the public demands in new film productions, of genuineness, originality and entertainment value.[11]

This review foreshadowed what the war film would become in the 1920s. For various reasons, films featuring war ceased to be melodramas reinforcing the traditional values of love, patriotism, and family devotion, seen in prominently during the 1910s, and shifted to showing the masculine terrain of war, which they presented as "realistic." However, during World War I the war genre was not yet assumed to be predominantly masculine. Men and women alike were used to promote patriotism and American entry into war, and the masculine and feminine character types of this era varied from disciplined men to slackers, and from active women to spoiled spenders. Most important for all of these characters, and for the audiences who learned from them, however, was that they proved heroic and did their parts in the end.

Even at the end of World War I the film industry still worked under the general assumption that a film must appeal to both men and women—and especially women. Thus, films about male heroism made at this time still required a love story or a doting mother in order to appeal to audiences and, equally important, to exhibitors. This study has analyzed the role played by active women in films from the early and mid-1910s, while demonstrating that the active woman existed alongside a variety of other female character types—the woman as moral center, the long-suffering love interest, the woman who waits at home. During U.S. participation in World War I, these suffering women grew to dominate the scene and the active women were removed from battle. Films such as *Victory of Conscience* (Reicher, 1916), *The Man Who Was Afraid* (Wright, 1917), *Fields of Honor* (Ince, Ralph, 1918), *Hearts of the World* (Griffith, 1918), *The Unbeliever* (Crossland, 1918), and *Woman* (Tourneur, 1918) exhibited women's suffering and sacrifice during war. However, the character type of the suffering woman took time to filter into popular film production. The 1920s saw a further divide between women's pictures (romances set during war) and war films—"he-men" pictures that used discourses of "realism" in promotion to suggest not only that war stripped away civilization to reveal some form of "real" masculinity but also that film was able to show audiences this process, in the next closest thing to actually being there. In other words, traits such as violence, virility, and sexual exploit were deemed the natural state of masculinity, which had been lost due to modernity and civilization. This privileging of men in the war genre, and subsequent displacement of women to the margins of that genre, reflects the masculinization of the industry and the nation that occurred in the decade following World War I.

A SHOCKING ENDING: *BEHIND THE DOOR*

American culture and the film industry were returning to the valorization of manly masculinity.[12] There was a sense that films for women were produced for general release, whereas "he-man" films were given more prestigious treatment. By the 1920s the war genre was primarily a genre of male heroics.[13] Women's pictures and American Girls in this period were romantic and melodramatic. "He-man" pictures were promoted as more realistic and gritty, and they had extended Broadway runs. A review for *Behind the Door* (Willat, 1919) echoed this sentiment:

> Do you enjoy a picture that gets out of the beaten path and presents men as they are under certain conditions, with the veneer of civilization stripped from them, shoved back a thousand years to the cavemen days when strength ruled and hate and love were the only two passions known? Do you wish to see a fight that passes anything in its intensity that has ever been staged? ... You may make some women stay at home but you will get other patrons to take their place if you bill it correctly and emphasize the fact that it is a "he" man story with more punch than find their way into a dozen pictures.[14]

This review encapsulated a trend that would dominate war films for the rest of the 1920s: a focus on strong, heroic men. Many of the characters bore physical and emotional scars, but these men were heroic nonetheless; in fact, their traumas made them all the more appealing. Concomitantly, representations of women saw the splintering of femininity between the exotic and active "other," and the sweet and yet modern American woman.[15]

The example of *Behind the Door* is useful in that it presents two character types: the tortured but rugged male hero who does a reprehensible act (skinning a man alive), and the chaste, vulnerable, and suffering American woman. The wife follows her husband to war, sneaking onto his ship and revealing herself only long after the boat has left the shore. The husband, the captain of the ship, cannot turn around to bring her home. He knows that the ocean is dangerous during wartime, and his prediction of danger is soon realized. A German U-boat surfaces, and raids the ship, kidnapping the wife. She is raped by the submariners and then shot from the torpedo tube after they are done with her (most of this is implied, not shown, but the film is still explicit in its intertitling and editing). She, of course, dies. Her husband vows vengeance; after a year he somehow finds the U-boat captain, brings him aboard the new ship, and takes the man "behind the door." The grieving husband later tells a friend: "I swore I'd skin him alive but he died on me—damn him." Revenge drives the husband's actions, but the murdered wife serves little more than to inspire male heroics and to signify his tortured relationship to the memory of war. The film ends with the American man returning to the town where he had met his wife; he then dies while resting his head on a table. He is reunited with the spirit of his wife and the two are finally together in the afterlife. As a somewhat happy ending to an entirely bitter tale, the reunion of the couple indicates that they have finally found peace together many years after the war. The woman's spirit acts as the man's savior, and the suffering wife conjures the archetype of woman-as-moral-center to the men of the nation.

I chose to discuss this film as the conclusion to this book because it has a shocking ending, and *not* because it is a shocking ending to the decade of war films about women. In the case of *Behind the Door*, the wife is not saved in the nick of time by a lover or by her own quick thinking and bravery. The fate of the wife, a sacrifice to move the narrative forward and to justify the husband's vengeance, signals what is to come for women in war films in future decades. If the wife had stayed home, her suffering would signal the kind of suffering expected of women on the home front. This wife's death by being shot from a torpedo tube should be startling but not surprising. The violence enacted upon her body is entirely the point. This kind of violence was always hinted at—and even explicit in the preparedness features of chapter 4—and always the threat against a vulnerable nation. Here, the violence is intentional and is meant to symbolically replace the idea of the "vulnerable woman" with the idea of a vulnerable nation. The women of this book represented ideals of nation; they represented its strength but they also represented what might befall a nation at the hands of the enemy. As in so many films, rape is used as a metaphor—the fear of the worst violation in patriarchal imagining. The foreign enemy—in this case the German enemy, with wartime propaganda still in recent memory—is capable of anything and, so the American nation and the American military must remain strong and vigilant. Many masculinized war films promote the same jingoism and xenophobia as the films with female protagonists. The major difference is the way the suffering of the female characters is shown.

Throughout the 1910s, women heroines served the American national mythos, valorizing militarism, expansionism, preparedness, and patriotism. The women in these films fulfilled their duty and embodied the vision of white America that was needed at the time. We are often told that after the war (both World War I and World War II), women who had taken jobs while the men were away were asked to return to their homes. In the case of women in the war genre, after World War I ended they were asked to hang up their soldier's uniforms and take up the roles of home-front sweethearts and suffering mothers. This book has shown that this was not always the case, and that women's presence in the war genre deserves a second watch.

APPENDIX 1
Civil War Films, 1908–1916

The following list was created from Paul Spehr's *The Civil War in Motion Pictures: A Bibliography of Films Produced in the United States since 1897* (Washington, DC: Library of Congress, 1961). For further analysis, see chapter 2.

1908

Barbara Frietchie, the Story of a Patriotic American Woman (Vitagraph)
The Blue and the Gray; or, The Days of '61 (Edison)
Charity Begins at Home: A Story of the South during the Civil War (Vitagraph)
The Days of '61 (Kalem)
The Guerrillas (American Mutoscope and Biograph)
In the Shenandoah Valley (Selig Polyscope)
Romance of a War Nurse (Edison)
Two Brothers of the G.A.R. (Lubin)

1909

Adventures of a Drummer Boy (Vitagraph)
Brother against Brother: A Story of the Civil War (Selig Polyscope)
The Bugle Call (Vitagraph)
The Escape from Andersonville (Kalem)
For Her Country's Sake (Vitagraph)
The Girl Spy (Kalem)
The Honor of His Family (Biograph)
An Hour of Terror (World Films)
In Old Kentucky (Biograph)
The Old Army Chest (Lubin)
The Old Soldier's Story (Kalem)
The Rally Round the Flag (Kalem)
Sheltered under Stars and Stripes (Bison)

A Telepathic Warning (Vitagraph)
A Wartime Sweetheart (Selig Polyscope)

1910

Abraham Lincoln's Clemency (Pathé American Co.)
All's Fair in Love and War (Capitol)
The Bravest Girl in the South (Kalem)
The Brother's Feud (Imp)
Brothers in Arms (Edison)
The Common Enemy (Selig)
The Confederate Spy: A Story of the Civil War (Kalem)
Corporal Truman's War Story (Kalem)
A Daughter of Dixie (Kalem)
Dixie (Imp)
A Dixie Mother (Vitagraph)
The Flag of His Country (Thanhouser)
The Fugitive (Biograph)
Further Adventures of the Girl Spy (Kalem)
The Girl Spy before Vicksburg (Kalem)
Her Soldier Sweetheart (Kalem)
His Yankee Girl (Powers)
The House with Closed Shutters (Biograph)
In the Border States; or, A Little Heroine of the Civil War (Biograph)
In War Time (Imp)
A Little Confederate (Powers)
The Love and Romance of the Girl (Kalem)
'Mid the Cannon's Roar (Edison)
The Nine of Diamonds (Vitagraph)
Ransomed; or, A Prisoner of War (Vitagraph)
The Road to Richmond (Selig Polyscope)
Uncle Tom's Cabin (Thanhouser)
Uncle Tom's Cabin (Vitagraph)
Under Both Flags (Pathé)
Under the Stars and Bars (Melies)
War (Powers)
War-Time Pals (Powers)
When Lovers Part (Kalem)

1911

Barbara Frietchie (Champion)
The Battle (Biograph)
The Battle Hymn of the Republic (Vitagraph)

The Blacksmith's Love (Selig Polyscope)
A Brother's Redemption (Lubin)
A Woman's Wit (Kalem)
Col. E.D. Baker, 1st. California (Champion)
The Colonel's Son (Kalem)
The Copperhead (Champion)
The Coward (Pathé)
The Coward's Flute (Champion)
Daddy's Boy and Mammy (Vitagraph)
A Daughter of Dixie (Champion)
A Daughter of the South (Pathé)
Driving Home the Cows (Kalem)
The Drummer Boy of Shiloh (Yankee Film Co.)
1861 (Selig Polyscope)
The Empty Saddle (Vitagraph)
The Exchange (Champion)
Fifty Years Ago (Powers)
The Fighting Schoolmaster (Vitagraph)
Flames and Fortune (Thanhouser)
Folks of Old Virginia (Champion)
For Her Sake (Thanhouser)
For the Love of the Enemy (Kalem)
The Fortunes of War (Imp)
From Wallace to Grant (Champion)
General Meade's Fighting Days (Champion)
A Girl and a Spy (Champion)
Grandmother's War Story (Kalem)
Grant and Lincoln (Champion)
He Fought for the U.S.A. (Essanay)
Hearts and Flags (Edison)
Her Little Slipper (Pathé)
His Last Parade (Lubin)
His Trust (Biograph)
His Trust Fulfilled (Biograph)
The Honoring of a Hero (Pathé)
The Imposter (Thanhouser)
Lieutenant Grey (Selig Polyscope)
A Lad in Dixie (Vitagraph)
A Little Rebel (Lubin)
The Little Soldier of '64 (Kalem)
The Little Spy (Vitagraph)
Longstreet at Seven Pines (Champion)

O'er Grim Fields Scarred (Reliance)
The Old Man and Jim (Champion)
On Kentucky Soil (Reliance)
One Flag at Last (Vitagraph)
The Perils of a War Messenger (Champion)
The Railroad Raiders of '62 (Kalem)
The Redemption of a Coward (Champion)
Right or Wrong (Melies)
The Rival Brothers' Patriotism (Pathé)
The Romance of a Dixie Belle (Kalem)
A Romance of the 60's (Lubin)
Service under Johnston and Lee (Champion)
Shenandoah (Champion)
A Southern Boy of '61 (Kalem)
A Southern Girl's Heroism (Champion)
A Southern Soldier's Sacrifice (Vitagraph)
Special Messenger (Kalem)
The Spy (Selig Polyscope)
Swords and Hearts (Biograph)
The Tale of a Soldier's Ring (Selig Polyscope)
To the Aid of Stonewall Jackson (Kalem)
Uncle Pete's Ruse (Imp)
Wages of War (Vitagraph)
War and the Widow (Champion)
A War Time (Kalem)
When North and South Met (Champion)
With Sheridan at Murfreesboro (Champion)
With Stonewall Jackson (Champion)

1912

Baby Betty (Selig Polyscope)
The Battle of Pottsburg Bridge (Kalem)
Blood Will Tell (Kay-Bee)
A Bluegrass Romance (Broncho)
The Bugler of Battery B (Kalem)
The Call of the Drum (Imp)
The Confederate Ironclad (Kalem)
The Darling of the C.S.A. (Kalem)
The Dead Pays (Kay-Bee)
The Defender of the Name (Rex)
The Dividing Line (Imp)

The Drummer Girl of Vicksburg (Kalem)
The Equine Spy (Film Supply Co.)
The Fighting Dan McCool (Kalem)
For the Cause (Kay-Bee)
For the Cause of the South (Edison)
Foraging on the Enemy (Champion)
Fortunes of War (Nestor)
The Grandfather (Edison)
Heroes of the Blue and Gray (Champion)
His Father's Bugle (Selig Polyscope)
The Informer (Biograph)
The Lie (Imp)
Love and War (Majestic)
Love, War and a Bonnet (Imp)
A Loyal Deserter (Selig Polyscope)
A Maid at War (Bison)
A Man's Duty (Reliance)
Me and Bill (Selig Polyscope)
The Medal of Honor (Gem)
None Can Do More (Rex)
On Secret Service (Kay-Bee)
On the Firing Line (101 Bison)
On the Line of Peril (Vitagraph)
Reflections by Firelight (Imp)
Saved from Court-Martial (Kalem)
The Seventh Son (Vitagraph)
Sheridan's Ride (101 Bison)
The Siege of Petersburg (Kalem)
The Soldier Brothers of Susanna (Kalem)
A Soldier's Duty (Edison)
A Spartan Mother (Kalem)
Stolen Glory (Keystone)
Sundered Ties (Broncho)
The Sunset Gun (Edison)
The Tide of Battle (Kalem)
The Two Spies (Kalem)
Under a Flag of Truce (Kalem)
United We Stand (Nestor)
A Wartime Romance (Selig Polyscope)
War's Havoc (Kalem)
When Lee Surrenders (Kay-Bee)

1913

At Shiloh (101 Bison)
Banty Tim (Lubin)
The Battle of Bloody Ford (Kalem)
The Battle of Bull Run (101 Bison)
Bell Boyd—A Confederate Spy (Selig Polyscope)
Between Home and Country (Reliance)
A Black Conspiracy (Kay-Bee)
The Blue or the Gray (Biograph)
The Boomerang (Broncho)
Bread Cast upon the Waters (Broncho)
The Carpenter, or the Stranger in Gray (Vitagraph)
A Child of War (Broncho)
Cohen Saves the Flag (Keystone)
The Colonel's Oath (Reliance)
The Coward's Atonement (Bison)
A Daughter of the Confederacy (Selig Polyscope)
Devotion (Domino)
A Dixie Mother (Mutual Film Corp)
Dixieland (Selig Polyscope)
The Drummer of the 8th (Broncho)
The Favorite Son (Kay-Bee)
The Fighting Chaplain (Kalem)
The Fire-Fighting Zouaves (Kalem)
The Girl and the Sunny South (American Kineto)
The Girl Spy's Atonement (Reliance)
Grand-Dad (Broncho)
The Great Sacrifice (Kay-Bee)
The Grey Sentinel (Broncho)
The Grim Toll of War (Kalem)
The Guerrilla Menace (101 Bison)
Heart Throbs (Broncho)
The Heritage of Eve (Broncho)
His Greatest Victory (Edison)
The Honor of a Soldier (Edison)
A House Divided (101 Bison)
The Imposter (Broncho)
In Love and War (101 Bison)
In the Battle's Smoke (Pilot)
In the Days of War (Pathé)
In the Secret Service (101 Bison)
The Ironmaster (Kay-Bee)

John Burns of Gettysburg (Kalem)
The Light in the Window (101 Bison)
The Little Turncoat (Kay-Bee)
The Lost Dispatch (Kay-Bee)
A Love of '64 (Lubin)
The Madcap (Broncho)
My Lady's Boot (Majestic)
Old Mammy's Secret Code (Broncho)
An Orphan of War (Kay-Bee)
The Patchwork Quilt (Edison)
Pauline Cushman—The Federal Spy (Selig Polyscope)
The Picket Guard (101 Bison)
The Price of Victory (Lubin)
Pride of the South (Broncho)
Prisoners of War (Kalem)
The Rose of Sharon (Essanay)
Saved by the Enemy (Edison)
The Sharpshooter (Broncho)
Shenandoah (Kalem)
Silent Heroes (Broncho)
The Sinews of War (Broncho)
A Slave's Devotion (Broncho)
Soldiers Three (101 Bison)
The Song Bird of the North (Vitagraph)
The Soul of the South (Kay-Bee)
A Southern Cinderella (Broncho)
Through Barriers of Fire (101 Bison)
The Toll of War (101 Bison)
A True Believer (Kay-Bee)
Uncle Tom's Cabin (Imp)
Uncle Tom's Cabin (Kalem)
Under Fire (101 Bison)
A War Time Mother's Sacrifice (Broncho)
The Wartime Siren (Kalem)
When Life Fades (Broncho)
When Lincoln Paid (Kay-Bee)
When Sherman Marched to the Sea (101 Bison)
With Lee in Virginia (Kay-Bee)
Within Enemy Lines (Edison)
The Woe of Battle (Kalem)
Women and War (101 Bison)

1914

The Baby Spy (Selig Polyscope)
The Battle of Shiloh (Lubin)
Between Two Fires (Lubin)
C.D. (Selig Polyscope)
Chest of Fortune (Kalem)
The Country Chairman (Famous Players)
Dan (All Stars Feature)
The Fair Rebel (Klaw and Erlanger)
Fitzhugh's Ride (Lubin)
His Brother Bill (Lubin)
In Old Virginia (Lubin)
In the Fall of '64 (Gold Seal)
The Last Man's Club (Selig Polyscope)
The Little Rebel (Warner's Features)
The Littlest Rebel (Photoplay Productions)
A Military Judas (Broncho)
A Mother of Men (Warner's)
Quantrill's Son (Vitagraph)
A Question of Courage (Majestic)
The Sleeping Sentinel (Lubin)
The Soul of Honor (Majestic)
The Southerners (Edison)
Stonewall Jackson's Way (Lubin)
Uncle Tom's Cabin (World Film Corp.)
A War Time Reformation (Gold Seal)
The Weaker Brother (Lubin)

1915

And They Called Him a Hero (Bison)
Barbara Frietchie (Metro Pictures)
Betty's Dream Hero (Laemmle)
The Birth of a Nation (D. W. Griffith)
Colonel Carter of Cartersville (Burr McIntosh)
The Coward (Kay-Bee)
The Heart of Lincoln (Gold Seal)
The Heart of Maryland (Tiffany Metro Pictures)
The Magistrate's Story (Edison)
The Memory Tree (Big U)
The Railroad Raiders of '62 [Episode 19, The Hazards of Helen] (Kalem)
Rivals (Kalem)

Sally Castleton, Southerner (Edison)
Shattered Memories (Gold Seal)
The Spy's Sister (Lubin)
Stepping Westward (Ideal)
The Tide of Fortune (Kay-Bee)
Tiny Hands (Powers)
Vain Justice (Essanay)
A War Baby (Lubin)
The Warrens of Virginia (Jesse Lasky Feature Play Co.)

1916
According to the Code (Essanay)
After the Battle (Big U)
Ashes of Remembrance (Rex)
The Crisis (Selig Polyscope)
A Daughter of Dixie (Big U)
A Gentle Volunteer (Rex)
Her Father's Son (Oliver Morosco Photoplay Co.)
His Mother's Boy (Rex)
Mammy's Rose (American)
Naked Hearts (Bluebird)
The Reunion (Thanhouser)
A Rose of the South (Blue Ribbon)
The Son of a Rebel Chief (Bison)
The Sting of Victory (Essanay)
The Suppressed Order (American)

APPENDIX 2
World War I Films, 1914–1919

The following list of films was compiled with reference to numerous important filmographies: the most important sources were Frank J. Wetta and Stephen J. Curley, *Celluloid Wars: A Guide to Film and the American Experience of War*; Larry Langman and Ed Borg, *Encyclopedia of American War Films*; and the American Film Institute online catalogue.

1914

Ordeal, The. Dir. Will S. Davis. Perf. William H. Tooker. Co. Life Photo.

1915

Battle Cry of Peace. Dir. J. Stuart Blackton. Perf. Charles Richman, L. Rogers Lytton. Co. Vitagraph.

Nation's Peril, The. Dir. George Terwilliger. Perf. Ormi Hawley, William H. Turner. Co. Lubin.

Patriot and the Spy, The. Dir. Edwin Thanhouser. Perf. James Cruze, Marguerite Snow. Co. Thanhouser Film Corp.

Via Wireless. Dir. George Fitzmaurice. Perf. Bruce McRae, Gail Kane. Co. Pathe.

1916

As in a Looking Glass. Dir. Frank H. Crane. Perf. Kitty Gordon, F. Lumsden Hare. Co. World.

Civilization. Dir. Thomas Ince. Perf. Barney Sherry, Howard Hickman, Enid Markey. Co. Thomas Ince.

Eagle's Wings, The. Dir. Rufus Steele. Perf. Grace Carlyle, Vola Smith. Co. Bluebird.

Fall of a Nation, The. Dir. Thomas Dixon. Perf. Lorraine Huling, Percy Standing. Co. National Films.

Flying Torpedo, The. Dir. John O'Brien, Christy Cabanne. Perf. John Emerson. Co. Fine Arts Film Co.

Hero of Submarine D-2, The. Dir. Paul Scardon. Perf. Charles Richman, James Morrison. Co. Vitagraph.

Joan the Woman. Dir. Cecil B. De Mille. Perf. Geraldine Farrar, Hobart Bosworth. Co. Jesse Lasky.

My Country First. Dir. Tom Terriss. Perf. Tom Terriss. Co. Terriss Film Corporation.

Patria. Dir. Leopold Wharton, Theodore Wharton, Jacques Jaccard. Perf. Irene Castle, Milton Sills. Co. International Film Service.

Paying the Price. Dir. Frank H. Crane. Perf. Gail Kane, Robert Cummings. Co. Paragon Films.

Pearl of the Army. Dir. Edward Jose. Perf. Pearl White, Ralph Kellard. Co. Astra Film Corp. Pathe.

Secret of the Submarine, The. Dir. George L. Sargent. Perf. Juanita Hansen, Tom Chatterton. Co. American Film Co.

Shell Forty-Three. Dir. Reginald Barker. Perf. H. B Warner. Co. Triangle

Somewhere in France. Dir. Charles Giblyn. Perf. Louise Glaum. Co. Thomas Ince

Three of Many. Dir. Reginald Barker. Perf. Clara Williams, Charles Gunn. Co. New York Motion Picture Corp.

Victory of Conscience, The. Dir. Frank Reicher. Perf. Cleo Ridgely, Lou-Tellegen. Co. Jesse L. Lasky

War Bride's Secret, The. Dir. Kenean Buel. Perf. Virginia Pearson, Walter Law. Co. Fox.

1917

Arms and the Girl. Dir. Joseph Kaufman. Perf. Billie Burke, Thomas Meighan. Co. Paramount

Dark Road, The. Dir. Charles Miller. Perf. Dorothy Dalton, Robert McKim, Jack Livingston. Co. Triangle.

Draft 258. Dir. William Christy Cabanne. Perf. Mabel Taliaferro, Walter Miller. Co. Metro.

For France. Dir. Wesley Ruggles. Perf. Edward Earle, Betty Howe. Co. Vitagraph.

For Liberty. Dir. Bertram Bracken. Perf. Gladys Brockwell. Co. Fox.

For the Freedom of the World. Dir. Ira M. Lowry. Perf. E.K. Lincoln, Barbara Castleton. Co. Ira M. Lowry and Frank J. Carrol Production Company.

For Valour. Dir. Albert Parker. Perf. Winifred Allen, Richard Barthelmess. Co. Triangle.

Gown of Destiny, The. Dir. Lynn F. Reynolds. Perf. Hal Lewis, Herrera Tejedde, Alan Sears. Co. Triangle.

Greatest Power, The. Dir. Edwin Carewe. Perf. Ethel Barrymore, William B. Davidson. Co. Metro.

Her Country's Call. Dir. Lloyd Ingraham. Perf. Mary Miles Minter, George Periolat. Co. American Film Co.

In Again–Out Again. Dir. John Emerson. Perf. Douglas Fairbanks, Arline Pretty. Co. Artcraft.

Little American, The. Dir. Cecil B. DeMille. Perf. Mary Pickford. Co. Mary Pickford Film Corp/Artcraft.

Little Patriot, The. Dir. William Bertram. Perf. Baby Marie Osborne, Herbert Standing. Co. Diando Film Co.

Maid of Belgium, A. Dir. George Archainbaud. Perf. Abbey Mitchell. Co. World Film Corp.

Miss Jackie of the Army. Dir. Lloyd Ingraham. Perf. Margarita Fischer, Jack Mower. Co. American Film Co.

On Dangerous Ground. Dir. Robert Thornby. Perf. Carlyle Blackwell, Gail Kane. Co. World Film Corp.

Over There. Dir. James Kirkwood. Perf. Charles Richman, Anna Q Nilsson. Co. Charles Richman Pictures Corp.

Paws of the Bear. Dir. Reginald Barker. Perf. William Desmond, Clara Williams. Co. New York Motion Picture Corp.

Secret Game, The. Dir. William C. De Mille. Perf. Sessue Hayakawa, Jack Holt, Florence Vidor. Co. Jesse L. Lasky Feature Play Co.

Slacker, The. Dir. William Christy Cabanne. Perf. Emily Stevens, Walter Miller. Co. Metro.

Spy, The. Dir. Richard Stanton. Perf. Dustin Farnum. Co. Fox Film Corp.

Volunteer, The. Dir. Harley Knoles. Perf. Madge Evans. Co. World.

Who Goes There? Dir. William P. S. Earle. Perf. Harry T. Morey, Corrine Griffith. Co. Vitagraph.

Who Was the Other Man? Dir. Francis Ford. Perf. Francis Ford, Duke Worne, Beatrice Van. Co. Universal.

Womanhood, the Glory of the Nation. Dir. J. Stuart Blackton. Perf. Alice Joyce, Harry T. Morey Co. Vitagraph.

Zeppelin's Last Raid. Dir. Irvin Willat. Perf. Enid Markey, Alfred Hickman. Co. Thomas Ince Productions.

1918

A Daughter of Uncle Sam

A Romance of the Air. Dir. Harry Revier; Franklin B. Coates. Perf. Florence Billings, Lieut Bert Hall, Edith Day. Co. En l'Air Cinema Ltd.

After the War. Dir. Joseph De Grasse. Perf. Grace Cunard, Edward Cecil. Co. Bluebird.

Birth of a Race, The. Dir. John W. Noble. Perf. Louis Dean, Harry Dumont, Carter B. Harkness. Co. Birth of a Race Photoplay Corp.

Bonnie Annie Laurie. Dir. Harry Millarde. Perf. Peggy Hyland, William Bailey. Co. Fox.

Border Wireless, The. Dir. William S. Hart. Perf. Wiliam S. Hart, Wanda Hawley. Co. William S. Hart Productions.

Claws of the Hun. Dir. Victor L. Schertzinger. Perf. Charles Ray, Jane Novak. Co. Thomas Ince Corp.

Come On In. Dir. John Emerson. Perf. Shirley Mason, Ernest Truex, Charles De Planta. Co. Famous Players-Lasky.

Cross Bearer, The. Dir. George Archainbaud. Perf. Montagu Love, Jeanne Engles.

Daughter Angele. Dir. William Dowlan. Perf. Pauline Starke, Walt Whitman. Co. Triangle Film Corp.

Daughter of Destiny. Dir. George Irving. Perf. Olga Petrova, Thomas Holding. Co. Petrova Picture Co.

Doing Their Bit. Dir. Kenean Buel. Perf. Jane Lee, Katherine Lee, Franklyn Hanna. Co. Fox.

Every Mother's Son. Dir. Raoul Walsh. Perf. Charlotte Walker, Percy Standing. Co. Fox.

Fields of Honor. Dir. Ralph Ince. Perf. Mae Marsh, Marguerite Marsh, George Cooper. Co. Goldwyn.

Flames of Chance, The. Dir. Raymond Wells. Perf. Margery Wilson, Jack Mulhall, Anna Dodge. Co. Triangle.

For the Freedom of the East. Dir. Ira M. Lowry. Perf. Lady Tsen Mei, Robert Elliot. Co. Betzwood Film Co.

Greatest Thing in Life, The. Dir. D. W. Griffith. Perf. Lillian Gish, Robert Harron. Co. Artcraft.

Hearts of the World. Dir. D. W. Griffith. Perf. Lillian Gish, Dorothy Gish, Robert Harron. Co. Artcraft.

Her Country First. Dir. James Young. Perf. Vivian Martin, John Cossar, Florence Oberle. Co. Famous Players-Lasky Corp.

Her Debt of Honor/The Debt of Honor. Dir. O.A.C. Lund. Perf. Peggy Hyland, Eric Mayne. Co. Fox.

Honest Man, An. Dir. Frank Borzage. Perf. William Desmond, Mary Warren. Co. Triangle.

Hun Within, The. Dir. Chester Withey. Perf. Dorothy Gish. Co. Paramount.

I'll Say So. Dir. Raoul Walsh. Perf. George Walsh, Regina Quinn. Co. Fox.

Inside the Lines. Dir. David M Hartford. Perf. Lewis S. Stone, Marguerite Clayton. Co. World.

Joan of Plattsburg. Dir. George Loane Tucker. Perf. Mabel Normand, Robert Elliot. Co. Goldwyn.

Johanna Enlists. Dir. William Desmond Taylor. Perf. Mary Pickford, Phiroz Nazir, Fred Huntley. Co. Pickford Film Co.

Kaiser, or the Beast of Berlin. Dir. Rupert Julian. Perf. Rupert Julian, Allan Sears, Lon Chaney. Co. Jewel Productions.

Kaiser's Finish, The. Dir. John Joseph Harvey. Perf. Earl Schenck, Claire Whitney. Co. Warner Brothers.

Kaiser's Shadow, The. Dir. Thomas Ince. Perf. Dorothy Dalton, Thurston Hall. Co. Thomas Ince Corp.

Kultur. Dir. Edward J. Le Saint. Perf. Gladys Brockwell, Georgia Woodthorpe. Co. Fox.

Lafayette, Here We Come! Dir. Leonce Perret. Perf. E.K. Lincoln, Dolores Cassinelli. Co. Perret Productions.

Lest We Forget. Dir. Leonce Perret. Perf. Rita Jolivet, Hamilton Revelle. Co. Rita Jolivet Film Corp/Metro Special.

Little Miss Hoover. Dir. John Stuart Robertson. Perf. Marguerite Clark, Eugene O'Brien. Co. Famous Players-Lasky.

Madame Spy. Dir. Douglas Gerrard. Perf. Jack Mulhall, Wadsworth Harris. Co. Butterfly.

Man Who Wouldn't Tell, The. Dir. James Young. Perf. Earle Williams, Grace Darmond. Co. Vitagraph.

Marriage Ring, The. Dir. Fred Niblo. Perf. Enid Bennett, Jack Holt. Co. Thomas Ince Corp.

Missing. Dir. James Young. Perf. Thomas Meighan, Sylvia Breamer. Co. J. Stuart Blackton.

Mr. Logan, U.S.A. Dir. Lynn F. Reynolds. Perf. Tom Mix, Kathleen Connors. Co. Fox.

Mrs. Slacker. Dir. Hobart Henley. Perf. Gladys Hulette, Creighton Hale. Co. Astra Film Corp/Gold Rooster Plays.

My Four Years in Germany. Dir. William Nigh. Perf. Halbert Brown, Willard Dashiell. Co. Warner Brothers.

No Man's Land. Dir. William S. Davis. Perf. Al Cole, Anna Q. Nilsson. Co. Metro.

On the Jump. Dir. Raoul Walsh. Perf. George Walsh, Frances Burnham. Co. Fox.

Over the Top. Dir. Wilfrid North. Perf. Arthur Guy Empey, Lois Meredith. Co. Vitagraph.

Private Peat. Dir. Edward Jose. Perf. Harold R. Peat, Miriam Fouche. Co. Famous Players-Lasky.

Road through the Dark, The. Dir. Edmund Mortimer. Perf. Clara Kimball Young, Jack Holt. Co. Clara Kimball Young Film Corp.

Road to France, The. Dir. Dell Henderson. Perf. Carlyle Blackwell, Evelyn Greeley. Co. World Film Corp.

Safe for Democracy (Life's Greatest Problem). Dir. J. Stuart Blackton. Perf. Mitchell Lewis, Ruby de Remer. Co. Blackton Productions.

Secret Code, The. Dir. Will Walling. Perf. Gloria Swanson, J. Barney Sherry. Co. Triangle.

Service Star, The. Dir. Charles Miller. Perf. Madge Kennedy, Clarence Oliver. Co. Goldwyn.

Shifting Sands. Dir. Will Walling. Perf. Gloria Swanson, Joe King. Co. Triangle Film Corp.

Shoulder Arms. Dir. Charlie Chaplin. Perf. Charlie Chaplin, Edna Purviance, Sydney Chaplin. Co. First National Pictures.

Spirit of '17, The. Dir. William Taylor. Perf. Jack Pickford, C. H. Geldert. Co. Jesse L. Lasky Feature Play Co.

Stolen Orders. Dir. George Kelson. Perf. Montagu Love, Kitty Gordon. Co. William A. Brady.

Suspicion. Dir. John M. Stahl. Perf. Grace Davison, Warren Cook. Co. M. H. Hoffman Co.

Till I Come Back to You. Dir. Cecil B. DeMille. Perf. Bryant Washburn, Florence Vidor. Co. Famous Players-Lasky.

To Hell with the Kaiser. Dir. George Irving. Perf. Lawrence Grant, Olive Tell. Co. Screen Classics.

Too Fat to Fight. Dir. Hobart Henley. Perf. Frank McIntyre, Florence Dixon. Co. Rex Beach Pictures.

Unbeliever, The. Dir. Alan Crosland. Perf. Marguerite Courtot, Raymond McKee. Co. Edison.

Vive La France. Dir. R. William Neill. Perf. Dorothy Dalton, Edmund Lowe. Co. Thomas Ince.

Wanted for Murder. Dir. Frank Crane. Perf. Elaine Hammerstein, Charles Raven. Co. Harry Rapf Productions.

Why America Will Win. Dir. Richard Stanton. Perf. A. Alexander, Harris Gordon. Co. Fox.

Wife or Country. Dir. E. Mason Hopper. Perf. Harry Mestayer, Gretchen Lederer. Co. Triangle.

Woman. Dir. Maurice Tourneur. Perf. Florence Billings, Warren Cook. Co. Maurice Tourneur Productions.

Woman the Germans Shot, The. Dir. John G. Adolfi. Perf. Julia Arthur, Creighton Hale. Co. Joseph L. Plunkett and Frank J. Carroll.

1919

A Regular Girl. Dir. James Young. Perf. Elsie Janis, Robert Lyton, Matt Moore. Co. Selznick Pictures Corp.

Adele. Dir. Wallace Worsley. Perf. Kitty Gordon. Co. United Picture Theatres of America.

Alias Mike Moran. Dir. James Cruze. Perf. Wallace Reid, Ann Little. Co. Famous Players-Lasky.

Behind the Door. Dir. Irvin Willat. Perf. Hobart Bosworth, Jane Novak, Wallace Beery. Co. Thomas Ince.

Beware. Dir. William Nigh. Perf. Maurine Powers, Regina Quinn. Co. Warner Brothers.

Dark Star, The. Dir. Patty Saks. Perf. Marion Davies, Dorothy Green. Co. Cosmopolitan Productions.

False Faces. Dir. Irvin Willat. Perf. Henry B. Walthall, Mary Anderson, Lon Chaney. Co. Thomas Ince Corp.

For Better, for Worse. Dir. Cecil B. DeMille. Perf. Elliot Dexter, Gloria Swanson. Co. Famous Players-Lasky.

Girl Who Stayed at Home, The. Dir. D. W. Griffith. Perf. Carol Dempster, Adolphe Lestina, Richard Barthelmess. Co. Famous Players-Lasky.

Heart of Humanity, The. Dir. Allen Holubar. Perf. Dorothy Phillips, William Stowell. Co. Universal.

Highest Trump, The. Dir. James Young. Perf. Earle Williams, Grace Darmond. Co. Vitagraph.

Light of Victory. Dir. William Wolbert. Perf. Monroe Salisbury, Bob Edmunds, Fred Wilson. Co. Bluebird.

Light, The. Dir. J. Gordon Edward. Perf. Theda Bera, Eugene Ormonde. Co. Fox.

Lost Battalion, The. Dir. Burton King. Perf. Major-General Robert Alexander, Lt. Col Charles Whittlesey. Co. MacManus Corp.

Love and the Law. Dir. Edgar Lewis. Perf. Glen White, Josephine Hill. Co. Edgar Lewis Productions.

Luck and Pluck. Dir. Edward Dillon. Perf. George Walsh, Virginia Lee. Co. Fox.

Pettigrew's Girl. Dir. George H. Melford. Perf. Ethel Clayton, Monte Blue. Co. Famous Players-Lasky.

This Hero Stuff. Dir. Henry King. Perf. William Russell, Winifred Westover. Co. William Russell Productions/American Film Co.

Unknown Love, The. Dir. Leonce Perret. Perf. Dolores Cassinelli, E.K. Lincoln. Co. Perret Productions.

Unpardonable Sin, The. Dir. Marshall Neilan. Perf. Blanche Sweet, Edwin Stevens. Co. Harry Garson.

Wanted for Murder. Dir. Frank Crane. Perf. Elaine Hammerstein, Charles Raven. Co. Harry Rapf Productions.

When Men Desire. Dir. J. Gordon Edwards. Perf. Theda Bera, Fleming Ward. Co. Fox.

Why Germany Must Pay/The Great Victory, Wilson or the Kaiser? The Fall of the Hohenzollerns. Dir. Charles Miller. Perf. Creighton Hale, Florence Billings. Co. Screen Classics, Inc.

Yankee Doodle in Berlin. Dir. Richard Jones. Perf. Bothwell Browne, Ford Sterling. Co. Mack Sennett Comedies.

ADDITIONAL FILMOGRAPHY

AMERICAN REVOLUTION:

For the Love of Country (Kalem 1908)
Spirit of '76 (Selig Polyscope 1908)
Army of Two (Edison 1908)
Brave Women of '76 (Lubin 1909)
Hessian Renegades (Biograph 1909)
The Old Hall Clock (Lubin 1909)
When the Flag Falls (Lubin 1909)
The Governor's Daughter (Kalem 1909)
A Daughter of the Revolution (Rex 1911)
For Washington (Thanhouser 1911)
A Revolutionary Romance (Solax 1911)
A Heroine of '76 (Rex 1911)
Before Yorktown (Republic 1911)
Flag of Freedom (Kalem 1912)
The Prison Ship (Kalem 1912)
A Revolutionary Romance (Selig Polyscope 1913)
The Swamp Fox (Kalem 1914)
Heart of a Woman (Domino 1914)
Washington at Valley Forge (Universal 1914)

MISCELLANEOUS:

A Mexican Joan of Arc (Kalem 1911)
The War Extra (Solax 1914)
The Captive (DeMille 1915)

ACKNOWLEDGMENTS

I gratefully acknowledge the financial support of the Social Sciences and Humanities Research Council of Canada (SSHRC) for funding this research. Without the aid of the SSHRC, the archival research necessary for this book would not have been possible. Thanks also go to my home institution, Brock University, and the Department of Communication, Popular Culture and Film for supporting my research and to my departmental colleagues for protecting the time of a pre-tenure researcher, which allowed this book to be possible. Thank you also to my editor at Rutgers University Press, Nicole Solano, and the series editor, Daniel Bernardi.

I would like to thank the mentors and advisors who have helped me throughout this journey. Philippa Gates has been a strong supporter of my work throughout my education and after, and it is her tireless work as a supervisor that helped this project find its shape. Katherine Spring, Christine Bold, Paul Heyer, Ute Lischke, and Paul Tiessen at Wilfrid Laurier University also deserve many thanks for their collective wisdom and support. At the University of California–Santa Cruz, Jenny Horne, Shelley Stamp, and Yiman Wang helped me greatly during the process of revisions. Thank you also to the archivists at the Library of Congress, George Eastman House, and Margaret Herrick Library.

Along with mentors, my colleagues and fellow researchers have provided generous feedback, shared ideas and work, and contribute to an academic community that is supportive and kind. Thank you to Laura Horak, Maggie Hennefeld, Topiary Landberg, Karen Ritzenhoff, Sarah Brand, Peter Mersereau, Michael Boyce, Joel Frykholm, Patrick Faubert, Stefanie Hunt-Kennedy, and Anna Cooper. In addition to researchers in various cities and towns across the globe, I am thankful for the friendships and supportive environment at my home institution of Brock University. Thank you to Adam Rappold, Sarah Matheson, Christie Milliken, Kate Cassidy, Lynn Arner, Tami Friedman, and Cristina Santos. An extra special thanks to my two writing partners at Brock: Amanda Bishop and Michele Donnelly. Without the writing sprints, this book might still be in process. Finally, thank you to my two editor-friends: Mandy Elliott and Lauren Winkler.

On a personal note, there are many people (some already listed above) whose friendship has been so necessary during what felt like long stretches of isolation while writing. Thank you to my friends Sarah Kelly, Jamie Van Gorkum, Marla Spain, Kyla Smith, Chris and Greg, and Tess McLernon. Thank you to my family, mom, dad (who I wish could see this book come out!), Steve, Kristy, Amos, Braedon, Bill Clarke, Richard Kline, and Pat Wimpenny. Thanks especially to my mom for walking Zeus while I wrote and to Zeus for endless laughs.

NOTES

NOTES TO INTRODUCTION

1. Laura Lee Hope, *The Moving Picture Girls in War Plays: Or, The Sham Battles at Oak Farm* (New York: Grosset and Dunlap, 1916), http://www.gutenberg.org/ebooks/20348.

2. See, for example, Shelley Streeby and Jesse Alemán, "Introduction," in *Empire and the Literature of Sensation: An Anthology of Nineteenth-Century Popular Fiction* (New Brunswick, NJ: Rutgers University Press, 2007), xiii–xxx; Shelley Streeby, *American Sensations: Class, Empire, and the Production of Popular Culture* (Berkeley: University of California Press, 2002); Alice Fahs, "The Feminized Civil War: Gender, Northern Popular Literature, and the Memory of War, 1861–1900," in *Unequal Sisters: An Inclusive Reader in U.S. Women's History*, 4th ed., ed. Vicki L. Ruiz and Ellen Carol DuBois (London: Routledge, 1990), 130–155.

3. The home-front representations of women during World War II—as seen in film, for which see Janine Basinger, "The Wartime American Woman on Film: Home-Front Soldier," *A Companion to the War Film*, ed. Douglas A. Cunningham and John C. Nelson (Malden, MA: Wiley, 2016), 89–105, and Michael Renov, *Hollywood's Wartime Women: Representation and Ideology* (Ann Arbor, MI: UMI Research Press, 1988), and as seen in other media, for which see Susan Ohmer, "Female Spectatorship and Women's Magazines: Hollywood, Good Housekeeping, and World War II," *Velvet Light Trap* 25 (March 1990), or Bilge Yesil, "'Who Said This Is a Man's War?': Propaganda, Advertising Discourse and the Representation of War Worker Women during the Second World War," *Media History* 10, no. 2 (August 2004): 103–117—are as diverse as the films in this study. However, two distinct messages regarding women were clear: that women should mobilize to join the workforce, such as in factory jobs, and that women should curb consumption in the homes, while keeping them running (Renov, *Hollywood's Wartime Women*, 33–46).

4. Recent books have expanded the scholarship on the war genre to include a consideration of gender: see Karen A. Ritzenhoff and Jakub Kazecki, eds., *Heroism and Gender in War Films* (New York: Palgrave Macmillan, 2014); Clémentine Tholas, Janis L. Goldie, and Karen A. Ritzenhoff, *New Perspectives on the War Film* (New York: Palgrave Macmillan, 2019); and Janine Basinger, "The Wartime American Woman on Film: Home-Front Soldier, in Cunningham and Nelson, *Companion to the War Film*, 89–105.

5. Steve Neale provides a succinct overview of debates surrounding definitions of the war film, in *Genre and Hollywood* (London: Routledge, 2000), 125–133. Included in these debates are discussions of whether war films should only include combat films, and whether they are only about conflicts from the twentieth century.

6. I will avoid calling these films the "Western" genre for the same reasons that the "War Film" is not yet defined.

7. Jenny Barrett, *Shooting the Civil War: Cinema, History and American National Identity* (London: I. B. Tauris, 2009), 5.

8. See Ben Singer, "Power and Peril in the Serial-Queen Melodrama," in *Melodrama and Modernity* (New York: Columbia University Press, 2001), 221–262.

9. Linda Williams, *Playing the Race Card: Melodramas of Black and White from Uncle Tom to O. J. Simpson* (Princeton, NJ: Princeton University Press, 2001), 12.

10. Jonna Eagle, *Imperial Affects: Sensational Melodrama and the Attractions of American Cinema* (New Brunswick, NJ: Rutgers University Press, 2017), 3.

11. Eagle, *Imperial Affects*, 3.

12. Streeby and Alemán, "Introduction," xviii.

13. Richard Abel, Giorgio Bertellini, and Rob King, "Introduction," in *Early Cinema and the "National"* (Bloomington, IN: John Libbey, 2008), 1.

14. Richard Dyer, *White: Twentieth Anniversary Edition* (New York: Routledge, 2017), 1.

15. Daniel Bernardi, "Introduction," in *The Birth of Whiteness: Race and the Emergence of U.S. Cinema* (New Brunswick, NJ: Rutgers University Press 1996), 7.

16. Daniel Bernardi, "The Voice of Whiteness: D. W. Griffith's Biograph Films," in *The Birth of Whiteness: Race and the Emergence of U.S. Cinema* (New Brunswick, NJ: Rutgers University Press, 1996), 107.

17. Guy Westwell, *War Cinema: Hollywood on the Frontline* (New York: Wallflower Press, 2006), 16.

18. This argument relies on the knowledge that a new aesthetic of war films emerges in the 1920s, with the "doughboy" films, such as *The Big Parade* (1925) and *What Price Glory* (1926), or the combat pilot movies, such as *Wings* (1927). *Hearts of the World* can be dismissed as a Griffith Civil War film only if one privileges the World War I pictures that are released in the mid-1920s onward. Conversely, situating *Hearts* within its actual context, produced during World War I, allows for a more nuanced understanding of the style and politics.

19. Westwell, *War Cinema*, 17.

20. David Bordwell, Kristin Thompson, and Janet Staiger's canonical text *The Classical Hollywood Cinema: Film Style and Mode of Production to 1960* (New York: Columbia University Press, 1985), designates 1917 as the beginning of classical style and production methods.

21. Bordwell et al., *The Classical Hollywood Cinema*, 29.

22. On the origins of film as masculinist and related to militaristic ideologies, see Stephen Bottomore, "Introduction: War and Militarism. Dead White Males," *Film History* 14, no. 3/4 (September 2002): 239–242. On women in the audience, see Miriam Hansen, *Babel and Babylon: Spectatorship in American Silent Film* (Cambridge, MA: Harvard University Press, 1991); Shelley Stamp, *Movie-Struck Girls: Women and Motion Picture Culture after the Nickelodeon* (Princeton, NJ: Princeton University Press, 2000); Charles Musser, "Before the Rapid Firing Kinetograph: Edison Film Production, Representation and Exploitation in the 1890s," in *Edison Motion Pictures, 1890–1900: An Annotated Filmography* (Washington, DC: Smithsonian Institution Press, 1997), 36.

23. Michael Isenberg, *War on Film: The American Cinema and World War I, 1914–1941* (London: Associated University Presses, 1981), 191.

24. Nan Enstad, *Ladies of Labor, Girls of Adventure: Working Women, Popular Culture, and Labor Politics at the Turn of the Century* (New York: Columbia University Press, 1999); Lauren Rabinowitz, *For the Love of Pleasure: Women, Movies, and Culture in Turn-of-the-Century Chicago* (New Brunswick, NJ: Rutgers University Press, 1998); and Kathy Peiss, *Cheap Amusements: Working Women and Leisure in New York City, 1880–1920* (Philadelphia: Temple University Press, 1986).

25. Stamp, *Movie-Struck Girls*.

26. Jennifer Bean, "Technologies of Early Stardom and the Extraordinary Body," in *A Feminist Reader in Early Cinema*, ed. Jennifer Bean and Diane Negra (Durham, NC: Duke University Press, 2002), 404–443.

27. Richard deCordova, *Picture Personalities: The Emergence of the Star System in America* (Champaign: University of Illinois Press, 1990), 11.

28. Jennifer Bean, "Toward a Feminist Historiography of Early Cinema," in *A Feminist Reader in Early Cinema*, ed. Jennifer Bean and Diane Negra (Durham, NC: Duke University Press, 2002), 8.

29. Frank Ninkovich, *Global Dawn: The Cultural Foundations of American Internationalism, 1865–1890* (Cambridge, MA: Harvard University Press, 2009), 2.

30. Ninkovich, *Global Dawn*, 16.

31. Ninkovich, *Global Dawn*, 48.

32. Alan Trachtenberg, *The Incorporation of America: Culture and Society in the Gilded Age* (New York: Hill and Wang, 1982), 7–8.

33. Gail Bederman, *Manliness and Civilization: A Cultural History of Gender and Race in the United States, 1880–1917* (Chicago: University of Chicago Press, 1995), 178.

34. Amy Kaplan, *The Anarchy of Empire in the Making of U.S. Culture* (Cambridge, MA: Harvard University Press, 2002).

35. Linda Frost, *Never One Nation: Freaks, Savages, and Whiteness in U.S. Popular Culture, 1850–1877* (Minneapolis: University of Minnesota Press, 2005), xv.

36. Yvonne Tasker, *Soldiers' Stories: Military Women in Cinema and Television since World War II* (Durham, NC: Duke University Press, 2011), 15.

37. Matthew Evangelista, *Gender, Nationalism, and War: Conflict on the Movie Screen* (Cambridge: Cambridge University Press, 2011), 1.

38. John Milton Cooper, *Pivotal Decades: The United States, 1900–1920* (New York: W. W. Norton, 1990), 2.

39. Cooper, *Pivotal Decades*, 221.

40. For more on the relationship between producers and the trade press, see William Uricchio and Roberta Pearson, *Reframing Culture: The Case of the Vitagraph Quality Films* (Princeton: Princeton University Press, 2014), 45.

NOTES TO CHAPTER 1

1. Louis Reeves Harrison, "Our American Girl," *Moving Picture World*, June 3, 1916, 1664.

2. Christy is also remembered for designing posters during World War I, promoting Liberty Bonds and enlistment. Women featured prominently in many of his posters.

3. Howard Chandler Christy, *The American Girl* (New York: Moffat, Yard, and Co., 1906), 15–16.

4. Christy, *The American Girl*, 16.

5. David Jeremiah Slater. "The American Girl, Her Life and Times: An Ideal and Its Creators, 1890–1930," PhD diss., University of Minnesota, 2005.

6. Ben Singer, *Melodrama and Modernity: Early Sensational Cinema and Its Contexts* (New York: Columbia University Press, 2001); Miriam Hansen, *Babel and Babylon: Spectatorship in American Silent Film* (Cambridge, MA: Harvard University Press, 1991); Sumiko Higashi, "The New Woman and Consumer Culture," in *A Feminist Reader in Early Cinema*, ed. Jennifer M. Bean and Diane Negra, 298–332 (Durham, NC: Duke University Press, 2002).

7. Vivien Gardner, "Introduction," in *The New Woman and Her Sisters: Feminism and Theatre, 1850–1914*, ed. Vivien Gardner and Susan Rutherford (Ann Arbor: University of Michigan Press, 1992), 6.

8. Jill Davis, "The New Woman and the New Life," in Gardner and Rutherford, *The New Woman*, 22.

9. Gardner, "Introduction," 4–5.

10. Leslie Ferris, "The Golden Girl," in Gardner and Rutherford, *The New Woman*, 42.

11. David Belasco, "The Girl of the Golden West," in *American Melodrama*, ed. Daniel Gerould (Cambridge, MA: Performing Arts Journal Publications, 1983), 183–274.

12. Belasco, "Girl of the Golden West," 47.

13. Vern L. Bullough and Bonnie Bullough, *Cross Dressing, Sex, and Gender* (Philadelphia: University of Pennsylvania Press, 1993), 156.

14. Nancy Woloch, *Women and the American Experience*, 4th ed. (Toronto: McGraw-Hill, 2006), 270.

15. Ferris, "Golden Girl," 42.

16. "In Defense of the American Girl," *San Francisco Call*, November 4, 1906, 12.

17. "In Defense of the American Girl," 12.

18. "How President Roosevelt's Cousin Established Ice Cream Soda in Berlin in Spite of the German Police," *San Francisco Call*, September 16, 1906, 11.

19. Mrs. Leslie, "The American Girl," *Middletown Daily Times*, August 27, 1892, 4.

20. "The Perfect American Woman," *Times Dispatch* (Richmond Virginia), January 22, 1905, magazine section 1.

21. Maude M. Fowler, "A Graduation Oration: The American Girl," *Jefferson Souvenir*, June 26, 1895, 4.

22. Ruth Lister, *Citizenship: Feminist Perspectives*, 2nd ed. (New York: NYU Press, 2003), 3.

23. Nira Yuval-Davis, "Gender and Nation," *Ethnic and Racial Studies* 16, no. 4 (1993): 621–632.

24. Yuval-Davis, "Gender and Nation," 622.

NOTES TO CHAPTER 2

1. See Appendix 1 for list of films.

2. See Richard Abel, "The 'Usable Past' of Civil War Films: The Years of the 'Golden Jubilee,'" in *Americanizing the Movies and "Movie-Mad" Audiences, 1910–1914* (Berkeley: University of California Press, 2006), 141–167.

3. Thomas Cripps, "The Absent Presence in American Civil War Films," *Historical Journal of Film, Radio and Television* 4, no. 4 (1994): para. 10.

4. Several films about loyal ex-slaves were released during this period, but these still represent a small percentage of the overall output. Additionally, the plot of each film is a variation on the theme of a loyal slave who somehow helps his or her former master. Titles include *The Common Enemy* (Selig, 1910), *The Confederate Spy* (Kalem, 1910), *Her Little Slipper* (Pathé, 1911), *His Trust* and *His Trust Fulfilled* (Biograph, 1911), *Swords and Hearts* (Biograph, 1911), *Uncle Pete's Ruse* (Imp, 1911), *None Can Do More* (Rex, 1912), *A Black Conspiracy* (Kay-Bee, 1913), *Devotion* (Domino, 1913), *Old Mammy's Secret Code* (Broncho, 1913), *A Slave's Devotion* (Broncho, 1913), *With Lee in Virginia* (Kay-Bee, 1913), *Dan* (All Stars Feature, 1914), *A Gentle Volunteer* (Rex, 1916), *Mammy's Rose* (American, 1916), and several adaptations of *Uncle Tom's Cabin*. See Appendix 1 for more detail.

5. Examples of films with women as protectors include *A Daughter of Dixie* (Champion, 1911), *1861* (Selig, 1911), *For Her Sake* (Thanhouser, 1911), *Romance of a Dixie Belle* (Kalem, 1911), *The Tale of a Soldier's Ring* (Selig, 1911), *When Lee Surrenders* (Kay-Bee, 1912), *The Ironmaster* (Kay-Bee, 1913), *Through Barriers of Fire* (101 Bison, 1913), *When Life Fades* (Broncho, 1913), *Between Two Fires* (Lubin, 1914), *Betty's Dream Hero* (Laemmle, 1915), and *A Daughter of Dixie* (Big U, 1916). Examples of films that depict active women as spies or participants of war—destroying bridges, delivering messages, etc.—include *For the Love of the Enemy* (Kalem, 1911), *From Wallace to Grant* (Champion, 1911), *A Little Rebel* (Lubin, 1911), *A Southern Girl's Heroism* (Champion, 1911), *War and the Widow* (Champion, 1911), *The Confederate Ironclad* (Kalem, 1912), *The Darling of the C.S.A.* (Kalem, 1912), *The Defender of the Name* (Rex, 1912), *For the Cause of the South* (Edison, 1912), *A Maid at War* (Bison, 1912), *On Secret Service* (Kay-Bee, 1912), *On the Firing Line* (101 Bison, 1912), *On the Line of Peril* (Vitagraph, 1912),

Saved from Court-Martial (Kalem, 1912), *The Soldier Brothers of Susanna* (Kalem, 1912), *The Two Spies* (Kalem, 1912), *War's Havoc* (Kalem, 1912), *At Shiloh* (101 Bison, 1913), *The Battle of Bull Run* (101 Bison, 1913), *Bell Boyd—A Confederate Spy* (Selig, 1913), *A Daughter of the Confederacy* (Selig, 1913), *The Little Turncoat* (Kay-Bee, 1913), *A Love of '64* (Lubin, 1913), *My Lady's Boot* (Majestic, 1913), *The Price of Victory* (Lubin, 1913), *The Toll of War* (101 Bison, 1913), *The Wartime Siren* (Kalem, 1913), *In the Fall of '64* (Gold Seal, 1914), *The Weaker Brother* (Lubin, 1914), *The Heart of Maryland* (Tiffany Metro, 1915), *Rivals* (Kalem, 1915), *The Spy's Sister* (Lubin, 1915), *Vain Justice* (Essanay, 1915), *A War Baby* (Lubin, 1915), *The Warrens of Virginia* (Lasky, 1915).

6. Donald Winkler, *Stealing Secrets: How a Few Daring Women Deceived Generals, Impacted Battles, and Altered the Course of the Civil War* (London: Sourcebooks, 2010); Lauren Cook Burgess, ed., *An Uncommon Soldier: The Civil War Letters of Sarah Rosetta Wakeman, Alias Pvt. Lyons Wakeman, 153rd Regiment, New York State Volunteers* (Oxford: Oxford University Press, 1996); Richard Hall, *Patriots in Disguise: Women Warriors of the Civil War* (St. Paul, MN: Paragon House, 1993); Elizabeth D. Leonard, *All the Daring of the Soldier: Women of the Civil War Armies* (New York: W. W. Norton, 1999).

7. Alice Fahs, "The Feminized War," in *The Imagined Civil War: Popular Literature of the North and South, 1861–1865* (Chapel Hill: University of North Carolina Press, 2001), 120–149.

8. Jenny Barrett, *Shooting the Civil War: Cinema, History and American National Identity* (London: I. B. Tauris, 2009), 2.

9. Barrett, *Shooting the Civil War*, 13.

10. Gary W. Gallagher, *Causes Won, Lost, Forgotten: How Hollywood and Popular Art Shape What We Know about the Civil War* (Chapel Hill: University of North Carolina Press, 2008), 2.

11. Daniel C. Gerould, "The Americanization of Melodrama," in *American Melodrama* (Cambridge, MA: Performing Arts, 1983), 7.

12. Jeffrey D. Mason, *Melodrama and the Myth of America* (Indianapolis: Indiana University Press, 1993), 1.

13. Mason, *Melodrama*, 16.

14. Mason, *Melodrama*, 13.

15. An examination of the chart given in Appendix 1 reveals that the Civil War films were not limited to these three character types. Indeed, passive women who existed only as love interests for soldiers and spies were also frequently seen in films of this era. Male heroes were equally as popular and it is not the aim of this chapter to suggest that women were the only heroes of the Civil War—in fact, of the over 300 films listed about 150 demonstrated heroic acts by women, or both and the remaining films concerned men in war (with one exception: *The Equine Spy* (1912) featured a heroic horse).

16. "The Spartan Mother," *Moving Picture World*, March 2, 1912, 770.

17. Henry Albert Phillips, "A Spartan Mother," *Motion Picture Story Magazine*, March 1912, 87.

18. Phillips, "A Spartan Mother," 89.

19. Phillips, "A Spartan Mother," 89.

20. Phillips, "A Spartan Mother," 81.

21. "A Dixie Mother," *Moving Picture World*, December 31, 1910, 1538.

22. *Two Brothers of the G.A.R.* (Lubin, 1908), *Brother against Brother* (Selig, 1909), *In Old Kentucky* (Biograph, 1909), *All's Fair in Love and War* (Capitol, 1910), *The Brother's Feud* (Imp, 1910), *A Daughter of Dixie* (Kalem, 1910), *Dixie* (Imp, 1910), *A Dixie Mother* (Vitagraph, 1910), *The Flag of His Country* (Thanhouser, 1910), *Under Both Flags* (Pathé, 1910), *Barbara Frietchie* (Champion, 1911), *The Colonel's Son* (Kalem, 1911), *The Copperhead* (Champion, 1911), *He Fought for the U.S.A.* (Essanay, 1911), *The Rival Brother's Patriotism* (Pathé, 1911), *A Southern Boy of '61* (Kalem, 1911), *A Southern Soldier's Sacrifice* (Vitagraph, 1911), *With Sheridan at*

Murfreesboro (Champion, 1911), *Blood Will Tell* (Kay-Bee, 1912), *A Bluegrass Romance* (Broncho, 1912), *The Informer* (Biograph, 1912), *A Man's Duty* (Reliance, 1912), *On the Line of Peril* (Vitagraph, 1912), *Sundered Ties* (Broncho, 1912), *United We Stand* (Nestor, 1912), *The Colonel's Oath* (Reliance, 1913), *Heart Throbs* (Broncho, 1913), *In the Days of War* (Pathé, 1913), *Pride of the South* (Broncho, 1913), *When Sherman Marched to the Sea* (101 Bison, 1913), *The Battle of Shiloh* (Lubin, 1914), *Between Two Fires* (Lubin, 1914), *Quantrill's Son* (Vitagraph, 1914), *The Tide of Fortune* (Kay-Bee, 1915), *According to the Code* (Essanay, 1916), *The Son of a Rebel Chief* (Bison, 1916), and *The Sting of Victory* (Essanay, 1916).

23. Henry Albert Phillips, "For the Cause of the South," *Motion Picture Story Magazine*, February 1912, 112.

24. Allen Stanhope, "The Informer," *Motion Picture Story Magazine*, December 1912, 156.

25. Louis Reeves Harrison, "Fighting Dan McCool," *Motion Picture Story Magazine*, May 1912, 89–96.

26. Elizabeth Heineman, "The Soldier Brothers of Susanna," *Motion Picture Story Magazine*, August 1912, 122–129.

27. "Battle of Pottsburg Bridge," *Moving Picture World*, January 27, 1912, 307.

28. "The Battle of Bloody Ford," *Moving Picture World*, March 8, 1913, 977.

29. In "High Fashion, Costume Design and Character Type: How Clothes Helped Billie Burke Become an American Girl," Leslie Midkiff DeBauche discusses the cooperation between the film industry and the fashion industry. In *La Decima Musa: Il Cinema e le Alltre Arti* (Udine, Italy: Universita degli studi di Udine, 2001), 163–169.

30. Marjorie Garber's *Vested Interests: Cross-Dressing and Cultural Anxiety* (London: Psychology Press, 1997) stands as a central text in the history of cross-dressing. More recently, Peter Boag's *Re-Dressing America's Frontier Past* (Berkeley: University of California Press, 2012), Alison Oram's *Her Husband Was a Woman! Women's Gender-Crossing in Modern British Popular Culture* (London: Routledge, 2013) and Deborah Cohler's *Citizen, Invert, Queer: Lesbianism and War in Early Twentieth-Century Britain* (Minneapolis: University of Minnesota Press, 2010) have addressed cross-dressing in national contexts. Laura Horak's *Girls Will Be Boys: Cross-Dressed Women, Lesbians, and American Cinema, 1908–1934* (New Brunswick, NJ: Rutgers University Press, 2016) is an extensive study of the practice of cross-dressing in American silent film.

31. Vern L. Bullough and Bonnie Bullough, *Cross Dressing, Sex, and Gender* (Philadelphia: University of Pennsylvania Press, 1993), 157.

32. For more on the transitional era, see Charlie Keil and Shelley Stamp, eds., *American Cinema's Transitional Era: Audiences, Institutions and Practices* (Berkeley: University of California Press, 2004). Horak, *Girls Will Be Boys*, 11, defines the other two waves as 1922–1928 and 1929–1934.

33. Horak, *Girls Will Be Boys*, 56.

34. On the distinction between cross-dressed women in early film and the concept of the New Woman, see Horak, *Girls Will Be Boys*, 5–11, and see 54–89 on heroic women as serving nationalistic ideologies.

35. Gene Gauntier, "Blazing the Trail," *Woman's Home Companion*, November 1928, 170.

36. The first *Girl Spy* film is available on the Kino DVD/Blu Ray collection *Cinema's First Nasty Women*. *The Girl Spy before Vicksburg* is available to view at the Eye Institute in Amsterdam.

37. "The Girl Spy," *Moving Picture World*, May 15, 1909, 643.

38. "The Darling of the C.S.A.," *Motion Picture Story Magazine*, September 1912, 59–68.

39. Winkler, *Stealing Secrets*, 131.

40. "Pauline Cushman, the Federal Spy," *Moving Picture World*, March 22, 1913, 1201–1202.

41. See also Abel, *Americanizing the Movies*, 148–149.

42. See also Bernardi, "The Voice of Whiteness: D. W. Griffith's Biograph Films," in *The Birth of Whiteness: Race and the Emergence of U.S. Cinema* (New Brunswick, NJ: Rutgers University Press, 1996), 103–128, for an in-depth discussion of Griffith's Biograph films, which similarly demonstrates that comparative analysis reveals the depth and breadth of racist practices that were in play before *Birth of a Nation* (1915) and *Broken Blossoms* (1919).

43. *Kalem Kalendars* included descriptions of all films released each week. It was only *War's Havoc* that included a black character.

44. Cripps, "The Absent Presence," para. 10.

45. Eileen Bowser, *The Transformation of Cinema: 1907–1915* (Berkley: University of California Press, 1990), 25.

46. In 1912 alone Kalem released *The Two Spies, The Battle of Pottsburg Bridge, A Spartan Mother, The Tide of Battle, War's Havoc, Under a Flag of Truce, The Drummer Girl of Vicksburg, The Bugler of Battery B, The Soldier Brothers of Susanna, The Siege of Petersburg, The Darling of the C.S.A., Saved from Court Martial, The Confederate Ironclad,* a handful of American Revolution films, and even one Spanish-American War film called *The Fillibusters.* In 1913 a smaller number of Civil War films were released by Kalem, including *The Woe of Battle, The Grim Toll of War, The Wartime Siren, The Deadly Battle at Hicksville,* and *Shenandoah.* By 1914 the *Kalendars* reveal a turn away from Civil War films, in favor of the "Indian" pictures evidenced in these titles: *Hopi Raiders; Reggie, the Squaw Man; The Tigers of the Hills; The Medicine Man's Vengeance; The Indian Ambuscade; Indian Fate; Indian's Honor; The Paleface Brave; Indian Blood; Red Hawk's Sacrifice;* and *The Indian Suffragettes.*

47. Features in 1912 referred to top billing, or films of special interest, rather than length. Kalem was still firmly committed to film lengths of one or two reels.

48. *Kalem Kalendar*, February 19, 1912, 4.

49. Simon's scores are available for view at the Library of Congress in the Performing Arts Reading Room.

50. *Kalem Kalendar*, February 12, 1912, 8.

51. *New York Dramatic Mirror*, January 31, 1912, 53.

NOTES TO CHAPTER 3

1. See Jonna Eagle, "Introduction," in *Imperial Affects: Sensational Melodrama and the Attractions of American Cinema* (New Brunswick, NJ: Rutgers University Press, 2017), 1–23, for a discussion of melodrama and identification with the victim.

2. See Amy Kaplan, "Introduction" and "Manifest Domesticity," in *The Anarchy of Empire in the Making of U.S. Culture* (Cambridge, MA: Harvard University Press, 2002), 1–22, 23–50, for a discussion of discursive practices of making expansionism a "domestic" issue.

3. Other films made during the transitional period include *A Daughter of the Revolution* (Rex, 1911), *For Washington* (Thanhouser, 1911), *A Revolutionary Romance* (Solax, 1911), *A Heroine of '76* (Rex, 1911), *Before Yorktown* (Republic, 1911), *Flag of Freedom* (Kalem, 1912), *The Prison Ship* (Kalem, 1912), *A Revolutionary Romance* (Selig Polyscope, 1913), *The Swamp Fox* (Kalem, 1914), *Heart of a Woman* (Domino, 1914), and *Washington at Valley Forge* (Universal, 1914).

4. These films include *For the Love of Country* (Kalem, 1908), *Spirit of '76* (Selig Polyscope, 1908), *Army of Two* (Edison, 1908), *Brave Women of '76* (Lubin, 1909), *Hessian Renegades* (Biograph, 1909), *The Old Hall Clock* (Lubin, 1909), *When the Flag Falls* (Lubin, 1909), and *The Governor's Daughter* (Kalem, 1909).

5. Because many of these films are unavailable to view, the assertions about the protagonists are based almost entirely on summaries and advertisements found in the trade press. In a

Kalem Kalendar the description of *The Prison Ship* opens with a romance but never mentions the female character again. However, in the accompanying film still, a woman is seen on the rowboat that rescues her lover from the prison ship (*Kalem Kalendar*, July 15, 1912, 13).

6. See also Liz Clarke, "A Band of Adventurers: Kalem's Gauntier-Olcott Film Unit in Egypt," *Historical Journal of Film, Radio and Television* 38, no. 4 (2018): 695–710.

7. "The Governor's Daughter," *Film Index*, November 27, 1909, 11–12.

8. "Advertisement for Washington," *Moving Picture News*, February 11, 1911, 28.

9. "The Spirit of '76," *Film Index*, July 4, 1908, pages unknown.

10. "Brave Women of '76," *Moving Picture World*, November 13, 1909, 695; "Brave Women of '76," *Variety*, November 6, 1909, 13.

11. "The Army of Two," *Film Index*, November 7, 1908, 9.

12. S. L. Rothapfel, "First Aid to Theater Men," *Motography*, November 18, 1916, 1122.

13. Rothapfel, "First Aid," 1122.

14. Rothapfel, "First Aid," 1122.

15. Jennifer Peterson, "'The Five-Cent University': Educational Films and the Drive to Uplift the Cinema," in *Education in the School of Dreams: Travelogues and Early Nonfiction Film* (Durham, NC: Duke University Press, 2013), 101–136.

16. Peterson, "'The Five-Cent University,'" 103.

17. See also William Uricchio and Roberta Pearson, *Reframing Culture: The Case of the Vitagraph Quality Films* (Princeton, NJ: Princeton University Press, 2014), 41–64; Constance Balides, "Cinema under the Sign of Money: Commercialized Leisure, Economies of Abundance, and Pecuniary Madness, 1905–1915," in *American Cinema's Transitional Era: Audiences, Institutions, Practices*, ed. Shelley Stamp and Charlie Keil (Berkeley: University of California Press, 2004), 285–313.

18. Danson Mitchell, "Washington at Valley Forge," *Motion Picture News*, March 21, 1914, 36.

19. Summary found in Mitchell, "Washington at Valley Forge."

20. "Latest Films of All Makers," *Film Index*, July 4, 1908, 10–11.

21. "Latest Films of All Makers," 10–11.

22. Nan Enstad, *Ladies of Labor, Girls of Adventure: Working Women, Popular Culture, and Labor Politics at the Turn of the Century* (New York: Columbia University Press, 1999), 186.

23. Virginia Wright Wexman writes about the concept of "blood" as synonymous with race at the turn of the century. Expanding from this concept was a hierarchy, which placed those of northern European descent at the top, followed by southern European, with Indigenous people at the bottom, and Mestizo Mexican in the middle. Following from this, we can see in the films about immigrant or European women, a proximity to the Anglo-American woman. Later in this chapter I will discuss the representation of Mexican women as well. However, African American women were never given roles such as the ones we see depicted as American and northern European women. Wexman, "The Family on the Land: Race and Nationhood in Silent Westerns," in *The Birth of Whiteness: Race and the Emergence of U.S. Cinema* (New Brunswick, NJ: Rutgers University Press, 1996), 132.

24. For more on the context of film spectacle in *Joan the Woman*, see Sheldon Hall and Steve Neale, *Epics, Spectacles and Blockbusters* (Detroit: Wayne State University Press, 2010), 34–40. For a detailed analysis of the preparation, production, promotion, and reception of the film, see Leslie Midkiff DeBauche, *Reel Patriotism* (Madison: University of Wisconsin Press), 5–28.

25. Robin Blaetz, *Visions of the Maid: Joan of Arc in American Film and Culture* (Richmond: University of Virginia Press, 2001), 42.

26. Robin Blaetz, "Joan of Arc and the War," in *Film and the First World War*, ed. Karel Dibbets and Bert Hogenkamp (Amsterdam: Amsterdam University Press, 1995), 120.

27. Blaetz, "Joan of Arc," 123.

28. Jerzey Toeplitz, "The Cinema in Eastern and Central Europe before the Guns of August," in Dibbets and Hogenkamp, *Film and the First World War*, 18.

29. "Cines and Eclipse Releases," *Moving Picture World*, February 1, 1913, 475.

30. J. Randolph Cox, *The Dime Novel Companion: A Source Book* (Westport, CT: Greenwood Press, 2000), 274.

31. "The Captive," *Moving Picture World*, May 1, 1915, 743.

32. "Battle, The," *Moving Picture World*, January 13, 1912, 112.

33. "Screen Magnetism Distinguishes Blanche Sweet," *Motion Picture News*, December 19, 1914, 34.

34. Richard deCordova, *Picture Personalities: The Emergence of the Star System in America* (Champaign: University of Illinois Press, 1990), 87.

35. "Reel Heroines in Real Life," *Day Book*, July 22, 1915, page unknown. Although the article is meant to highlight brave deeds performed by familiar on-screen heroines, the rescue performed by Sweet seems to have consisted of nothing more than going to look for the missing woman and then possibly ending up in the same predicament of being stuck at the bottom of a steep embankment.

36. "Biograph Reissues Equal to Present Day Films," *Motion Picture News*, May 29, 1915, 41.

37. Stephen Bush, "The Mexican Joan of Arc (Kalem)," *Moving Picture World*, July 15, 1911, 19.

38. Dominique Bregent-Heald, *Borderland Films: American Cinema, Mexico, and Canada during the Progressive Era* (Lincoln: University of Nebraska Press, 2015), 3.

39. Jennifer Keene, *Americans and the First World War* (Essex: Pearson Education, 2000), 11.

40. Keene, *Americans*, 11.

41. Keene, *Americans*, 12.

42. Stephen Bush, "Mexican War Pictures," *Moving Picture World*, February 7, 1914, 657.

43. Bush, "Mexican War Pictures," 657.

44. Bush, "Mexican War Pictures," 657.

45. The plot summary was paraphrased from a summary provided in *Moving Picture World*, August 22, 1914, 1152.

46. Shelley Streeby, *American Sensations: Class, Empire, and the Production of Popular Culture* (Berkeley: University of California Press, 2002), 103.

NOTES TO CHAPTER 4

1. Jonna Eagle, *Imperial Affects*, 6.

2. Wilson's efforts are still the subject of debate. See, for example, John Milton Cooper Jr., "Introduction," in *Making a Case for Wilson* (Baltimore: Johns Hopkins University Press, 2008), 4.

3. John Milton Cooper Jr., *Pivotal Decades: The United States, 1900–1920* (New York: W. W. Norton, 1990), 227.

4. See John M. Cooper Jr.'s edited collection, *Reconsidering Woodrow Wilson* (Baltimore: Johns Hopkins University Press, 2008), in particular Cooper, "Making a Case for Wilson" (9–23), and Mark T. Gilderhus, "Revolution, War, and Expansion: Woodrow Wilson in Latin America" (165–188). Both provide detailed analyses of the shifting approach to foreign policy that defined Wilson's two terms as president.

5. See Jennifer D. Keene, *The United States and the First World War* (London: Pearson Education, 2000), 9–12.

6. Cooper, *Pivotal Decades*, 252.

7. Oscar King Davis, "Warns Nation War Is Danger at All Times," *Chicago Daily Tribune*, January 31, 1915, 1.

8. The film is considered a lost film. The analysis will be based on synopses from the trade press and from the full scenario that was submitted to the Library of Congress for copyright (Copyright number: LP6935). The phrase "fanatic women and silly-looking men" was used in the scenario to describe the crowd at the Peace Conference.

9. Joyce Berkman, "Feminism, War, and Peace Politics," in *Women, Militarism, and War: Essays in History, Politics, and Social Theory*, ed. Jean B. Elshtain and Sheila Tobias (Savage, MD: Rowman and Littlefield, 1990), 147.

10. Berkman, "Feminism, War," 149.

11. Edward Weitzel, "The Nation's Peril," *Moving Picture World*, November 27, 1915, 1675.

12. "'Civilization' Makes Profound Impression in East," *Motion Picture News*, June 17, 1916, 3717–3718.

13. "'Civilization' Makes Profound Impression," 3717.

14. "'Civilization' Makes Profound Impression," 3717.

15. Stephen Bush, "Civilization," *Moving Picture World*, June 17, 1916, 2056.

16. "'Fall of a Nation' Is Gripping Play," *New York Telegraph*, November 6, 1916, page unknown.

17. Lynde Denig, "The Fall of a Nation," *Moving Picture World*, June 24, 1916, 2256.

18. "'Fall of a Nation' Depicts Conspiracy against Liberty," *Motion Picture News*, June 10, 1916, 3551.

19. "'The Fall of a Nation' Rises to Dramatic Heights," *Motion Picture News*, June 24, 1916, 3877.

20. Lynde Denig, "Thomas Dixon Lauds the Cinema," *Moving Picture World*, June 3, 1916, 1671.

21. Advertisement, *Moving Picture World*, August 28, 1915, 1514–1515.

22. Advertisement, *Moving Picture World*, August 28, 1915, 1516.

23. See William Uricchio and Roberta Pearson, *Reframing Culture: The Case of the Vitagraph Quality Films* (Princeton, NJ: Princeton University Press, 2014); and Anthony Slide, *The Big V: A History of the Vitagraph Company* (Metuchen, NJ: Scarecrow Press, 1976).

24. Hudson Maxim, "The Argument for Preparedness," in *Reform, War, and Reaction*, ed. Stanley Coben (Columbia: University of South Carolina Press, 1972), 69.

25. Library of Congress, Copyright LP6935. It is unclear if this was the final shooting script, but evidence from synopses found in the trade press suggest the film is very similar to that laid out in the scenario. Example synopsis: "'The Battle Cry of Peace' Is Epic Patriotism," *Motion Picture News*, August 21, 1915, 82.

26. Sheldon Hall and Stephen Neale, *Epics, Spectacles, and Blockbusters: A Hollywood History* (Detroit: Wayne State University Press, 2010), 21. For more on this, see also Eileen Bowser, "The Feature Film," in *The Transformation of Cinema* (Berkeley: University of California Press, 1990), 191–215.

27. For more on the difficulty of incorporating expansionism into American politics, when the founding myth of the nation is predicated on notions of "freedom," see this book's Introduction; also see Amy Kaplan, *The Anarchy of Empire* (Cambridge, MA: Harvard University Press, 2002).

28. Advertisement, "The Battle Cry of Peace," *Motion Picture News*, August 28, 1915, 27.

29. V-L-S-E was the distributor created through the partnership of Vitagraph, Lubin, Selig, and Essanay film producers.

30. "V-L-S-E Will Handle Dixon's 'The Fall of a Nation,'" *Motion Picture News*, September 2, 1916, 1356.

31. Julian Stringer, "Introduction," in *Movie Blockbusters*, ed. Julian Stringer (London: Routledge 2003), 3.

32. Altman, quoted in Stringer, "Introduction," 2.

33. Steve Neale, "Hollywood Blockbusters: Historical Dimensions," in Stringer, *Movie Block-busters*, 47.

34. See Hall and Neale, *Epics, Spectacles, and Blockbusters*, 31–35; and Eileen Bowser, "Scene Dissection, Spectacle, and Film as Art," in *The Transformation of Cinema* (Berkeley: University of California Press, 1990), 255–272.

35. G. P. Von Harleman and Clarke Irvine, "Harbingers of 'Civilization,'" *Moving Picture World*, June 3, 1916, 1693.

36. Leslie Midkiff DeBauche, *Reel Patriotism: The Movies and World War I* (Madison: University of Wisconsin Press, 1997), 35–44.

37. "Rally Industry to Country's Call," *Motography*, April 14, 1917, 764; "Theaters Aid Patriotism," *Motography*, April 14, 1917, 758. For a scholarly discussion of filmic promotion during World War I, see also Fabrice Lyczba, "Hoaxes, Ballyhoo Stunts, War, and Other Jokes: Humor in the American Marketing of Hollywood War Films during the Great War," in *Humor, Entertainment, and Popular Culture during World War I*, ed. Clémentine Tholas-Disset and Karen A. Ritzenoff (New York: Palgrave Macmillan, 2015), 59–76.

38. "Films Used by U.S.," *Motography*, April 14, 1917, 790.

39. "Film Brings Recruits," *Motography*, May 19, 1917, 1034.

40. "U.S. Endorses 'Womanhood,'" *Motography*, May 19, 1917, 1058.

41. A weekly section in *Motography* entitled "What the Picture Did for Me" provided brief responses from exhibitors about how the films were received by their patrons. Edward Trinz (owner of a West End middle-class theater) stated, "During wartime this picture, although praised by the critics, was not praised by the audience. This is because it shows too many battle scenes, with people being killed, scenes which at this time do not appeal to the people, especially not to women and children. . . . We ran it two days with fair results." *Motography*, June 2, 1917, 1133–1134.

42. "'Womanhood' Smashes Precedents," *Motography*, June 9, 1917, 1216.

43. Library of Congress Copyright Record 10406.

44. Louis Reeves Harrison, "Womanhood, the Glory of the Nation," *Moving Picture World*, April 21, 1917, 449–450.

45. "'Womanhood' Patriotically Shown in New York," *Motion Picture News*, April 14, 1917, 2316.

46. Peter Milne, "Womanhood, the Glory of the Nation," *Motion Picture News*, April 21, 1917, 2513.

47. "Patriotism Aroused at 'Womanhood' Showings," *Motion Picture News*, November 28, 1917, 2665.

48. "'Womanhood' to Have Showing April 1," *Motion Picture News*, April 7, 1917, 2163; "'Womanhood' Patriotically Shown in New York," *Motion Picture News*, April 14, 1917, 2316; "Choose 'Womanhood' as Recruiting Stimulus," *Motion Picture News*, April 14, 1917, 2324.

49. "Roosevelt Applauded in Film," *Motography*, April 21, 1917, 821.

50. "'Womanhood' Billed Nationwide," *Motography*, May 26, 1917, 1110.

51. "Roosevelt Applauded in Film," 821.

52. "$1000 Greater Vitagraph Prize," *Motography*, April 21, 1917, 822.

53. "Essays Flood Vitagraph," *Motography*, July 28, 1917, 188.

54. "Essays Flood Vitagraph," 188.

55. "Film Aids Enlistment," *Motography*, April 21, 1917, 834.

56. "Film Aids Enlistment," 834.

57. "Navy Recruits by Film," *Motography*, April 28, 1917, 893.

58. DeBauche, *Reel Patriotism*, 9.

59. "Lobby Girl Advertises Theater," *Motography*, April 21, 1917, 872.

60. "Presenting Geraldine Farrar Picture," *Motography*, April 17, 1917, 815.

61. "Presenting Geraldine Farrar Picture," 815.

62. "Theater Girls Aid Uncle Sam," *Motography*, April 21, 1917, 815.

63. Robin Blaetz, *Visions of the Maid: Joan of Arc in American Film and Culture* (Richmond: University of Virginia Press, 2001), 46.

NOTES TO CHAPTER 5

1. Advertisement, "Universal Preparedness Pictures," *Moving Picture Weekly*, May 12, 1917, 2.

2. Jennifer Bean, "Technologies of Early Stardom," in *A Feminist Reader in Early Cinema*, ed. Jennifer Bean and Diane Negra (Durham, NC: Duke University Press, 2002), 403–443; Ben Singer, *Melodrama and Modernity* (New York: Columbia University Press, 2001); Shelley Stamp, *Movie-Struck Girls: Women and Motion Picture Culture after the Nickelodeon* (Princeton, NJ: Princeton University Press, 2000).

3. See Stamp's chapter "Ready-Made Customers: Female Movie Fans and the Serial Craze" in *Movie Struck Girls*, 102–153.

4. Justin Morris, "Read It Today, See It Tonight: Extratextuality and the Silent Film Serial," *Cineaction*, no. 94 (2014): 45–50.

5. See Ilka Brasch, *Film Serials and the American Cinema, 1910–1940* (Amsterdam: Amsterdam University Press, 2018); Rudmer Canjels, *Distributing Film Serials: Local Practices, Changing Forms, Cultural Transformation* (New York: Routledge, 2011).

6. Brasch, *Film Serials*, 15.

7. Richard Abel, "Movie Stars and Seriality in the 1910s," *Velvet Light Trap* 79 (Spring 2017): 83–84.

8. Paul S. Moore, *Now Playing: Moviegoing and the Regulation of Fun* (Albany: SUNY Press, 2008), 158.

9. None of these serials have survived in their entirety. The Library of Congress contains several segments of *Pearl of the Army*, and the Museum of Modern Art's film collection contains segments of *Patria*. In addition to viewing the existing footage from both serials, my research was augmented by the fictional tie-ins published in newspapers to coincide with the screenings, as well as by copyright records that summarize each episode in full. These records are held in the Library of Congress's Motion Picture and Television Reading Room. For *Liberty* and *The Secret of the Submarine*, I have relied on newspaper tie-ins and plot synopses in the trade press.

10. In "Story Papers," Lori Merish discusses the originally intended male audience of popular story papers of the nineteenth century, which were enthusiastically read by girls and working-class female readers. Soon after realizing that they had a female readership, publishers started to incorporate stories about "factory women, seamstresses, cigar girls, servants, prostitutes, and—after midcentury—the renowned 'sewing machine girls.'" Lori Merish, "Story Papers," in *The Oxford History of Popular Print Culture: U.S. Popular Print Culture, 1860–1920*, ed. Christine Bold (Oxford: Oxford University Press, 2011), 43–62.

11. Roger Hagedorn, "Doubtless to Be Continued: A Brief History of Serial Narrative," in *To Be Continued . . . : Soap Operas around the World*, ed. Robert C. Allen (New York: Routledge, 1995), 27–48.

12. See Stamp, *Movie-Struck Girls*; Singer, *Melodrama and Modernity*; Morris, "Read It Today'"; Moore, *Now Playing*.

13. "'Fangs of the Wolf,' 1st Episode of 'Liberty,'" *Moving Picture Weekly*, August 5, 1916, 20–27, 47.

14. Advertisement, *Moving Picture Weekly*, May 12, 1917, 4.

15. In his chapter on "Serial Queens," Singer emphasizes that even though the female heroine demonstrated active and admirable qualities reflective of the "New Woman," the dangerous situations also led to the depiction of women in peril. Singer, *Melodrama and Modernity*, 222.

16. "Pathé's New Serial Ready for Release Dec. 3," *Motion Picture News*, November 25, 1916, 3313.

17. Robin Blaetz, *Visions of the Maid: Joan of Arc in American Film and Culture* (Richmond: University of Virginia Press, 2001), 42.

18. Blaetz, *Visions of the Maid*, 33. For more on Joan of Arc in American film, see chapters 3 and 4 (on *Joan the Woman*) and chapter 6 (on *Joan of Plattsburg*).

19. "Pathé's New Serial Ready for Release Dec. 3," *Motion Picture News*, November 25, 1916, 3313.

20. "Pathé's New Serial," 3313.

21. Mark T. Gilderhus, "Revolution, War, and Expansion: Woodrow Wilson in Latin America," in *Reconsidering Woodrow Wilson*, ed. John Milton Cooper Jr. (Baltimore: Johns Hopkins University Press, 2008), 170.

22. Gilderhus, "Revolution, War, and Expansion," 171.

23. Roland Usher, "'The American Problem and the War,'" *Chicago Daily Tribune*, March 14, 1915, A5.

24. "Star Rides in Mid-Air," *Motography*, April 28, 1917, 896.

25. "Pearl White in Christy Army Poster," *Moving Picture World*, July 21, 1917, 462.

26. *Toledo Times*, May 4, 1918, no page. Information for Pearl White and Irene Castle was found in scrapbooks in the Robinson Locke Collection at the New York Public Library. Many of the clippings contain only partial bibliographic information, which often does not include original page numbers or titles. The *Toledo Times* article was found on page 57 of the Pearl White scrapbook.

27. Bean, "Technologies," 405.

28. Singer, *Melodrama and Modernity*, 231; Stamp, *Movie-Struck Girls*, 126.

29. Singer, *Melodrama and Modernity*, 231.

30. Louis Joseph Vance, "Patria: A Romance of Preparedness," *Washington Post*, April 22, 1917, SM6.

31. Vance, "Patria," SM8.

32. Library of Congress, Copyright Record 10346.

33. Richard Slotkin, *Gunfighter Nation: The Myth of the Frontier in Twentieth-Century America* (Norman: University of Oklahoma Press, 1998), 88.

34. Slotkin, *Gunfighter Nation*, 88–91.

35. "Patria," 14.

36. Stamp, *Movie-Struck Girls*, 108.

37. *Cosmopolitan*, September 1916, 65.

38. Leslie Midkiff Debauche, "High Fashion, Costume Design and Character Type: How Clothes Helped Billie Burke Become an American Girl," *La Decima Musa: Il Cinema e Le Altre Arti* (Udine, Italy: Universita degli studi di Udine, 2001), 164.

39. Edward Speyer, "Saving the U.S.A. Is the Lady's Simplest Task in New Serial," *Detroit News Tribune*, November 12, 1916, 12.

40. This article was found in the Robinson Locke Collection at the New York Public Library: series 2, vol. 37, p. 52.

41. From Irene Castle scrapbook, New York Public Library, 57.

42. C. Blythe, "Mrs. Castle Will 'Carry On,'" *Motion Picture Classic*, October 1918, 20–21, 79.

43. Nan Enstad, *Ladies of Labor, Girls of Adventure: Working Women, Popular Culture, and Labor Politics at the Turn of the Twentieth Century* (New York: Columbia University Press, 1999), 55.

44. Enstad, *Ladies of Labor*, 50, 163.

45. Moore, *Now Playing*, 187–188; Kathy Peiss "Making Faces: The Cosmetics Industry and the Cultural Construction of Gender, 1890–1930," in *Unequal Sisters: An Inclusive Reader in U.S. Women's History*, ed. Vicki L. Ruíz and Ellen Carol DuBois (New York: Routledge, 1990), 353; Enstad, *Ladies of Labor*, 17–20.

46. DeBauche, "High Fashion," 168.

47. DeBauche, "High Fashion," 167.

NOTES TO CHAPTER 6

1. From the outbreak of World War I in Europe in 1914 until April 1917, the United States remained neutral and isolationist regarding the European conflict. Debates in American politics during this period were divided between the view that the United States should be preparing an army—usually promoted as a form of defense—and the view that the United States should remain a peaceful, isolationist country.

2. Leslie Midkiff DeBauche, *Reel Patriotism: The Movies and World War I* (Madison: University of Wisconsin Press, 1997), xvi.

3. Perhaps not surprisingly, the lines for marriage licenses were shockingly long during the short period this rule was in place. Helen Ketchum, the lobby girl noted for her promotion of *Womanhood* and *Joan the Woman*, was also said to dress as Joan of Arc in order to "heckle the 'war bridegrooms' and drive them from the altar to the colors." "Lobby Girl Advertises Theater," *Motography*, April 21, 1917, 872.

4. Plot summary found in Joseph L. Kelley, "The Slacker," *Motion Picture News*, August 11, 1917, 1020.

5. "'The Slacker' Production De Luxe," *Motography*, July 14, 1917, 85.

6. Kelley, "The Slacker," 1020.

7. One notable advertising gimmick for *The Slacker* was used while the film was shown in Boston. The gimmick was described in full in the *Moving Picture World*: On a rope stretched between the roofs of two skyscrapers travels an airplane in which is seated a dummy. The airplane is brilliantly illuminated by a powerful searchlight that follows it as it speeds through the air over the business district. Each night thousands of people gasp with surprise and fear when they see the realistic-looking dummy fall from the plane and drop like a stone toward the earth. After the dummy falls about 150 feet, a thin cord hoists it back into its seat in the plane. Thanks to this startling advertising device, few Bostonians could have been ignorant of the fact that *The Slacker* was being shown in the city. "Startling Advertising Stand for 'The Slacker,'" *Moving Picture World*, August 11, 1917, 971.

8. "New Metro Feature," *Motography*, October 13, 1917, 786.

9. "New Metro Feature," 786.

10. Edward Weitzel, "Draft 258," *Moving Picture World*, December 15, 1917, 1644.

11. Weitzel, "Draft 258," 1644.

12. "'Draft 258' Successor to 'The Slacker,'" *Motography*, October 20, 1917, 820.

13. Peter Milne, "Mrs. Slacker," *Motion Picture News*, April 13, 1918, 2258.

14. Mary Pickford, *The Little American* (DeMille, 1917); Billie Burke, *Arms and the Girl* (Kaufman, 1917); Mabel Normand, *Joan of Plattsburg* (Tucker, 1917); Emily Stevens, *The Slacker* (Cabanne, 1917); Lillian and Dorothy Gish, *Hearts of the World* (Griffith, 1918).

15. DeBauche, *Reel Patriotism*, 34.

16. In addition to DeBauche on Pickford in *Reel Patriotism*, see also Clémentine Tholas-Disset, "Mary Pickford's WWI Patriotism: A Feminine Approach to Wartime Mythical Americanness," in *Heroism and Gender in War Films*, ed. Karen A. Ritzenhoff and Jakub Kazecki (New York: Palgrave Macmillan, 2014), 9–21.

17. "Mary Pickford Starts Ambulance," *Motography*, July 28, 1917, 184.

18. "Mary Pickford Doing 'Bit,'" *Motography*, July 7, 1917, 33.

19. "Plans for Mary Pickford," *Motography*, May 26, 1917, 1101.

20. Quoted in DeBauche, *Reel Patriotism*, 50.

21. Major Funkhouser, the head of the Chicago censor board, prevented the film from playing in Chicago because it could be perceived as anti-German. "Pickford Film Held Up," *Motography*, July 21, 1917, 120.

22. Ine van Dooren and Peter Kramer, "The Politics of Direct Address," in *Film and the First World War*, ed. Karel Dibbets and Bert Hogenkamp (Amsterdam: Amsterdam University Press, 1995), 105.

23. Louis Reeves Harrison, "Johanna Enlists," *Moving Picture World*, September 14, 1918, 1610.

24. Tholas-Disset, "Mary Pickford's WWI Patriotism," 13.

25. Clémentine Tholas-Disset and Karen A. Ritzenhoff, "Introduction," *Humor, Entertainment, and Popular Culture during World War I*, ed. Clémentine Tholas-Disset and Karen A. Ritzenhoff (New York: Palgrave Macmillan, 2015), 1–22.

26. Kristen Anderson Wagner, *Comic Venus: Women and Comedy in American Silent Film* (Detroit: Wayne State University Press, 2018), 185.

27. Edward Weitzel, "Her Country First," *Moving Picture World*, September 14, 1918, 1608.

28. "As to 'Joan of Plattsburg,'" *Motion Picture News*, May 11, 1918, 2831.

29. Robin Blaetz, *Visions of the Maid: Joan of Arc in American Film and Culture* (Richmond: University of Virginia Press, 2001), 68.

30. Maggie Hennefeld, *Specters of Slapstick and Silent Film Comediennes* (New York: Columbia University Press, 2018), 170.

31. "'Joan' Intended as Spy-Brake," *Motion Picture News*, May 18, 1918, 2944.

32. Peter Milne, "Daughter of Destiny," *Motion Picture News*, January 12, 1918, 291.

NOTES TO CONCLUSION

1. For the war genre in the 1920s, see Jeanine Basinger, *The World War II Combat Film: Anatomy of a Genre* (Middleton, CT: Wesleyan University Press, 2003), 80–97; Michael Isenberg, *War on Film: The American Cinema and World War I, 1914–1941* (Rutherford, NJ: Fairleigh Dickinson University Press, 1981); Robert Eberwein, *Armed Forces: Masculinity and Sexuality in the American War Film* (New Brunswick, NJ: Rutgers University Press, 2007). For the masculinization of the genre throughout the 1920s, see Liz Clarke, "Ladies Last: Masculinization of the American War Film in the 1920s," *Journal of Popular Film and Television* 43, no. 4 (2015): 171–187.

2. The phrase is also a reference to Susan Jeffords's book on Vietnam War films, *The Remasculinization of America: Gender and the Vietnam War* (Bloomington: Indiana University Press, 1989).

3. According to *Motography*, *Uncle Sam at Work* was a series of films released by "Universal Film Manufacturing Company which show the government in operation" ("Recruits Obtained by Film," *Motography*, April 21, 1917, 813–814). The third film of the series was used for recruitment purposes.

4. "How Uncle Sam Prepares," *Motography*, April 28, 1917, 889.

5. "Recruits Obtained by Film," 813.

6. From the Library of Congress, George Kleine Manuscript Collection.

7. Library of Congress, George Kleine Manuscript Collection.

8. "Edison Stars Miss Courtot," *Motion Picture News*, January 26, 1918, 571.

9. An October 23, 1926, article in the *Moving Picture World*, entitled "Ladies Last . . . On Broadway," states that "earlier in the season Paramount made Broadway sit up and gasp by presenting a picture in which there was practically no love interest. Here was a direct defiance of the primary rule of picture production that the lead must be thrown to a woman star if success was to be assured" (475). The films of 1917–1918 were still produced with this "primary rule of picture production" in mind.

10. Joseph Kelley, "Unbeliever," *Motion Picture News*, March 2, 1918, 1320.

11. "Warm Praise for War Film," *Moving Picture World*, January 17, 1920, 439.

12. By "manly masculinity" I mean virile, rugged—defined by action, violence, and athleticism. See Gail Bederman's *Manliness and Civilization* (Chicago: University of Chicago Press, 1996).

13. Clarke, "Ladies Last," 181–186.

14. "Behind the Door," *Motion Picture News*, January 17, 1920, 915.

15. For a discussion of the 1920s war films that feature female protagonists, see Liz Clarke, "Vamps and Virgins: The Women of 1920s Hollywood War Romances," in *New Perspectives on the War Film*, ed. Clementine Tholas, Janis L. Goldie, and Karen A. Ritzenhoff (London: Palgrave Macmillan, 2019), 39–57.

SELECTED BIBLIOGRAPHY

Abel, Richard. *Americanizing the Movies and "Movie-Mad" Audiences, 1910–1914*. Berkeley: University of California Press, 2006.

———. "Movie Stars and Seriality in the 1910s." *Velvet Light Trap*, no. 79 (Spring 2017): 81–90.

Abel, Richard, Giorgio Bertellini, and Rob King. "Introduction." In *Early Cinema and the "National,"* 1–7. Bloomington, IN: John Libbey, 2008.

Balides, Constance. "Cinema under the Sign of Money: Commercialized Leisure, Economies of Abundance, and Pecuniary Madness, 1905–1915." In *American Cinema's Transitional Era: Audiences, Institutions, Practices*. Edited by Shelley Stamp and Charlie Keil, 285–313. Berkeley: University of California Press, 2004.

Barrett, Jenny. *Shooting the Civil War: Cinema, History and American National Identity*. London: I. B. Taurus, 2009.

Basinger, Janine. "The Wartime American Woman on Film: Home-Front Soldier." In *A Companion to the War Film*. Edited by Douglas A. Cunningham and John C. Nelson, 89–105. Malden, MA: Wiley, 2016.

———. *The World War II Combat Film: Anatomy of a Genre*. Middletown, CT: Wesleyan University Press, 2003.

Bean, Jennifer. "Technologies of Early Stardom and the Extraordinary Body." In *A Feminist Reader in Early Cinema*. Edited by Jennifer Bean and Diane Negra, 404–443. Durham, NC: Duke University Press, 2002.

———. "Toward a Feminist Historiography of Early Cinema." In *A Feminist Reader in Early Cinema*. Edited by Jennifer Bean and Diane Negra, 1–26. Durham, NC: Duke University Press, 2002.

Bederman, Gail. *Manliness and Civilization: A Cultural History of Gender and Race in the United States, 1880–1917*. Chicago: University of Chicago Press, 1996.

Belasco, David. "The Girl of the Golden West." In *American Melodrama*. Edited by Daniel Gerould, 183–247. New York: Performing Arts Journal Publications, 1983.

Berkman, Joyce. "Feminism, War, and Peace Politics." In *Women, Militarism, and War: Essays in History, Politics, and Social Theory*. Edited by Jean Bethke Elshtain and Sheila Tobias, 141–160. Savage, MD: Rowman and Littlefield, 1990.

Bernardi, Daniel. "Introduction." In *The Birth of Whiteness: Race and the Emergence of U.S. Cinema*, 1–11. New Brunswick, NJ: Rutgers University Press, 1996.

———."The Voice of Whiteness: D. W. Griffith's Biograph Films." In *The Birth of Whiteness: Race and the Emergence of U.S. Cinema*, 103–128. New Brunswick, NJ: Rutgers University Press, 1996.

Blaetz, Robin. "Joan of Arc and the War." In *Film and the First World War*. Edited by Karel Dibbets and Bert Hogenkamp, 116–124. Amsterdam: Amsterdam University Press, 1995.

———. *Visions of the Maid: Joan of Arc in American Film and Culture*. Richmond: University of Virginia Press, 2001.

Boag, Peter. *Re-Dressing America's Frontier Past*. Berkeley: University of California Press, 2012.

Bordwell, David, Kristin Thompson, and Janet Staiger. *The Classical Hollywood Cinema: Film Style and Mode of Production to 1960*. New York: Columbia University Press, 1985.

Bottomore, Stephen. "Introduction: War and Militarism. Dead White Males." *Film History* 14, no. 3/4 (September 2002): 239.

Bowser, Eileen. *The Transformation of Cinema, 1907–1915.* Berkeley: University of California Press, 1994.

Brasch, Ilka. *Film Serials and the American Cinema, 1910–1940: Operational Detection.* Amsterdam: Amsterdam University Press, 2018.

Bregent-Heald, Dominique. *Borderland Films: American Cinema, Mexico, and Canada during the Progressive Era.* Lincoln: University of Nebraska Press, 2015.

Bullough, Vern L., and Bonnie Bullough. *Cross Dressing, Sex, and Gender.* Philadelphia: University of Pennsylvania Press, 1993.

Canjels, Rudmer. *Distributing Silent Film Serials: Local Practices, Changing Forms, Cultural Transformation.* London: Routledge, 2011.

Christy, Howard Chandler. *The American Girl.* New York: Moffat, Yard and Co., 1906.

Clarke, Liz. "A Band of Adventurers: Kalem's Gauntier-Olcott Film Unit in Egypt." *Historical Journal of Film, Radio and Television* 38, no. 4 (December 2018): 695–710.

———. "Ladies Last: Masculinization of the American War Film in the 1920s." *Journal of Popular Film and Television* 43, no. 4 (2015): 171–187.

———. "Vamps and Virgins: The Women of 1920s Hollywood War Romances." In *New Perspectives on the War Film.* Edited by Clémentine Tholas-Disset, Janis L. Goldie, and Karen A. Ritzenhoff, 39–57. Cham, Switzerland: Palgrave Macmillan, 2019.

Cohler, Deborah. *Citizen, Invert, Queer: Lesbianism and War in Early Twentieth-Century Britain.* Minneapolis: University of Minnesota Press, 2010.

Cooper Jr., John Milton. "Introduction." In *Reconsidering Woodrow Wilson.* Edited by John Milton Cooper, 1–8. Baltimore: Johns Hopkins University Press, 2008.

———. "Making a Case for Wilson." In *Reconsidering Woodrow Wilson.* Edited by John Milton Cooper, 9–24. Baltimore: Johns Hopkins University Press, 2008.

———. *Pivotal Decades: The United States, 1900–1920.* New York: Norton, 1990.

Cox, J. Randolph. *The Dime Novel Companion: A Source Book.* Westport, CT: Greenwood Press, 2000.

Cripps, Thomas. "The Absent Presence in American Civil War Films." *Historical Journal of Film, Radio and Television* 14, no. 4 (January 1994): 367–376.

Davis, Jill. "The New Woman and the New Life." In *The New Woman and Her Sisters: Feminism and Theatre, 1850–1914.* Edited by Vivien Gardner and Susan Rutherford, 17–36. Ann Arbor: University of Michigan Press, 1992.

DeBauche, Leslie Midkiff. "High Fashion, Costume Design and Character Type: How Clothes Helped Billie Burke Become an American Girl." In *La Decima Musa: Il Cinema e Le Alltre Arti,* 163–169. Udine, Italy: Universita degli studi di Udine, 2001.

———. *Reel Patriotism: The Movies and World War I.* Madison: University of Wisconsin Press, 1997.

DeCordova, Richard. *Picture Personalities: The Emergence of the Star System in America.* Urbana: University of Illinois Press, 1990.

Denson, Shane. "The Logic of the Line Segment: Continuity and Discontinuity in the Serial-Queen Melodrama." In *Serialization in Popular Culture.* Edited by Rob Allen and Thijs van den Berg, 77–91. New York: Routledge, 2014.

Dooren, Ine van, and Peter Kramer. "The Politics of Direct Address." In *Film and the First World War.* Edited by Karel Dibbets and Bert Hogenkamp, 97–107. Amsterdam: Amsterdam University Press, 1995.

Dyer, Richard. *White: Twentieth Anniversary Edition.* New York: Routledge, 2017.

Eagle, Jonna. *Imperial Affects: Sensational Melodrama and the Attractions of American Cinema.* New Brunswick, NJ: Rutgers University Press, 2017.

Eberwein, Robert. *Armed Forces: Masculinity and Sexuality in the American War Film.* New Brunswick, NJ: Rutgers University Press, 2007.

Enstad, Nan. *Ladies of Labor, Girls of Adventure: Working Women, Popular Culture, and Labor Politics at the Turn of the Twentieth Century.* New York: Columbia University Press, 1999.

Evangelista, Matthew. *Gender, Nationalism, and War: Conflict on the Movie Screen.* Cambridge: Cambridge University Press, 2011.

Fahs, Alice. *The Imagined Civil War: Popular Literature of the North and South, 1861–1865.* Chapel Hill: University of North Carolina Press, 2010.

Ferris, Leslie. "The Golden Girl." In *The New Woman and Her Sisters: Feminism and Theatre, 1850–1914.* Edited by Vivien Gardner and Susan Rutherford, 37–58. Ann Arbor: University of Michigan Press, 1992.

Frost, Linda. *Never One Nation: Freaks, Savages, and Whiteness in U.S. Popular Culture, 1850–1877.* Minneapolis: University of Minnesota Press, 2005.

Gallagher, Gary W. *Causes Won, Lost, and Forgotten: How Hollywood and Popular Art Shape What We Know about the Civil War.* Chapel Hill: University of North Carolina Press, 2008.

Garber, Marjorie. *Vested Interests: Cross-Dressing and Cultural Anxiety.* London: Psychology Press, 1997.

Gardner, Vivien. "Introduction." In *The New Woman and Her Sisters: Feminism and Theatre, 1850–1914.* Edited by Vivien Gardner and Susan Rutherford, 1–16. Ann Arbor: University of Michigan Press, 1992.

Gerould, Daniel Charles. *American Melodrama.* Cambridge, MA: Performing Arts Journal Publications, 1983.

Gilderhus, Mark T. "Revolution, War, and Expansion: Woodrow Wilson in Latin America." In *Reconsidering Woodrow Wilson.* Edited by John Milton Cooper Jr., 165–188. Baltimore: Johns Hopkins University Press, 2008.

Hagedorn, Roger. "Doubtless to Be Continued: A Brief History of Serial Narrative." In *To Be Continued . . . Soap Operas around the World,* 27–48. New York: Routledge, 1995.

Hall, Richard. *Patriots in Disguise: Women Warriors of the Civil War.* St. Paul, MN: Paragon House, 1993.

Hall, Sheldon, and Stephen Neale. *Epics, Spectacles, and Blockbusters: A Hollywood History.* Detroit: Wayne State University Press, 2010.

Hansen, Miriam. "Adventures of Goldilocks: Spectatorship, Consumerism and Public Life." *Camera Obscura,* no. 22 (January 1990): 50–71.

———. *Babel and Babylon: Spectatorship in American Silent Film.* Cambridge, MA: Harvard University Press, 1991.

Hennefeld, Maggie. *Specters of Slapstick and Silent Film Comediennes.* New York: Columbia University Press, 2018.

Higashi, Sumiko. "The New Woman and Consumer Culture: Cecil B. DeMille's Sex Comedies." In *A Feminist Reader in Early Cinema.* Edited by Jennifer M. Bean and Diane Negra, 298–332. Durham, NC: Duke University Press, 2002.

Horak, Laura. *Girls Will Be Boys: Cross-Dressed Women, Lesbians, and American Cinema, 1908–1934.* New Brunswick, NJ: Rutgers University Press, 2016.

Isenberg, Michael T. *War on Film: The American Cinema and World War I, 1914–1941.* Rutherford, NJ: Fairleigh Dickinson University Press, 1981.

Jeffords, Susan. *The Remasculinization of America: Gender and the Vietnam War.* Bloomington: Indiana University Press, 1989.

Kaplan, Amy. *The Anarchy of Empire in the Making of U.S. Culture.* Cambridge, MA: Harvard University Press, 2002.

Keene, Jennifer D. *The United States and the First World War*. London: Pearson Education, 2000.

Keil, Charlie, and Shelley Stamp. "Introduction." In *American Cinema's Transitional Era: Audiences, Institutions, Practices*, 1–11. Berkeley: University of California Press, 2004.

Kelly, Andrew. *Cinema and the Great War*. London: Routledge, 1997.

Kemp, Niver. *Early Motion Pictures: The Paper Print Collection in the Library of Congress*. Washington, DC: Library of Congress, 1985.

Langman, Larry, Ed Borg, and R. L. Langman. *Encyclopedia of American War Films*. New York: Garland, 1989.

Leonard, Elizabeth D. *All the Daring of the Soldier: Women of the Civil War Armies*. New York: W. W. Norton, 1999.

Lister, Ruth. *Citizenship: Feminist Perspectives*. 2nd ed. New York: NYU Press, 2003.

Lyczba, Fabrice. "Hoaxes, Ballyhoo Stunts, War, and Other Jokes: Humor in the American Marketing of Hollywood War Films during the Great War." In *Humor, Entertainment, and Popular Culture during World War I*. Edited by Clémentine Tholas-Disset and Karen A. Ritzenhoff, 59–76. New York: Palgrave Macmillan, 2015.

Mason, Jeffrey Daniel. *Melodrama and the Myth of America*. Bloomington: Indiana University Press, 1993.

Massey, Mary Elizabeth. *Women in the Civil War*. Lincoln: University of Nebraska Press, 1994.

Maxim, Hudson. "The Argument for Preparedness." In *Reform, War, and Reaction*. Edited by Stanley Coben, 62–73. Columbia: University of South Carolina Press, 1972.

Merish, Lori. "Story Papers." In *The Oxford History of Popular Print Culture: U.S. Popular Print Culture, 1860–1920*. Edited by Christine Bold, 43–62. Oxford: Oxford University Press, 2011.

Moore, Paul S. *Now Playing: Moviegoing and the Regulation of Fun*. Albany: SUNY Press, 2008.

Morris, Justin. "Read It Today, See It Tonight: Extratextuality and the Silent Film Serial." *Cineaction*, no. 94 (2014): 45–50.

Musser, Charles. "Before the Rapid Firing Kinetograph: Edison Film Production, Representation and Exploitation in the 1890s." In *Edison Motion Pictures, 1890–1900: An Annotated Filmography*, 43–45. Washington, DC: Smithsonian Institution Press, 1997.

Neale, Steve. *Genre and Hollywood*. London: Routledge, 2000.

———. "Hollywood Blockbusters: Historical Dimensions." In *Movie Blockbusters*. Edited by Julian Stringer, 47–60. London: Routledge, 2003.

Ninkovich, Frank A. *Global Dawn*. Cambridge, MA: Harvard University Press, 2009.

Ohmer, Susan. "Female Spectatorship and Women's Magazines: Hollywood, Good Housekeeping, and World War II." *Velvet Light Trap* 25, no. March (1990): 53.

Oram, Alison. *Her Husband Was a Woman! Women's Gender-Crossing in Modern British Popular Culture*. London: Routledge, 2013.

Peiss, Kathy. *Cheap Amusements: Working Women and Leisure in New York City, 1880 to 1920*. Philadelphia: Temple University Press, 1986.

———."Making Faces: The Cosmetics Industry and the Cultural Construction of Gender, 1890–1930." In *Unequal Sisters: An Inclusive Reader in U.S. Women's History*. Edited by Vicki L. Ruíz and Ellen Carol DuBois, 342–362. New York: Routledge, 1990.

Peterson, Jennifer Lynn. *Education in the School of Dreams: Travelogues and Early Nonfiction Film*. Durham, NC: Duke University Press, 2013.

Rabinovitz, Lauren. *For the Love of Pleasure: Women, Movies, and Culture in Turn-of-the-Century Chicago*. New Brunswick, NJ: Rutgers University Press, 1998.

Renov, Michael. *Hollywood's Wartime Woman: Representation and Ideology*. Ann Arbor, MI: UMI Research Press, 1988.

Ruhs, Alice. "The Feminized Civil War: Gender, Northern Popular Literature, and the Memory of War, 1861–1900." In *Unequal Sisters: An Inclusive Reader in U.S. Women's History*, 4th ed. Edited by Vicki L. Ruíz and Ellen Carol DuBois, 130–155. New York: Routledge, 1990.

Singer, Ben. *Melodrama and Modernity: Early Sensational Cinema and Its Contexts*. New York: Columbia University Press, 2001.

Slater, David Jeremiah. "The American Girl, Her Life and Times: An Ideal and Its Creators, 1890–1930." PhD diss., University of Minnesota, 2005.

Slide, Anthony. *The Big V: A History of the Vitagraph Company*. Metuchen, NJ: Scarecrow Press, 1976.

Slotkin, Richard. *Gunfighter Nation: The Myth of the Frontier in Twentieth -Century America*. New York: Atheneum,1992.

Spehr, Paul C. *The Civil War in Motion Pictures: A Bibliography of Films Produced in the United States since 1897*. Whitefish, MT: Literary Licensing, 2012.

Stamp, Shelley. *Movie-Struck Girls: Women and Motion Picture Culture after the Nickelodeon*. Princeton, NJ: Princeton University Press, 2000.

Streeby, Shelley. *American Sensations: Class, Empire, and the Production of Popular Culture*. Berkeley: University of California Press, 2002.

Streeby, Shelley, and Jesse Alemán. "Introduction." In *Empire and the Literature of Sensation: An Anthology of Nineteenth-Century Popular Fiction*. New Brunswick, NJ: Rutgers University Press, 2007. xiii–xxxx.

Stringer, Julian. "Introduction." In *Movie Blockbusters*, 1–14. London: Routledge, 2003.

Tasker, Yvonne. *Soldiers' Stories: Military Women in Cinema and Television since World War II*. Durham, NC: Duke University Press, 2011.

Tholas-Disset, Clémentine. "Mary Pickford's WWI Patriotism: A Feminine Approach to Wartime Mythical Americanness." In *Heroism and Gender in War Films*. Edited by Karen A. Ritzenhoff and Jakub Kazecki, 9–21. New York: Palgrave Macmillan, 2014.

Tholas-Disset, Clémentine, and Karen A. Ritzenhoff, "Introduction." In *Humor, Entertainment, and Popular Culture during World War I*. Edited by Clémentine Tholas-Disset and Karen A. Ritzenhoff, 1–22. New York: Palgrave Macmillan, 2015.

Toeplitz, Jerzy. "The Cinema in Eastern and Central Europe before the Guns of August." In *Film and the First World War*. Edited by Karel Dibbets and Bert Hogenkamp, 17–27. Amsterdam: Amsterdam University Press, 1995.

Trachtenberg, Alan. *The Incorporation of America: Culture and Society in the Gilded Age*. 1st ed. New York: Hill and Wang, 1982.

Uricchio, William, and Roberta E. Pearson. *Reframing Culture: The Case of the Vitagraph Quality Films*. Princeton, NJ: Princeton University Press, 2014.

Wagner, Kristen Anderson. *Comic Venus: Women and Comedy in American Silent Film*. Detroit: Wayne State University Press, 2018.

Wakeman, Sarah Rosetta. *An Uncommon Soldier: The Civil War Letters of Sarah Rosetta Wakeman, Alias Private Lyons Wakeman, 153rd Regiment, New York State Volunteers*. New York: Oxford University Press, 1995.

Welsh, James M. "The Great War and the War Film as Genre: Hearts of the World and What Price Glory." In *Hollywood's World War I: Motion Picture Images*. Edited by John E. O'Connor and Peter C. Rollins, 27–38. Bowling Green, OH: Bowling Green State University Popular Press, 1997.

Westwell, Guy. *War Cinema: Hollywood on the Front Line*. London: Wallflower, 2006.

Wetta, Frank Joseph, and Stephen J. Curley. *Celluloid Wars: A Guide to Film and the American Experience of War*. New York: Greenwood, 1992.

Wexman, Virginia Wright. "The Family on the Land: Race and Nationhood in Silent Westerns." In *The Birth of Whiteness: Race and the Emergence of U.S. Cinema*. Edited by Daniel Berardi, 129–169. New Brunswick, NJ: Rutgers University Press, 1996.

Williams, Linda. *Playing the Race Card: Melodramas of Black and White from Uncle Tom to O. J. Simpson*. Princeton, NJ: Princeton University Press, 2001.

Winkler, H. Donald. *Stealing Secrets: How a Few Daring Women Deceived Generals, Impacted Battles, and Altered the Course of the Civil War*. London: Sourcebooks, 2010.

Woloch, Nancy. *Women and the American Experience*. 4th ed. Toronto: McGraw-Hill, 2006.

Yesil, Bilge. "'Who Said This Is a Man's War?': Propaganda, Advertising Discourse and the Representation of War Worker Women during the Second World War." *Media History* 10, no. 2 (August 2004): 103–117.

Yuval-Davis, Nira. "Gender and Nation." *Ethnic and Racial Studies* 16, no. 4 (1993): 621–632.

INDEX

Note: Page numbers in italics refer to illustrations

ABOUT THE AUTHOR

LIZ CLARKE is an assistant professor in communication, popular culture, and film at Brock University, Canada. Her research is focused on feminist media history, including women in silent American film and women screenwriters. She has published articles in *Camera Obscura* and *Feminist Media Histories*, as well as papers in the edited anthologies *New Perspectives on the War Film* and *Martial Culture, Silver Screen: War Movies and the Construction of American Identity.*

Aaron Michael Kerner, *Torture Porn in the Wake of 9/11: Horror, Exploitation, and the Cinema of Sensation*

Ahmed Al-Rawi, *Cyberwars in the Middle East*

Brenda M. Boyle, *American War Stories*

Brenda M. Boyle and Jeehyun Lim, eds., *Looking Back on the Vietnam War: Twenty-First-Century Perspectives*

David Kieran and Edwin A. Martini, eds., *At War: The Military and American Culture in the Twentieth Century and Beyond*

Delia Malia Caparoso Konzett, *Hollywood's Hawaii: Race, Nation, and War*

H. Bruce Franklin, *Crash Course: From the Good War to the Forever War*

Jonna Eagle, *Imperial Affects: Sensational Melodrama and the Attractions of American Cinema*

Jon Simons and John Louis Lucaites, eds., *In/visible War: The Culture of War in Twenty-First-Century America*

Katherine Chandler, *Unmanning: How Humans, Machines and Media Perform Drone Warfare*

Liz Clarke, *The American Girl Goes to War: Women and National Identity in U.S. Silent Film*

Martin A. Danahay, *War without Bodies: Framing Death from the Crimean to the Iraq War*

Mary Douglas Vavrus, *Postfeminist War: Women and the Media-Military-Industrial Complex*

Matt Sienkiewicz, *The Other Air Force: U.S. Efforts to Reshape Middle Eastern Media Since 9/11*

Nan Levinson, *War Is Not a Game: The New Antiwar Soldiers and the Movement They Built*

Roger Stahl, *Through the Crosshairs: The Weapon's Eye in Public War Culture*

Simon Wendt, ed., *Warring over Valor: How Race and Gender Shaped American Military Heroism in the Twentieth and Twenty-First Centuries*

Tanine Allison, *Destructive Sublime: World War II in American Film and Media*